THE MASSIVE ADULT JOKE BOOK

THE MASSIVE ADULT JOKE BOOK

JOHNNY SHARPE

Capella

Published by Capella,
an imprint of
Arcturus Publishing Limited
For Bookmart Limited
Registered Number 2372865
Desford Road, Enderby, Leicester LE9 5AD

ISBN 1-84193-122-5
This edition published 2002

Printed in Denmark by Norhaven Paperbacks, Viborg

Cover design by Alex Ingr

Johnny Sharpe is a fictional character.

© Arcturus Publishing Limited
1–7 Shand Street, London SE1 2ES

CONTENTS

A

ACCIDENTS

The restaurant was packed full with diners when all of a sudden, there was a terrible commotion and a woman began to choke on a piece of food. Quick as a flash, a man ran forward grabbed the woman and put her face-down on the floor. Then he pulled down her knickers and licked her bottom. Immediately, the woman coughed up the piece of food and stood up fully recovered. As the man walked back to his table, his companion looked at him in astonishment. "Bloody hell, I've never seen anything like that before!" he exclaimed."That's called the Hindlick manoeuvre," the man replied.

The boarding house was well known in the district, not least for the fact that the woman who ran the establishment acted like a mother to all her 'bachelor boys.' As well as feeding them the best home cooking, she would wash and iron their clothes and help them as much as she could. One day, young Charlie asked her if she would sew a button on his flies but she was just in the middle of cooking dinner.

"Mrs McGregor's upstairs, she won't mind doing it for you," said the woman.

So Charlie went upstairs and the woman continued with her cooking when all of a sudden there was an almighty yell and the poor man hurtled downstairs in blind panic.

"What happened?" asked the woman looking alarmed.

"Mr McGregor!" he gasped. "Mr McGregor came in just as his wife was biting off the thread!"

The foreman was just wondering why one of his men was so late getting back from making a delivery, when the phone rang.

"Sorry boss," said the man. "I had a bit of an accident on the way back, I hit a pig."

"Well, just put it on the side of the road and we'll pick it up later."

"But boss, it's not dead. It just keeps squealing."

"Okay, get the rifle from the back of the truck and put it out of its misery. Then throw it in the ditch until later."

Five minutes went by and the phone rang again.

"Boss, it's me. I'm still here."

"Why? Did you do as I said?"

"Yeah, I shot it and put it in the ditch, but his motorbike is still stuck under the truck!"

For the third time that week, Ben had been late home from work and his wife was sick and tired of reheating his food.

"Next time this happens," she threatened, "your dinner will be in the bin and the bed will be made up in the spare room."

"Don't worry darling," he promised, "nothing will stop me from getting home on time tonight."

True to his word, Ben left work 10 minutes early to make sure he caught the train but alas, as he was crossing the road, a double-decker bus swerved around the corner and knocked him to the ground. Fortunately, he only had cuts and bruises but he was taken to hospital for a check up and eventually arrived home three hours late.

"So much for promises!" yelled the wife. "You've done it this time."

"But darling!" protested Ben, "it wasn't my fault. I got hit by a bus."

"Oh yeah!" she replied scornfully, "and that took three hours, did it?"

A man rushed into a bar, shouting out in anguish,

"Does anyone here have a black cat with a white collar?"

No one replied. He repeated his question more loudly, but still there was no response.

"Oh bloody hell!" he muttered to himself, "I've just run over a vicar."

A man dressed in pyjamas went up to the hotel reception and asked for the key to room 402.

"I'm sorry Sir, the room's taken," came the reply.

"I know it is," replied the man impatiently, "it's mine. I just fell out of the window!"

Two cars crashed head-on on a narrow lane just outside a small village. One of the drivers jumped out and ran over to the other car to discover it was the Captain of a rival pub cricket team.

"George, are you OK?" he asked.

"A bit groggy," came the reply.

The first man went back to his car and returned with a hip flask of whisky.

"Here," he said to George, "take a sip of this, it'll make you feel better."

"Why thanks," said the second man, "that's really kind of you, considering we're both up to win the inter-pub cricket trophy."

He handed the hip flask back

"Aren't you going to have a sip?"

"What! You're kidding," said the first man, "the police will be here any moment."

A man drove too fast down a country lane, skidded on some black ice and ended up in a ditch. Fortunately, a farmer appeared moments later, leading a big black horse. When he saw the man's predicament, he offered to help.

"If we tie a rope around the car, I think old Black Bess here will be able to help get it out."

So they tied the rope from the horse to the car and the farmer shouted,

"Come on Starlight, pull as hard as you can!" but the horse didn't move.

Then the farmer shouted,

"Come on Silky, one, two, three. Pull!"

But still the horse didn't move. So for a third time the farmer yelled,

"OK, Dobbin, pull now."

Nothing happened. Then he called,

"Go on Black Bess, my beauty, pull hard."

This time, the horse took the strain and slowly pulled the car out of the ditch. The motorist was very grateful but also a little puzzled.

"Don't mind me asking," he said, "but why did you call the horse by all those different names?"

"Well, it's like this," explained the farmer. "Old Black Bess is blind and if she thought she was the only one pulling, she'd never have bothered trying."

The window cleaner missed his footing and plunged ten feet to the ground where he lay nursing a broken ankle.

"Quick!" shouted a passerby, "get this man a glass of water while I call an ambulance."

"Listen mate," groaned the window cleaner, "how far do I have to fall to get a shot of whisky?"

"And don't come back 'til you've got a good story," yelled the editor to his lazy reporter.

Two hours later, the hapless man was still looking for something to write about when he came across a road accident. A large crowd of people had gathered round the incident and there was no way he could get to see what had happened. Then he had an idea.

"Let me through, let me through!" he called, pushing people out of the way. "I'm the victim's son."

Eventually he got to the front to find a dead donkey lying on the ground in front of the truck. Ho ho ho.

A window cleaner is working at the top of the tallest building in the world when his cradle breaks and he's left hanging on by his fingertips.

"Oh Lord, please help me," he says in sheer terror, "please don't let me die."

All of a sudden, a voice booms out from the clouds,

"Have faith my son. Let go and I will lift you up to safety."

Stunned, the window cleaner looks down at the sheer drop below him and whimpers,

"Is there anyone else up there I can speak to?"

"Is that Belle's Florist?" said the man angrily on the end of the phone.

"Yes, it is," came the reply. "How may I help you?"

"Now listen here. I'm just celebrating the launch of my new company and I get a wreath delivered saying 'Rest in Peace.' Have you any idea what a bad impression that can make?"

"Well that *is* bad!" said the florist, "but it's not as bad as the impression that your 'Congratulations on Your New Location' bouquet will make at that funeral."

The crowd cheered and cheered as the man stood dripping wet on the riverbank.

"Well done!" they all shouted to him. "What a hero! What a rescue!"

"Hero, bollocks," muttered the man. "Who the hell pushed me in?"

ANIMALS

"Right you bloody good for nothing horse, you lose here today and it'll be the milk round for you tomorrow morning," said the angry jockey.

The race began and by the fifth jump it was obvious that the horse was going to be an also ran. The jockey took out his whip and gave it a sharp thwack.

"Steady on there," said the horse, "I've got to be up at four o'clock in the morning."

Little Red Riding is walking through the forest on the way to meet her Grandma when she spots someone moving.

"Mr. Wolf, Mr. Wolf," she trills, "I can see you! Come out from behind that tree."

"Bugger off," he replies angrily and disappears deeper into the forest.

Moments later, Red Riding Hood spots him again.

"Mr. Wolf, Mr. Wolf!" she calls. "I can see you behind the bush."

The wolf glowers at her and runs off. A short while later she sees him hiding behind a big rock.

"I can see you, I can see you," she says, pointing her finger at him.

"Now look here," says the wolf, "who the hell are you and what are you doing in the forest?"

"I'm Little Red Riding Hood and I'm on my way to see Grandma," she replies.

"Then fuck off and do it," yelled the wolf, "and let me have a crap in peace."

A toad and a rabbit sought pleasure at a brothel but it was a pretty miserable place and they both picked up a nasty infection. Two days later, the toad's willy had turned a horrible yellow colour and the rabbit's had turned purple.

"I've got to get help," said the worried toad and he disappeared into the forest where he met a kindly witch. She told him the only cure was to seek out Dr. Marvel in the Land of Oz.

A few hours later, the rabbit met the same witch and told her of his plight. Again, she told him he needed to go to the Land of Oz.

"But how do I get there?" he asked.

"It's quite simple," she replied. "Just follow the yellow dick toad."

"Mummy, mummy," said the baby camel. "Why have we got big flat feet?"

"So that we can walk across the sand easier when we're trekking through the desert," she replied.

"And why have we got such thick hides?" he continued.

"That's to protect us from the desert's fierce sun," she replied.

"But why have we got long eyelashes?"

"That's to protect our eyes against sand storms."

"So mum, what the fuck are we doing in Bristol Zoo?" he said.

"Get the carriage ready," says the King to his groom. "I've just had a telegram to say the Queen is arriving home today."

So the groom polishes the carriage, grooms the horse, puts beautiful purple plumes on its harness and then notices the animal has a huge erection.

"Hey," admonishes the groom. "Who got the telegram, you or the King?"

A cow went down to the pond for water and noticed three ducks swimming about on the surface.

"Hello," she said to the first duck, "who are you?"

"My name's Quack and I'm blowing bubbles," replied the duck.

A second duck came swimming by and the cow greeted it also.

"Hi there, what's your name?"

"Hello," replied the second duck, "my name's Quack Quack and I'm blowing bubbles."

A little later she spotted the third duck.

"Hi" she said, "I bet I can guess your name. It's Quack Quack Quack isn't it?"

"No," replied the duck, "my name's Bubbles."

Dirty Jake is playing poker in the saloon but the game is not going well. Every time he loses, he kicks the puppy lying underneath the table, until the poor thing is black and blue. Eventually, it comes to the final hand and Jake, now desperate to recoup some of his losses, bets all the money he has left. Alas, he loses and is so angry, he takes his gun out of its holster and shoots the poor dog in the foot. A few years later, Dirty Jake is once again playing poker in the salon when suddenly the doors fly open and in walks a huge dog, standing on his hind legs, he's over six feet tall. The bar goes quiet as the dog takes out a gun and growls,

"I'm looking for the man that shot my paw."

The ancient Roman animal trainer released the lions into the Colosseum, and turned to his assistant with a sigh.

"They're a poor lot, this week," he said glumly, "even worse than the ones last year."

"I know," replied his assistant, "the Christians aren't up to much either, are they?"

"No," said the trainer. "Bloody awful shower."

"Still, look on the bright side," said his assistant, "at least we don't get pitch invasions like they do at the chariot races."

Two snakes are creeping through the undergrowth when one says to the other

"What kind of snakes are we? Do we kill our prey by squeezing them to death or give them a bite of our deadly poison?"

"We're the poisonous ones," replied the second snake, "why do you ask?"

"Because I've just bitten my lip."

Two lions were walking through the jungle and the male kept licking the female's arse.

"I wish you'd stop that," she complained.

"Sorry," he replied, "I've just eaten an estate agent and I'm trying to get the taste out of my mouth."

When the away team turned up for the match, they were amazed to see that the goalkeeper for the opposing side was a Great Dane. The dog performed incredibly and stopped the away team scoring.

After the match, the away Captain asked the opposing team how they ever managed to get the dog to play so well.

"Well, it's the same for everyone," replied the manager, "practice, practice, practice."

After a long hot summer, the rat infestation becomes critical and the Mayor of London, Red Ken, is at his wits end. He broadcasts a plea for help and the call is answered by a wizened old woman dressed in black. She tells him she will rid the city of rats for £1,000. The Mayor agrees and the woman begins her task. From a huge bag she takes out a bright purple rat and places it on the ground. Then, as they set off down the street, rats appear from everywhere and follow the purple creature. Soon there are millions of them and as the purple rat walks into the Thames, all the others follow and disappear until there are none left. The Mayor is overjoyed and pays up gladly, but just as the old woman is about to leave he whispers in her ear, "You haven't got a purple Tory in that bag have you?"

A young soldier was sent to a remote outpost deep in the desert. After 3 months, he awoke one morning to loud cheers and banging of drums.

"What's happening?" he asked his colleague.

"The goat herd is passing through again. Someone's spotted them on the horizon and is letting everyone know. Come on or we'll be late."

The newest recruit was hurried along and pushed through the fort gates.

"But why is everyone rushing?" he exclaimed. "There's still plenty of time before they get here."

"Maybe," replied his friend, "but if you're too late, all the good looking ones have gone."

"Welcome home Brian!" said the banner over the pub door as the intrepid explorer returned from his safari in darkest Africa. After a few pints, his crowd of well-wishers asked him to tell them some of his more hair-raising stories.

Brian sat back and began

"There was this one day when I went out alone into the jungle and strayed into unknown territory. Suddenly I heard a loud roar behind me and turning round, I saw a huge lion ready to pounce. Well, I just ran for it, with this beast right behind me. Luckily, just as it was about to get me, it slipped and I was able to run on. But next moment, he was breathing down my neck again. Then just as I thought it was curtains, he slipped again and I managed to run back into the camp."

His audience listened spellbound until a voice from the back remarked,

"Bloody hell, Brian, if that had been me, I'd have shit my pants.

Brian turned to the speaker and replied,

"What do you think the lion kept slipping on?"

A lion is walking through the jungle in an awful mood, ready to take it out on anyone he meets. As he turns a corner he sees a baboon.

"Bloody hell, you're ugly," he says. "I've never noticed before just how ugly you are with your flat nose and red arse. Go on, get out of here."

"Yeah, yeah, alright," says the baboon and disappears as fast as he can.

Later, he catches sight of a sloth lounging in a tree.

"Ugh, you really are weird," says the lion. "Look at the way you move and what long arms you've got. Go on, bugger off."

"Sorry," mutters the sloth, as he slinks away.

By this time the lion is feeling in a much better mood and is starting to enjoy himself. He sees a frog sitting on a lily pad and shouts at him,

"Oi you ugly get! Your skin doesn't fit properly and you're covered in warts. Ugh! I can hardly bear to look at you."

"Well fuck you," replies the frog. "I haven't been well."

The hedgehog made his way down to the riverbank and very slowly walked into the water. As it got deeper, he soldiered on, gasping for breath but suddenly he disappeared under and it was only by rolling himself up into a ball that he was able to get back to the bank. After lying panting on the side for 10 minutes, the hedgehog tried again. But after going under twice, did he manage to get back to dry land before collapsing. This time it took him much longer to recover but once he felt fit enough, he started back into the water. Two ducks were watching from the other side of the bank and one said to the other,

"Come on George, don't you think it's time we told him he was adopted?"

A couple are walking around the zoo when they come to the gorilla cage. There's no one around so the man says to his wife,

"Sharon, take your blouse off and let's see if it has any effect on the gorilla."

She hesitates.

"Go on!" he urges, "no one will see."

So she takes her blouse off and the gorilla starts jumping up and down in excitement.

"Now take your bra off," he says.

She does this and the gorilla gets even more excited.

"Right, take your skirt off" he says.

"Oh no, I couldn't, how would we explain it if someone came along?" she asks.

"There's no one around, it'll be fine."

So over the next few minutes the woman gradually takes all her clothes off and by this time, the gorilla is going berserk. Then the husband opens the door of the cage and pushes her inside.

"Now tell him you have a headache!" he says.

A man walked into a nightclub and asked to see the manager.

"If I show you a unique act, can I have a free drink please?"

"I shouldn't think so," replied the manager, "but go on, impress me."

So the man took a small toad out of his pocket and placed it at the piano. To everyone's delight and amazement the toad started to play some wonderful blues. At the end of the piece the audience erupted into loud applause.

"Yeah, pretty good," admitted the manager. "What do you want to drink?"

Ten minutes later, the man approached the manager again.

"Listen, if I show you another great act, can I have another free drink?"

"Go on then."

From his pocket, the man brought out a white hamster. He put it on top of the piano and while the toad played, the hamster sang the blues.

Once more, the audience went wild.

Suddenly, there was a tap on the man's shoulder and turning round he saw a guy in a fancy waistcoat.

"Hi, my name's Louis and I'm a top theatrical agent. Here's my card. How much do you want for the act?"

The man shrugged, "Sorry, it's not for sale."

"Come on now, you look like you could do with some money, how about £10,000?"

The man refused. "I'm not selling at any price."

"OK, how about I just buy the hamster, say £6,000."

"Well, that sounds fair. Okay, the hamster for £6000 it is."

The man handed over the hamster and received the £6,000. After the agent had left, the club manager came up to the man.

"You idiot! You had a great act there, worth a fortune, and you split it up for six grand. That could have made you rich."

"Oh, that's alright," grins the man. "The toad's a ventriloquist."

A woman arrived home from work to discover her dog had the next door neighbour's hamster in its mouth. Horrified, she ordered the dog to drop it but the poor little creature was well and truly dead.

"Oh damn!" she cursed, "what will Mr Jones say about this!"

Then she had a great idea. She took the hamster inside, bathed it and combed its fur then crept quietly next door and put the animal back in its cage.

Some days passed before she met up with her neighbour and as they chatted, the hamster came up in conversation.

"You won't believe this," said Mr Jones, "but a week ago our hamster died and we buried him in the garden."

"Oh really!" replied the woman.

"Yes, but some sick bugger dug him up and put him back inside his cage."

So this lion is in the bush, shagging an antelope when suddenly he spots his lioness coming towards him.

"Quick!" he whispers to the antelope, "pretend I'm killing you."

A game of poker was being played on a bench in the park and a passer-by was amazed to see that one of the players was a dog. As he stopped to watch, the dog won three hands in a row.

"Wow!" he exclaimed, "that's fantastic. I've never seen such a clever dog."

One of the other players replied,

"Oh come on, he's not that clever. Whenever he gets a good hand, he wags his tail."

A woman walked past a pet shop on the way to work and outside on a perch was a beautiful parrot. As she passed by, he squawked loudly,

"Oh Madam, you are so ugly."

Upset, the woman hurried on, but the next day as she passed the shop, he called out loudly

"Madam, madam, you are so ugly," causing other passers-by to look at her with interest.

Now after enduring this humiliation for a week, she could take it no longer. She walked angrily into the shop and confronted the manager.

"Any more abuse from that parrot and I'll wring its neck," she raged.

The owner promised it wouldn't happen again and when she passed the following morning, she looked for any reaction from the bird. At first he never spoke a word and then just as she began to relax he called out,

"Oh, Madam, Madam… you know, don't you?"

Dave was early for his date with Sonia so while she went off to get ready, he started to play with her little dog on the living room carpet. He found a ball and began throwing it around the room for the dog to chase. However, he got a little over-enthusiastic and the ball flew out of the open door onto the 10th floor balcony and over the railings to the ground below. The dog followed.

Stunned, Dave just sat there until his girlfriend appeared.

"Erm... Sonia," he said hesitantly, "have you noticed how depressed your dog has become recently?"

A man had been crossing the desert by camel for over three months. Lacking any female company, he suddenly had a most awful urge – one that had to be satisfied straight away. He backed the camel over to a pile of rocks, stood on top of the rocks and undid his flies. Alas, as he moved towards the animal, it walked further away. Undaunted, he backed up the camel again and got on top of the rocks but once more the animal walked a few feet away.

"Damn, damn, damn!" he muttered as he got down to bring the camel back to the rocks for a third time. Now this farce went on for another fifteen minutes or so, when out of the blue appeared a gorgeous young girl.

"I can't believe it," he said as he looked her up and down.

"Excuse me Miss," he said, smiling with satisfaction, "would you mind holding the camel for me?"

A rabbit was hopping through the jungle when he came across a pile of bones. As he stopped to look at them, he caught sight of a lion creeping up behind him and knew he was in deep shit. Suddenly having an idea, he said loudly to himself,

"Mmm, that sure was a tasty lion."

Hearing this, the lion slunk away.

Up in a tree, a monkey had been watching the events below and realised the rabbit had played a trick. He thought this was a chance to get on the lion's good side, so he went in search of the animal and described how he had been fooled. The lion was most annoyed and decided to hunt the rabbit down, taking the monkey with him. A couple of hours later, they discovered the rabbit in a clearing, taking a snooze. As they crept towards him, the rabbit became aware of the movement and saw them through the slits in his eyes.

"Oh bugger," he thought to himself, "I'm for it this time." Then he realised, maybe there was one chance left. He turned over and said loudly,

"How much longer am I going to have to wait? Where's that bloody monkey with my next lion?

A dog was terrorising the neighbourhood.

"If you don't keep him under better control, he'll have to be taken away," the owner was told, so they had him neutered.

However, on the following day the postman was walking up the garden path when the dog jumped out and sunk his jaws deep into the man's leg.

"Get him off, get him off!" yelled the postman frantically as the owner rushed out to drag the dog away.

"I'm so sorry," apologised the owner. "I can't understand why he's still so aggressive; I've just had him neutered."

"Well you should have had all his teeth taken out instead," retorted the postman angrily. "As soon as I saw him I knew he wasn't going to screw me."

"Oh Jack," said mum, "our Julie wants to take the dog for a walk but the dog's on heat."

"Don't worry," replied dad, "I know what to do about that." He went into the garage and doused a cloth with some petrol, which he then rubbed all over the dog's bum. "That'll disguise the smell, so the dogs won't be attracted," he said. However, 40 minutes later the daughter returned without the dog.

"Where's the dog?" asked her parents anxiously.

"We ran out of fuel half way round," replied Julie, "but it's okay, there's a big Alsatian pushing her home."

"Oh Father," wailed the distraught woman. "My little dog has died. He's been my companion for over 13 years and I'd like to give him a wonderful funeral."

"I'm sorry," replied the priest, "but we don't conduct funerals for animals. Maybe the church down the road will oblige."

"Okay," she replied. "I'll try there because I really want this and I've saved up £500 for the service."

"Oh, now wait a minute," said the priest quickly, "of course we'll do the funeral here. Why didn't you tell me the dog was Catholic?"

Two men were boasting about their dogs.

"Mine can carry out four orders all at the same time," said the first man. "Watch, I'll show you."

"Rover, pop down the paper shop, get me the racing post and on the way back pick up a betting slip and a pen from the bookies. Oh, and pick up last week's winnings."

Sure enough, the dog arrived back 10 minutes later with everything the man asked for.

"Very good," said the second man, "but watch this."

"Springer, get me some food."

The dog disappeared and arrived back 15 minutes later with an egg and a saucepan of water. He gathered together some sticks, lit a small fire and placed the saucepan of water on top of it. When the water boiled, he put in the egg and then stood on his head.

"That's fantastic," remarked the first man, "but why is he standing on his head?"

"Because he broke the eggcup last week," came the reply.

A woman had a beautiful carpet but it was badly stained because of her dog that kept peeing all over it. So she cut out the stains and took the pieces along to the carpet shop.

"I'm no fool," she said. "Can I have a carpet the colour of these stains, please."

A woman was in the cinema when she noticed a man and his dog sitting in front of her. The dog was glued to the screen. He would cry at the sad bits and bark joyously when it was funny.

After the film was over, she tapped the man on the shoulder and commented on his remarkable dog.

"Yes, I'm amazed at his reaction," replied the man, "because he didn't like the book at all."

One day the beautiful princess was walking through the woods when she came across a frog sitting on a lily pad.

"Good day to you," said the frog, "do not be alarmed. I am really a handsome prince who was turned into a frog by a wicked old witch. If you kiss me, I will turn back into my former self and we can live happily ever after. We'll get married and live in a mighty castle. You can set up home, learn to cook, wash my clothes and have my children."

Later that night, the Princess sat down to a plate of frog's legs lightly sautéed in white wine and onions. She looked at it and smiled.

"I don't think so," she said.

ANNIVERSARIES

The couple had been married for 20 years and the husband asked his wife how she would like to celebrate their latest anniversary.

"How about a new car for you to get around in?" he suggested.

"No thanks."

"OK, what about a 6-month world cruise, stopping off at all the Seven Wonders of the World?"

"No."

"Well, what would you like?"

"I'd like a divorce," she said.

"What!" he exclaimed, "come on Doris, I wasn't planning to spend *that* much."

ARISTOCRACY

First and foremost, Sir Henry Pennington was a true aristocrat who believed in the stiff upper lip, true patriotism and right and proper etiquette.

One night he returned early from his club to discover his eldest daughter writhing around on the floor with a young earl.

"Dorothy!" he yelled, "let's do it right. Arch your back immediately and lift that gentleman's balls off the cold floor."

The butler was very keen to impress his new employers so he was working hard to stay alert to all the guests' wishes. Suddenly, as a female guest leant over to reach for the salt, her tits fell out of her low cut dress. Quick as a flash, the butler picked up two serving spoons and placed them back inside before anyone had noticed what had happened. Later that night, as the final guests left, the host turned to his butler and commended him on his quick thinking.

"But I think if it happens again, a warm spoon may be more acceptable."

Lady Matilda only had a dressing gown on when her butler entered unannounced to tell her that the guests were arriving.

"Henry!" she scolded, "You must knock and wait for me to answer before you come into my bedroom. For all you know, I may have just got out of the bath."

"No need to worry Ma'am," replied Henry, "I always look through the keyhole before I come in."

Cynthia had invited the Women's Institute round to her country estate for afternoon tea. As she offered them cakes, her 14-year-old son came hurtling into the room, chasing a black and white cat. As he disappeared through the window, he could be heard to yell at the top of his voice,

"When I get hold of that cat, I'll fuck it."

Unperturbed, Cynthia turned to her guests and remarked

"And he will you know, he's a randy little bugger."

B

BAD TASTE

Two men were in the park watching a woman sunbathing on the grass. Her skirt was very short so she hadn't left much to the imagination.

"I bet we're looking at her black knickers," said the first man.

"No, I don't think so," said his mate, "I think it's her pubes."

At that moment a young boy went past.

"Listen," said the first man, "let's have a bet to see who's right and get that boy to go over and check."

So the bet was made and the boy walked over to the woman. A few moments later he returned.

"Well, who was right?" they asked. "Was it panties or hair?"

"Neither," said the boy. "Flies."

A man joins a group of war veterans listening to a brass band in the park. All of a sudden the man in front of him begins to twitch his head backwards and forwards in sudden jerky movements.

"I'm sorry," he says, "it's an old injury I got from the war."

A few moments later, the man to the left of him begins to throw his arms around in the air.

"Sorry," he gasps, "can't help it. I got it in the war."

Then the man on his right starts to shake his hand about, faster and faster it goes.

"Did you get that in the war as well?" he asks.

"No," comes the reply. "I got it from my nose and now I can't get it off my finger."

BARS

A customer walks up the bar and attracts the barman's attention.

"Can I have a packet of helicopter flavour crisps, please?" he asks.

"Sorry, mate," says the barman, "we've only got plane."

"Bloody women!" cursed the man at the bar. "I think my wife is having an affair with a travelling salesman. Last night I found a case of brushes under the bed!"

"Yeah, bloody women," agreed the bartender. "I think my wife's having an affair with a pet shop owner. When I got home, I found two budgies, 1 parrot and three gerbils under our bed."

A man further down the bar had been listening to this conversation and he spoke up.

"That's nothing, I think my wife's having an affair with a horse. I came home last night and found a jockey under our bed!"

A man walked up to a bar and the landlord said,

"Sir, you know you've got a steering wheel shoved down your trousers?"

"I know," replied the man. "It's driving me nuts!"

A blind man went into a cocktail bar and said to the barman,

"Can you let me smell the empty glass of the person who just left?"

Puzzled, the barman handed him the glass and the blind man sniffed it saying,

"I'll have the same please. That's two shots of vodka, a dash of lemonade, twist of lime and 3 drops of cherry brandy."

The barman was amazed that the blind man had described the drink so perfectly.

The following week, he came in again and went through the same ritual. He smelled the empty glass next to him and ordered exactly the same.

"May I have 1 shot of brandy, 1 shot of Martini, four drops of pure orange juice, a touch of soda and 2 ice cubes."

"Clever little bugger," thought the barman to himself.

When the blind man appeared a few days later, the barman decided to have some fun. He found his wife Maureen in the office and asked her to rub a glass round her fanny. Then he took the glass to the blind man for him to smell.

"Well, I don't believe it!" exclaimed the blind man.

"How long has Maureen been working here?"

A shepherd's pie walks up to the bar and orders a pint of bitter.

"Sorry, mate," says the barman, "we don't serve food in here."

A stranger walks into a crowded bar and asks for a pint of beer. As he stands sipping it, someone suddenly shouts out '53' and the whole pub collapses in laughter. Someone else calls '46' and the crowd bursts into further merriment.

"Hey, what's going on?" asks the stranger.

The bartender replies,

"It's a local crowd in here and because everyone knows each other, they don't bother to tell their jokes anymore, they just call out the number of their joke."

"I see," says the stranger, and later when there's a sudden lull in the laughter, he calls out '19'.

There's a hushed silence. Bewildered, the stranger calls out '51'. Again there's no reaction. He turns to the bartender in amazement.

"I don't understand," he says, "Why aren't they laughing?"

The bartender gives a knowing shake of the head.

"Ah well, you see, it's the way you tell them."

After downing his 12th pint, the man's mood changed from happy to quarrelsome. Suddenly, he stood up and shouted to everyone in the room.

"Alright, you tossers! Everyone on this side of the room is a dirty bastard and everyone on that side is queer."

The room went quiet as everyone stared at him in astonishment. And then a man quietly got up and walked to the other side of the room.

"Where the hell are you going?" demanded the drunk, "looking for trouble, are you?"

"No, no," replied the man hastily, "it's just that I'm on the wrong side of the room."

Two men are drinking at a bar, one is Chinese, the other is Jewish. All of a sudden the Jewish man leans over and kicks the Chinese man on the leg.

"Hey! What was that for?" splutters the Chinese man.

"That's for Pearl Harbour," replies the Jewish man.

"Pearl Harbour? You silly sod, I'm Chinese. Pearl Harbour was the Japanese."

"So what?" comes the reply. "Chinese, Japanese, it's all the same to me."

The two men return to their drinks but five minutes later, the Chinese man leans over and punches the other in the arm.

"Hey! What's your game?" says the Jewish man angrily.

"That was for the Titanic," replies the Chinese man.

"The Titanic!" he says in astonishment, "but that was an iceberg."

"Iceberg, Goldberg, it's all the same to me."

Two men, off the oilrigs, arrive back in Aberdeen and head for the nearest bar. They order two pints of heavy and two whisky chasers which they down in a couple of minutes. Another round of drinks is ordered and then another five minutes later, followed by a third round five minutes after that. After the next round of drinks are placed in front of them, one man turns to his mate, lifts his glass and says 'Cheers!'

The other man replies impatiently,

"Hey, did we come here for a drink or just to talk crap all night?"

A stranger was sitting morosely at the end of the bar, staring into his pint of beer.

"Looks like you've got the whole world on your shoulders," remarked the barman sympathetically. "Are you alright?"

The stranger looked up sadly and replied,

"It's the curse of the drink. Booze makes you angry. It makes you want to pick a fight. It makes you want to shoot your wife. It makes you miss!"

A bear walks into a pub and asks for a pint of beer.

"Sorry, we don't serve beer to bears," comes the reply.

"I want a beer," demands the bear again.

"I've told you, we don't sell beer to bears," comes the equally forceful reply.

"Listen, if you don't give me a beer, I'll eat that woman at the other end of the bar," snarls the bear.

"You're still not having a beer."

So the bear eats the woman and says to the barman, "Right, now give me a pint of beer."

This time he is told "We don't serve beer to bears on drugs."

"What do you mean, on drugs?" asks the bear, scratching his head.

"Well, that was a barbitchuate!"

A woman goes into a bar and asks for a double entendre.

So the barman gives her one.

A man walked into a bar and saw a sign that said 'ham sandwiches £2.50, cheese sandwiches £2.00, hand job £12.'

"Do you do the hand jobs?" he asked the girl behind the bar.

"Yes," she said.

"Well, wash your hands and get me a cheese sandwich," he replied.

"What's up Steve?" asked the barman. "You're looking a bit pissed off."

"I am," replied Steve. "I just passed that new sperm bank that's opened round the corner and it's paying £25 for every sample."

He shook his head sadly. "I've let a fortune run through my fingers!"

A man walks into a bar and orders a pint of beer. He drinks half of it and pours the other half over his hand. As the evening progresses, he orders another five pints and each time drinks half of it and pours the rest over his hand. Eventually, the barman asks him why he does this.

"I'm getting my date drunk," comes the reply.

BLONDES

A blonde goes into a hotel room and its more than 3 hours before she comes out again.

"What happened to you?" asks her friend. "We all had dinner ages ago."

"I couldn't get out," she replies. "There were 3 doors in the room, one went into the bathroom, one into the wardrobe and the third had a 'do not disturb' notice hanging on the door."

A blonde was giving details of a car accident she'd had the day before.

"Now miss, can you tell me what gear you were in at the time of the collision?"

"Oh yes," she replied, "a beautiful blue trouser suit with matching shoes and handbag in navy blue."

What's the difference between an ironing board and a blonde?

It's hard to open the legs of an ironing board.

"Everyone on the floor!" screamed the robbers as they ran into the bank, armed with sawn-off shotguns.

"Get your clothes off and lie face down on the ground!"

Everyone did as they were ordered except a young blonde girl who lay down on her back.

"Psst!" whispered her friend, "turn over, this is a bank robbery, not the office party!"

What do you get when you turn three blondes upside down?

Two brunettes.

A brunette was walking down the middle of the road saying 74 to herself over and over again. A blonde spotted her and called out,

"What are you doing?"

"Don't you know?" replied the brunette. "It's great fun. You should try it."

So the blonde walked into the middle for the road and began chanting '74, 74,74...'

Suddenly, a lorry appeared and knocked her down.

The brunette continued,

"75, 75, 75..."

A blonde got stuck in some quicksand and it wasn't long before only her head and shoulders were left above the ground. Fortunately, one of the strongest men from the local village was passing by and he heard the blonde's cries for help.

"Don't panic!" he called, "just grab my hand and I'll soon pull you out."

But no matter how hard he pulled, the poor blonde just sank lower and lower.

"I can't understand it," said the strongman. "I'll have to go and get some help."

"No wait," shouted the blonde in panic. "Would it help if I took my feet out of the stirrups?"

A ventriloquist is doing his act at the summer show and telling a few blonde jokes. Suddenly, a blonde woman stands up at the back and shouts out angrily,

"You bastard, it's always the same, telling everyone that blondes are stupid. Well, we're not."

"Look, I'm sorry," says the ventriloquist, apologetically. "It's just the act; I didn't mean to…"

"I'm not talking to you," interrupts the blonde heatedly, "it's that little bastard on your knee who's telling all the jokes."

BRAINLESS

"Doctor, doctor," said the anguished man. "I can't satisfy my wife in bed any more, what shall I do?"

The doctor sent him along to see a big black man who specialised in helping couples with this type of problem.

"When you're making love," he was told, "the black man will wave a fan above your heads and this will help stimulate your wife into having an orgasm."

So the scene was set for the following evening. As the black man waved the fan, the couple did their bit, but alas the woman remained unsatisfied. Heartbroken, the embarrassed husband said to the black man, "I bet you couldn't do any better!", so they changed places and as the husband waved the fan, the couple writhed beneath him. In no time at all the woman had a marvellous orgasm, and the husband said bitterly,

"You see, that's how you're supposed to wave the fan!"

An old couple were having breakfast and listening to the 7 o'clock news.

"… And finally a weather warning. There will be 2-6 inches of snow today so everyone is asked to park on the odd numbered side of the street."

The old man went off and parked his car. The following morning, there was another weather report.

"The snow will continue to fall today, up to 6 inches, so people are asked to park on the even numbered side of the street."

The old man did as requested. On the third day, the old man looked out of his window and exclaimed, "Martha, the weather's even worse today. I don't fancy going outside."

"Well don't," replied his wife, "leave the car in the garage today."

Three hillbillies walked into a fast food restaurant and took a table by the window. One of them drew his friends' attention to a sign above the counter and the next moment, they all had their todgers out, wanking away as fast as possible. The waitress came over and looked at them in amazement.

"What the hell do you think you're doing?" she demanded.

They replied,

"We saw the sign up there saying 'first come, first served' and we're starving."

Two men were walking down the street when one said,

"Look out Sean, that looks like dog shit."

Sean bent down and touched it with his finger.

"It feels like dog shit," he said, "hold on," and the next moment, he put some to his lips.

"Yes, it tastes like dog shit as well. It's a good thing we didn't step in it!"

Three men were chatting in the pub and the conversation turned to children.

"We were going to call our son Gerald," said the first man, "but he was born on April 23 so we called him George, after St. George."

"Well, that's a coincidence," said the second man, "because our son was born on St. David's Day, we called him David."

"Would you believe it!" exclaimed the Irishman. "The same thing happened with my son, Pancake."

Patrick and Stan are walking down the lane when they see Molloy swimming around in a field of grass.

"Now look at that," remarks Patrick, "what a stupid bugger, have you ever seen anything so silly. He shouldn't be there."

"Don't you think you ought to go and get him?" says Sean.

"I would," replies Patrick, "only I can't swim!"

A lorry driver and his mate were driving down a country lane when they came to a sign that said 'Caution: low bridge 9'10".

"What shall we do?" asked the driver's mate, "this truck has got to be at least 10'6"."

The driver got out of the cab and had a good look round.

"Come on," he said furtively. "I can't see any cops around, we'll chance it."

Three simple men scooped the prizes in the local raffle. The first won a crate of beer, the second won a side of pork and the third won the booby prize, a toilet brush. The following week they met for a drink and the first remarked,

"Well, that was a bit of luck last week, I really enjoyed my beer."

"Yes, indeedy," said the second man, nodding his head, "the pork was great, especially the crackling."

"And what about you?" they said, looking at the third man.

"Well, I was a bit disappointed, to be honest," he replied. "I think I'll just go back to using paper."

An Englishman, a Scotsman and an Irishman escape from Dartmoor Prison and disappear into the surrounding countryside hotly pursued by a group of prison officers with tracker dogs.

"Quick!" whispers the Englishman. "If we don't do something soon, those dogs are going to hunt us down. Get up a tree as soon as you can."

The Englishman scrambles up a beech tree and lies very still. Suddenly, there's an excited barking of dogs and the prison officers burst through the undergrowth and surround the tree.

"I think there's something up there!" one of them says excitedly

"Hey, who's up there?" he yells.

The Englishman mimics the sound of a pigeon.

"Damn, it's only a bird," they say and leave disappointed.

Moments later, the dogs start barking again and surround another tree.

"Who's up there?" shout the officers."

The Scotsman, hiding in the branches, calls 'twit twoo, twit twoo.'

"A bloody owl," they grumble and continue on their way. Then for a third time the dogs start barking frantically.

"Right, gotcha!" shouts one of the officers. "Who's up there?"

The Irishman replies, "neigh, neigh…"

Did you hear about Marvin, the actor?

He cut his leg off to play Long John Silver. He didn't get the part though. He had the wrong leg amputated.

"Bob!" called the newspaper editor, "did you go and check out that story about the woman who could sing soprano and alto at the same time?"

"Yeah," replied Bob. "But there was no story. The woman had two heads."

A huge man walked into the bar and shouted at the top of his voice,

"OK you lot, which one of you is John Austin?"

A little man called out,

"Over here, it's me."

The big man went over and punched him in the mouth, knocking out one of his teeth. The little man just stood there and laughed, so the huge man hit him again and broke his nose. Still the little man laughed. This made the huge man even more angry.

"What the hell are you laughing at?" he roared.

"Cos I've been kidding you," he replied. "I'm not really John Austin at all. I'm Derek Fuckwitt."

Said the weak wally to his wife,

"Now come on dear, the boss is being very fair. He said he'd really like to give me the day off, but if he did, then he'd have to do it for everyone whose wife had just given birth to sextuplets!"

Two simple men decide to go on a weekend fishing trip. They pop down to the local store and get fully kitted out with all the right gear for good weather and bad... plus hundreds of pounds worth of fishing tackle and camping equipment.

After fishing for two days on the bank of the river, they manage to catch just one small fish between them.

"Bloody hell!" exclaims one, "that damned fish has cost us nearly £1,000."

"Well then," says the other, "it's a good thing we didn't catch anymore!"

An attractive young woman answers the telephone one night and is confronted by an obscene caller. In great detail he tells her all the sexual perversions he would like to perform on her but after 10 minutes of this she interrupts him, saying,

"This is amazing. You mean you can tell all this just by me saying hello?"

Two simple men park up outside the cinema and jump out of the car. They've just closed the doors when the driver curses,

"Bloody hell, I've left the keys in the car and the door's locked."

"Well, let's call the garage," said the other.

"No, that's no good. All the phones round here are broken."

"OK, let's smash a window."

"Oh no, I couldn't bear to do that, it'll cost a fortune."

"Well you'd better hurry up and think of something 'cos it's beginning to rain and the hood's down!"

Two simple-minded men stopped for a meal at a motorway cafe and discovered it was running a special competition. If you picked the correct number from that day's menu, you won a session of free sex.

"Come on Jake, let's have a go!" urged Dan.

"I'll have number 14, the tomato soup," said Dan, "and my mate will have number 5, egg and chips."

The waiter took down the order and looked at their expectant faces.

"I'm sorry," he said shaking his head, "you've picked the wrong numbers."

During the following two weeks, the men went back on six occasions but failed every time to pick the winner.

"I think this whole competition is a fake!" complained Jake on his seventh try.

"Oh no," replied Dan, "it's on the level. My wife won twice last week."

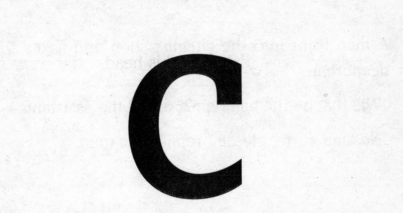

CHEMIST

A man walked into a chemist shop and asked the feisty young salesgirl for one hundred condoms.

"Well fuck me!" she exclaimed.

"In that case, make it 101," he replied.

A man went into the chemist shop and asked for a deodorant.

"Will that be the ball type?" asked the assistant.

"No, underarm, please," replied the man.

"Do you sell extra large condoms?" the woman asked the chemist.

"Yes we do," he said, "would you like a packet?"

"No thanks, but do you mind if I wait here until somebody does?"

CHURCH

A woman was in church one Sunday morning when she had a terrible coughing fit.

Later, a friend turned to the woman's husband and commented,

"That's a bad cough your wife has, it certainly drew everyone's attention."

"Oh yes," replied the husband. "She was wearing a new hat."

A rich man moved into the neighbourhood and went to church on the Sunday morning where he listened to a spellbinding sermon. After the service was over, he took the vicar by the hand and shook it vigorously.

"That was the best damned sermon I've ever heard," he said forcefully.

"Well thank you very much," replied the vicar somewhat taken aback by the man's gushing enthusiasm. "But erm... I'd rather you didn't curse," he said.

The rich man continued,

"Yes, you can count on me to be at this service every week, it was bloody marvellous."

"Good, good," replied the vicar, "but please don't swear."

"In fact, it was so damned great, I put £1,000 in the collection," he added.

"Fuck me!" said the vicar.

After Sunday service, the vicar greeted his congregation as they left the church. Last to leave was Martha who was obviously quite distressed.

"Martha, my dear, what's wrong?" he asked, looking concerned.

"It's my husband," she replied, sobbing, "he's dead."

"Oh I'm sorry to hear that!" exclaimed the vicar. "Did he say anything before he died? What were his last words?"

"Put that gun down," she replied.

A churchman was celebrating 25 years in the parish and as a special thank you, the congregation arranged for him to spend two weeks in Florida. He arrived at the hotel and was shown to his room where he found a naked girl lying across the bed. Immediately, he rang up his parish and told them how angry he was at what they had done. On hearing this, the girl got up to go but the man said quickly, "Hold on, I'm angry at them, I'm not angry at you."

The vicar's sermon had been going for 15 minutes when a man in the congregation stood up and walked out. After the service a woman came up to the vicar, full of apologies.

"I'm so very sorry my husband walked out," she said, "but he's been sleepwalking ever since he was a little boy."

COMPANY MATTERS

John was only 19 when he suffered terrible injuries that left him without any ears. He was determined to become successful despite the disability and by the time he was 40 he had built up a prestigious international company and was a millionaire many times over.

The time came when he needed a good 'right hand' man so from all the applications received, he whittled it down to 3.

The first man was interviewed and showed great business acumen. John was impressed. However at the end of the interview he asked the final, important question.

"Do you notice anything different about me?"

"You've got no ears," came the reply.

Poor John, he was so touchy about his appearance that he dismissed the man immediately.

The second candidate was interviewed and she was even more impressive than the first. Then he came to the final question.

"And how would you describe me?" he asked.

"You've got no ears," she replied, so she didn't get the job either.

So it came to the third person. The man strode in confidently and did a perfect interview. John was extremely impressed. He asked the final question.

"And what about me, is there anything you notice?"

"Yes," replied the man "you wear contact lenses."

John was overjoyed. "That's right, how did you know?"

"Because it would be hard to wear glasses without any fucking ears," answered the man.

Two men went for a job at a computer company and had to fill in application forms and complete a short test. Afterwards, the personnel officer called them in and remarked,

"Well, you both answered all the questions very well, except for one question which neither of you knew. So I am pleased to offer the job to Mr. Copeland and I wish Mr. Forester good luck on his future endeavours."

"But how can you choose between us?" asked Mr. Forester, "if you say we both answered all the other questions so well."

"Well, it was the way you didn't answer the question you didn't know," came the reply.

"Mr. Copeland wrote 'I don't know' and you, Mr. Forester, wrote 'neither do I'."

A builder was at the top of a high scaffold, when he realised he needed a saw. Two floors below him, he spotted his mate so he called to him.

"Pete!" he hollered "I" he said pointing to his eye, "need" he continued, pointing to his knee "a saw" he finished, making a sawing movement with his hands.

But then to his astonishment, his mate took out his willy and began masturbating. So quickly, the builder came down to where his mate was standing and said,

'Bill, what the hell are you doing?"

"Listen, I was just letting you know I'm coming," replied his mate.

The husband returned from work and enthused about his new secretary.

"You know, she wears a blue and yellow bra," he said, "the colours of my favourite football team." Then, seeing his wife's face, he added hastily, "but it's no big deal. It just makes me feel good."

The following night, he returned home and said to his wife,

"You won't believe this but she told me she also wears blue and yellow knickers. Of course, it's no big deal, but it makes me feel good."

A couple of days went by before his wife greeted him at the door with the words,

"I've got a new boss at work. His dick's three inches longer than yours. But it's no big deal, it just makes me feel good!"

A lady who sold household goods door-to-door had just finished visiting a block of flats and called for the lift. As she stepped inside and pressed for ground level, she was forced to let rip an almighty fart.

"Oh well, never mind," she thought, "at least there's no one else in here."

Nevertheless, she got some pine air freshener from her bag and sprayed it around the lift. Then, to her horror, the lift stopped on the 12th floor and a dishevelled man got in. Immediately, he began to make loud sniffing noises and the woman felt obliged to remark upon his behaviour.

"Is there something wrong?" she asked innocently.

"I'm not sure," he replied, "but it smells like someone just shit a Christmas tree."

A man was walking along the street with two screaming babies under his arm.

"Dear me!" exclaimed a passer-by. "They must be hungry, why don't you feed them? You can't be much of a father."

"Listen lady," said the man impatiently. "I'm not their father. I'm a condom salesman and I'm taking these two complaints back to the company."

A man had started work in a clothing factory but after being there 6 weeks, the boss noticed that he always had Fridays off.

"Now look here Pete," said the boss, "you've fitted in here very well and you're a good worker, but you're never here on Fridays. Why is that? Are you sick?"

"Yeah," replied Pete, "I am." He hesitated for a moment and then continued. "It's my brother-in-law. Every Thursday, he gets paid, goes down the pub, drinks till he's really pissed then goes home and beats up my sister. On my way to work on Friday morning, I always pop in to see how she is and after comforting her, somehow we always end up in bed."

"What!" exclaimed the boss in horror. "Are you telling me you shag your sister?"

"Well, I told you I was sick," replied Pete.

The General Manager of a local company prided himself on knowing what was going on with the workforce. However, one evening he returned home from work in a foul mood.

"What's wrong?" asked his wife.

"Bloody Jenkins, in packing," he replied. "Asked for the afternoon off to go to his uncle's funeral. Well, I wasn't having that. I thought it was the old trick to get to see the football match, so I followed him."

"So what happened? Did your team lose?"

"What team? It was his uncle's bloody funeral!"

A delivery truck arrives at the gates of a science laboratory and the driver is directed to a building on the far side of the factory site.

"I've got a batch of cages outside for you," he tells the scientist, "where shall I put them?"

The scientist points to a separate room and is just walking away when the deliveryman calls to him,

"Hey, mate, what do you want all these cages for anyway?"

"We're going to be keeping some lawyers in them," he replies. "They're going to be used for a number of experiments."

The deliveryman scratches his head in puzzlement,

"Don't you normally use rats for that?"

"Yeah, but we get so attached to rats."

★

An English businessman was invited to a state banquet while on a visit to Moscow. He was relieved to find himself sitting next to a stunning blonde who smiled warmly at him as he sat down. Halfway through the meal, having drunk a few vodkas, he knocked his napkin on the floor and fondled the girl's ankle as he picked it up. Much to his

disappointment, the girl did not react. A little later, the man dropped his knife and this time when he picked it up, he fondled the girl's knee. Again, there was no reaction. But then suddenly, as his hand moved further up her leg, she began scribbling furiously on the back of her serviette, which she passed over to him.

It read, "When you get to where you want to be, please show no surprise, whatsoever. Yours sincerely, Arthur St.John Parkinson MI5."

The Managing Director rose to his feet and glared at the men sitting round the boardroom table.

"Right!" he demanded, "who's been having an affair with my secretary?"

The room went silent.

"Okay," continued the M.D, "who hasn't had an affair with my secretary?"

Again, there was silence and then a hand was slowly raised.

"Actually Sir, I haven't," said a small, shaky voice.

"In that case, you sack her," ordered the M.D.

A girl came out of the interview room looking very pleased with herself.

"I think I've got the job," she told the receptionist, "there's only one other person waiting."

"Well let me just give you a word of warning," replied the receptionist, "your new boss thinks he'd God's gift to women. He'll have you over the desk, ripping your dress off, in less than an hour."

"Thanks for the tip," she replied, "I'll just have to make sure I'm wearing old clothes."

The managing director called for his chief accountant.

"Andrew, I'm very disappointed," he said. "I have a report in front of me here, describing your disgraceful behaviour at the office party last night. It says, and I quote, Andrew was seen dancing naked around a tree in the company courtyard. Tied to the tree was another man singing at the top of his voice! Now, what have you to say for yourself? What were you doing?"

"Well, you ought to know," retorted Andrew. "You were the one tied to the tree!"

A very obese man had been dieting for three months but one day he arrived at work carrying a huge jam and double cream doughnut. His work friends admonished him.

"Come on Bill, you're on a diet, you shouldn't be having that."

Bill replied, "It was just meant to be. This morning, as I drove to work, I saw this doughnut in the baker shop and I thought to myself, if there's a parking place nearby then it's God's wish that I should have it. And guess what, after driving round 10 times, there was a parking place!"

A woman was drinking in the company bar when 3 of her male colleagues came to join her.

"Damn this bloody audit," said one. "I'm really screwed."

"Me too," said another. "I'm bloody screwed as well."

The third man shook his head in despair.

"And I'm really fucked," he said sorrowfully.

In the silence that followed, the woman said,

"Hey, guys, can you tell me how I can get audited?"

CONFESSION

The priest had been in his new parish for 18 months and already he was fed up with the number of people coming to him in confession and talking about their affairs. Eventually he told his congregation to use another word.

"From now on, I would like you to say you have fallen, instead of telling me you're having an affair," he said.

The new word worked well. Then it came to the priest's summer holiday and another priest came to stand in for a month but was not made aware of the new arrangement. After 2 weeks of listening to the daily confessions, he was astonished at what he was being told so he went to see the Lord Mayor.

"I'm very pleased with the local people's morals," he said. "They have very little to confess to me. I think something should be done about the state of the pavements, though, because people seem to be falling down all the time."

The Lord Mayor smiled, knowingly.

"Oh, there's nothing to worry about there, Father," he replied.

"Well I think there is," persisted the priest. "Your wife has fallen 3 times this week."

An old woman of 86 hobbled into confession and told the priest she had sinned.

"I have committed adultery with a 22 year old boy," she said.

"My goodness!" exclaimed the priest. "When was this?"

"Fifty years ago," replied the old woman, "I just like to tell people about it from time to time."

"Forgive me Father, for I have sinned," said the man in the confessional.

"What is it my son?"

"During the war I hid a resistance fighter in my attic."

"But that's not a sin. That's a very courageous act," said the priest.

"But I charged him 20 francs every week of his stay."

"Hmm," mused the priest. "That's not something to be proud about, but at least you risked your life and saved his."

"Just one more thing," continued the man, "do you think I ought to tell him the war's over?"

"Forgive me Father for I have sinned," said the man in the confessional.

"What is it, my son?" came the reply.

"Well, last week I went round to my girlfriend's flat but she wasn't in. The only person there was her flat mate and we ended up having sex."

"Oh dear," replied the priest.

"And then a couple of days later, I popped round to my mate's house but he'd gone down the pub. The only person there was his wife and we ended up having sex."

"Oh dear," remarked the priest again.

The man continued

"So then last night, I went into the local pub and it was empty. Everyone had gone to watch the darts team playing away. There was only Mandy serving behind the bar so we ended up having sex. What shall I do?"

But there was no answer from the other side of the screen.

"Father, are you there?" demanded the man. No answer came, so he began looking for the priest and eventually found him hiding in the pews.

"What are you doing there?" he exclaimed.

"Well, I suddenly realised that you and I were alone together," replied the priest.

A man went to the confessional and told the priest he'd almost had sex with a married woman the night before.

"I don't understand," said the priest, "what do you mean by almost?"

"Well, we rubbed our naked bodies together but I didn't actually put it in."

"Well, in God's sight rubbing together is the same as putting it in, so you will say 20 Hail Marys and put £20 in the collecting box for the poor."

So on the way out, the man went up to the box with his £20 note but after a moment put the money back in his wallet and walked out.

"Hey," said the priest, who had see this, "why didn't you put the £20 in the box?"

"Well I rubbed the £20 against the box," replied the man, "and in God's sight rubbing is the same as putting it in."

COUPLES

It was Friday night and Bob was down the pub with his mate Pete.

"Going to the match tomorrow?" asked Bob

"Oh, I dunno," replied Pete, "my wife's not keen on me being out every Saturday."

"Listen, that's no problem. On Saturday morning, take her upstairs, strip her naked and give her the best shagging you can. When she's really enjoying herself then tell her you're going to the match."

On Monday, the two men met up for a lunchtime pint.

"Didn't see you on Saturday," remarked Bob, "did you try what I said?"

"Yeah!" replied Pete. "I took the wife upstairs, ripped her clothes off, saw her lying there on the bed and thought 'Oh bugger it, the team's not been playing that well anyway'!"

A couple were at the cinema.

"Are you comfortable there?" he asked her.

"Yes thanks," she replied.

"I hope the seat's not torn and covered in crumbs," he continued.

"Oh no, it's fine," she said.

"And have you got a good view?" he persisted.

"Yes, it's fine," she replied.

"Great," said her date. "Swap seats."

The unfaithful husband went to pick up his wife Connie from a conference and was startled to see her leaving the building with his mistress. He hid from sight until his mistress had gone, then picked up his wife and drove home casually remarking, "Did I see you leaving with a friend?"

"Oh no," she replied, "she was just one of the delegates. What a tart! Flirted with anything in trousers and kept a few beds warm at night."

The husband was dismayed to hear this and was determined to find out from his mistress about his wife's behaviour. The next time he saw her, he casually asked about the conference and the sort of people that were there.

"I think I heard that one of the speakers came from my neck of the woods," he said.

"Oh yes," replied the mistress, "that would be Connie. She wasn't much fun. She came with her husband and they spent most of the time in their room!"

A couple went to the marriage guidance councillor.

"What's the problem?" he asked.

The wife answered, "Well thingie, here, complains that I don't pay him enough attention."

The wife nagged him relentlessly.

"It's just not good enough, Arthur. Every night you're down the pub and you never get back before midnight, leaving me here all alone time and time again. I've had just about enough!" she exclaimed.

So on this one particular night, Arthur took his wife along with him.

"What'll you have?" he asked.

"I'll have what you have," she replied.

A few minutes later, two pints of bitter were placed before them. Arthur took a sip, then his wife took a sip.

"Urrgh, this is awful!" she spluttered, "How the hell can you drink it?"

"You see!" replied Arthur triumphantly, "and you think I come out each night to enjoy myself."

A hillbilly husband and wife had been picked to appear on a late night quiz programme about married couples. The quiz had been going well until the compere asked,

"And where was the strangest place you ever made out?"

"That's got to be up the ass," they replied innocently.

A woman walked into a tattoo parlour and asked the tattooist if he would put a picture of a turkey on her left buttock and a picture of Father Christmas and a reindeer on her right buttock.

Now the tattooist was used to the strangest requests but this was so unusual he had to ask why.

"Well," replied the woman, "My husband's always complaining that there's never anything to eat between Thanksgiving and Christmas."

In her courting days, Jackie went out with a sailor and as a sign of her love she had his face tattooed on her left breast. But the passion went out of their relationship and they parted. The following year she met a soldier and had his face tattooed on her right breast but again, their love was short-lived.

Some years later, she met and married a pilot and one day as she emerged from the shower, he looked at her and laughed.

"What's that for?" she said angrily.

"I was just imagining the long faces on those two fellas in 10 years time!" he replied.

A newcomer to the neighbourhood was shocked and alarmed to see a couple acting outrageously in the field outside their house. The woman was tugging her tits up and down while the man was masturbating.

"Oh don't worry about them, they're deaf," said a voice behind him.

"She's telling him to milk the cow and he's telling her to go fuck herself."

A middle-aged couple were getting ready for bed. As she stood there naked, she said,

"Oh Tony, do you remember when we first met, you said you'd fuck my brains out and suck my tits dry?"

"Oh yes," he replied, looking at her, "and it seems I did a good job."

A woman was determined to lose 2 stones in weight and to help her keep to the strict diet, she put a pin-up of a supermodel in the fridge. It worked well. Every time she opened the fridge door and saw the picture, it would stop her from taking out any food. Unfortunately, it didn't work for her husband. He put on weight because he was forever opening the fridge door!

COURTING

Poor Doreen! She's had no luck. A few months ago a man asked if he could change her name to his. Of course she was delighted and said, yes.

Now he calls her Jimmy!

A man was desperate to meet someone of the opposite sex but he had low self-esteem because one of his eyes was made of wood. He got more and more despairing of the situation until his friends urged him to join a dating club. So he took the plunge and signed up. As luck would have it, a woman joined at the same time, and like him, she lacked confidence because she was very fat. Photos were exchanged and although both could see the other's shortcomings, they decided to meet and go for dinner. It was a great success. They found many shared interests and there was never an awkward moment.

"Would you like another glass of wine?" he asked.

"Oh yes, please," she replied.

"Would you like a coffee?" he asked later.

"Thank you," she replied happily.

As they left the restaurant, the man plucked up the courage to ask her for a kiss.

"Oh yes," she agreed.

As they kissed and cuddled, the man then asked the big question.

"Would you like to come back to my place?" he said nervously.

"Oh wouldn't I!" she enthused.

"What!" he exclaimed angrily "what gives you the right to call me wooden eye, you fat bitch?"

A widow of only a few months goes out on her first date since the death of her husband. They have a great evening but when he makes a move, she holds him back saying, "I can't. I'm wearing black knickers because I'm still in mourning for my husband."

They continue to date, although it never goes past a goodnight kiss at the end of the evening.

Then a few weeks later in the middle of a passionate embrace, he gets out a packet of black condoms.

"What are those for?" she asks.

"I'd like to give you my condolences!" he replies.

A man met a beautiful girl in the pub and couldn't believe his luck when she invited him back to her place. Very soon, they were upstairs, stripping off but just as he was about to throw himself at her she suddenly stopped and said,

"Oh, I should have told you, I went to the doctors today and he told me I had either VD or TB, but I can't remember which."

Even this news couldn't dampen the man's ardour. He rang up the girl's doctor straight away.

"I'm sorry," said the doctor. "I had two girls in today so I can't remember."

"Oh no!" exclaimed the man, "what shall I do?"

"Well chase her around the room a few times and if she starts to cough then go ahead and make love," came the reply.

Melvin was comforting his old friend.

"Don't worry," he said "I'll find a woman for your son to marry, bring him down to the club next week."

The following Saturday his friend's son arrived and was introduced to Moira. The boy turned away in disgust.

"Ugh, she's awful," he said. "She's got a face like the back of a bus, a big moustache, one eye and very little hair."

"You don't have to whisper," said Melvin. "She's deaf as well."

The man pulled up outside his girlfriend's house and turned to give her a goodnight kiss. As he did so, he also pulled out his John Thomas and put it into her hand.

"How dare you!" she exclaimed, getting out of the car quickly. When she'd walked up the garden path to her front door, she turned and shouted angrily,

"I've only got two words to say to you, get lost!"

"Aarrgh!" he screamed back. "I've got two for you, LET GO."

The man parked the car in Lovers' Lane and for a few moments the young couple just sat and listened to the countryside noises.

"Oh it's lovely here," enthused the girl. "I think I can even hear the crickets."

"That's not a cricket," replied the man, "that's a zip."

It was 1965 and Melvyn had arrived at his girlfriend's house to take her out for the evening. While he was waiting, he chatted to her father.

"We're going to meet some friends at the coffee bar," he said "and then go on to the flicks."

"Don't you fancy going off to screw?" asked the father.

Melvyn looked shocked as he replied,

"Screw sir? Do you really approve of that?"

"Oh yes," said the father "I'm not old fashioned and I know my daughter really enjoys a good screw. She can do it for hours on end."

"Well in that case, we will," replied Melvyn eagerly, and some moments later he and his girlfriend left the house.

But it wasn't long before she returned in tears.

"Oh dad!" she sobbed. "It's called the twist, you fool!"

The courting couple were looking for somewhere private but the gates of the park had been locked for the night.

"Never mind," said the boy, "if you stand on this (showing her his erect John Thomas) you'll be able to get over the wall."

"That may be so," she replied, "but how will I get back?"

A young couple were parked in lovers lane and after a bout of heavy petting, the boy whispered urgently.

"Go on Cath, let me put it in."

"Oh no", she replied, "We said we'd wait until we were married."

"Well just a little" he gasped "let me just put the head in to see what it's like."

She finally agreed but as soon as he began, he got carried away and thrust as far as he could go, in and out frantically.

"Oh George!" exclaimed the girl, "I can't wait, I can't wait, put it all in, please!"

George thought quickly and replied,

"Oh no Cath, we can't, remember our promise."

The young man walked his girlfriend to her front door and started to kiss her.

"How about a quick blow job?" he said, "before I go."

"Oh no," she replied, "not here, anyone could pass and see us."

"Oh come on," he coaxed, "it won't take long, just a tiny little blow job."

"No, it wouldn't be right," she said adamantly.

For the next couple of minutes the man tried unsuccessfully to change her mind, then suddenly the front door was yanked open and a young girl stood there sleepy-eyed, obviously just having got out of bed.

"Dad says hurry up and give him a blow job, or he'll come down and do it, or I will, or someone will just as long as you take your bloody hand off the intercom."

The couple had been out on their first date and finished the evening back at her place in bed. As he struggled with her clothes, she said,

"You know I'm not that sort of girl really."

"I know," he replied, somewhat distracted. The girl burst into tears.

"What's wrong?" he asked looking alarmed.

"You… You're the first one," she sobbed.

"What? The first one to make love to you?"

"No, the first one to believe I'm not that kind of girl," she replied.

COURTROOM DRAMA

"Before I come to a decision on these divorce proceedings, does anyone wish to speak?" asked the judge.

The lawyer for the husband stood up and replied,

"M'lud, may I just bring to your attention once again, that what my client did was out of chivalry. Since when was it wrong to open a door for a lady?"

"I'm not disputing a chivalrous act," replied the judge, "but I think you're overlooking the fact that the car was travelling at 70 mph at the time."

The judge looked at the old woman and said, "Before I pass sentence, do you have anything to say in your defence?"

The old woman got to her feet and replied,

"Yes Your Honour. The evening that it happened, I was sitting quietly on my porch when this beautiful young man came up to me and started to kiss my hand. Then he kissed my face and began rubbing himself up against me. He put his hands underneath my blouse and fondled my breasts. It was so wonderful, I opened my legs, Your Honour, and asked him to go all the way."

The old woman shook her head sadly as she remembered that evening. She continued, "That's when he laughed and said April Fool! So I picked up my rifle and shot him."

Just before the jury retired to contemplate the case, the judge summed up the evidence and finished by saying,

"Let us not forget that if someone's statement in court is different from their original interview with the police, this does not necessarily indicate a sign of dishonesty.

Why, even I have found myself in a similar situation. For instance, this morning I could have sworn that I was wearing my gold watch, but after some thought, realised I'd left it on the washstand in the bathroom."

The jury left the courtroom and were out all day, so the judge did not return home until late. When he walked through the door, he was surprised to see policemen all over the house.

"Oh Ronald, your gold watch has been stolen!" exclaimed his wife. "Nothing else, just the watch."

"My watch!" he exclaimed. "Now how would anyone know it was there!"

"I don't know," sobbed the wife. "It's just been one of those days. There's been any amount of people wanting to check the water pressure in the bathroom."

"All rise!" called the clerk of the court as the judge arrived for the proceedings.

"Jeffrey Duvall, you are accused of murdering your wife on the night of January 6 by hammering her to death. How do you plead?" asked the judge.

"Guilty, M'lud."

Hearing this, a man at the back of the court shouted out, "You bastard!"

"Quiet!" demanded the judge, who continued, "You are also accused of murdering your mother-in-law, on the same night, at the same address, by using a hammer on her skull. How do you plead?"

"Guilty M'lud."

Again, there was a commotion at the back of the court as the same man stood up and shouted abuse. "You bastard!" he yelled again.

"You Sir!" said the judge, pointing at him, "one more outburst like that and you'll be in contempt of court. Who are you?"

"I'm his neighbour," replied the man, "and he swore blind he hadn't borrowed my hammer!"

"Now madam," said the judge, "you are requesting a divorce on the grounds that your husband is a flat slob. What exactly do you mean?"

The woman thought for a moment and replied,

"Well, for instance, when we're in a café, he always drinks with his pinkie sticking out."

"Madam, there's nothing wrong with that. In some circles it's thought the height of good manners to drink tea with your little finger sticking out."

"Who said anything about his little finger?" she replied.

The judge looked over his glasses at the man standing before him.

"You are filing for divorce on the grounds of your wife's adultery. Is that so?"

"Yes, Your Honour."

"And do you have proof of this adultery. Can you name the man involved? Have you seen him?"

"Well erm, no, not exactly, Your Honour. But I can tell you when I first knew about it," he added confidently. "It was one weekend 3 months ago. I had been away all week on a conference and didn't arrive home until late on Friday night. In the morning, we made mad passionate love when suddenly the woman in the flat next to us started banging on the wall and shouting, "Don't start all that again, for fuck's sake! Have you not had enough this week?"

"The priest was walking home from morning service when he passed a toad sitting on the edge of the road. To his amazement, the toad began to speak.

'Help me please, help me,' said the toad. 'A wicked spell has been cast over me. I'm not a toad at all, but a 16-year-old boy. Please help me break the spell. All you have to do is show me some kindness by taking me home with you and putting me in your nice warm bed.' The priest being of course a charitable man he naturally obliged.

And that, Your Honour, is the case for the defence."

"Will the defendant please rise," said the judge.

"Madam, you have been found guilty of killing your husband by pushing him off a 10 storey balcony. Before I pass sentence, is there anything you would like to say?"

"Yes, Your Honour," said the 84 year old woman. "When I came home and found my husband in bed with another woman I guessed that if he could make love aged 96 years old, he could also fly."

"Do you have any questions?" the judge asked learned counsel.

"Yes, M'lud. Mrs Smith, is it true that you committed adultery on the day of the 27 March, on the roof of the Dome, dressed in a baby doll outfit with a 60 year old man wearing nothing but a necktie."

Mrs Smith smiled and replied,

"Can you repeat the date, please?"

"This is a very serious matter Miss X. Please answer truthfully," urged the judge.

"We have been told that you spent the night with this man in a hotel outside Leeds. Have you anything to say?"

"Yes m'lud. It wasn't my fault. I was deceived."

"Really! What do you mean?"

"Well, he told the receptionist I was his wife!"

Paddy was walking down by the canal when he saw a man throw himself in the water. Quick as a flash he jumped in after him and dragged the man to the side. But no sooner had he loosened his grip than the man plunged back in. Three times, Paddy dragged the man out and after the third time the man gasped,

"Okay, okay, I won't go back in."

True enough, he didn't go back in. He ran to the nearest tree and hanged himself.

On the day of the inquest, the coroner remarked to Paddy,

"I don't understand. You'd saved him three times from the canal, why didn't you cut him down from the tree?"

"Well, your honour Sir, I thought he was hanging himself up to dry," replied Paddy sadly.

"So, Mr. Smith, you want a divorce. On what grounds?" asked the Judge.

"On the grounds that I live in a 2-storey house," he replied.

"I fail to see the significance of that," questioned the Judge, "please explain."

"Well, Your Honour, one story is 'I've got a headache' and the second story is 'It's the wrong time of the month!"

D

DEATH

Two women were taking tea at the Ritz and catching up on family news.

"I was so sorry to hear your Stanley had died," remarked the first woman. "I hope you've been able to carry on life without him."

"Yes, thank you," came the reply. "He was such a kind and thoughtful man. Do you know, hours before he died he gave me three envelopes which he told me would ease the burden once he'd gone."

"How thoughtful!" remarked the first woman. "What was in them?"

"Well, the first had £700 in it to buy a coffin. The second had £3,000 in it and a note saying 'Use this to give me a good send-off'. And let me tell you, they'll be talking about his funeral for years to come!"

"And what about the third envelope?"

"Oh that said 'Use this cheque for £4,000 to buy a nice stone.' So I did," she said, holding out her finger to show a diamond ring, "what do you think of it?"

"I'm afraid to tell you Mr. Jones, that you're dying."

"Oh no, how long have I got?"

"20…"

"20 what? Twenty weeks, twenty days, 20 minutes?"

"20, 19, 18, 17…"

A woman dies and her grieving family come to the funeral parlour to pay their last respects.

"Oh no!" gasps her daughter. "I really wanted you to bury my mother in her red dress but this one is blue!"

The funeral director looks aghast, excuses himself and pops next door. To his horror he realises they've made a mistake when he sees a second body clothed in the red dress. He returns and says apologetically

"I am so sorry. If you'd just like to go back to the lounge, I'll have this problem sorted as soon as possible."

In less than five minutes, he calls the family back and they are delighted to find the woman is dressed in the right clothes. A little while later, the family leave and the assistant undertaker turns to his boss and says,

"Good gracious, that was the quickest change of clothes I've ever seen. How did you manage to do it so fast?"

"I didn't," replies the funeral director, "I just changed heads."

"I'm so sorry Bob, I hear you buried your wife last week."

"Had to," replied Bob, "She was dead."

Half way through the morning shift the manager of the warehouse noticed one of his men was crying.

"What's wrong Paddy?" he asked.

"It's my father," said Paddy. "I got a phone call this morning from Dublin to say he'd died."

"Oh that's terrible," replied the manager. "Why don't you take the rest of the day off."

"That's very kind of you Sir, but no thanks. It's easier to keep working."

A couple of hours later, the manager was concerned to see that Paddy was crying again.

"What's happened?" he asked.

"I've just had a phone call from my brother and his father has died as well," replied Paddy, wiping his eyes.

An old woman was seriously ill and decided she didn't want to live any longer. Hidden under the floorboards was a rifle that used to belong to her dear departed husband, so she decided to end it all and shoot herself in the heart. But not being too sure where her heart was, she rang up her best friend and asked her.

"It's about 2" under your left tit," came the reply, so she shot herself in the kneecap.

As the coffin was carried out of the church on the way to its final resting place, it was bumped against the wall and a moan was heard.

"Quick," someone said, "Charlie's still alive."

And indeed, Charlie was not only alive but he lived for another 10 years.

On the occasion of his second funeral, as the coffin was once again being carried out of the church his wife said to the pallbearers,

"For goodness sake, make sure you don't bump the wall again."

The youth turned to his friend and said,

"When it's time for me to go, I want to die in my sleep like Grandpa... not screaming and carrying on like the passengers on his bus."

What do you call a woman who knows where her husband is all the time?

A widow.

The doctor came out of the consulting room looking very serious.

"I'm sorry, Mrs Powers," he said, shaking his head, "but I'm afraid your husband is at death's door."

"Really!" she replied. "Is it possible to open the door and push him through?"

A man was lying on his deathbed, and as his life was slipping away, he beckoned his wife to come closer.

"Jenny, darling, I have something to confess. During our married life I was unfaithful to you six times. In fact, I even slept with your best friend. I hope you can forgive me."

"I know exactly what you did," she replied coldly. "Why do you think I poisoned you?"

It was the day of Charlie's funeral. His wife and two children were sitting in the front row listening to the vicar's sermon.

"...and so, brothers and sisters, we say farewell to Charles, a good and kind man, loving husband, devoted father, always ready to lend a helping hand..."

At that point, the wife, looking slightly shocked, whispered to her eldest son.

"John, quick, we must be at the wrong funeral. Take a peek in the coffin. I don't know who this man is that the vicar is talking about."

Two women talking over the garden wall.

"So what do you think, Beryl? Would it be fatal if your husband ran away with another woman?"

Beryl thought for a moment. "Yes, it could be. They say the shock of sudden intense happiness can be bad for the heart."

Following the death of her husband, a woman rang up the local newspaper to put a notice of his death in the obituaries.

"Yes, madam," said the newspaperman, "what would you like to say?"

"John is dead," she replied.

Startled by the abrupt wording, he informed her, "Actually madam, you are allowed up to twelve words for the same price. Is there anything else you'd like to say?"

The woman thought for a moment and then replied,

"John is dead. Set of brand new golf clubs for sale."

"Jack, it's your brother, Bob, here," came the voice down the telephone line. "I'm not going to be able to get back for dad's funeral because I'm stuck in the outback. Do something nice for him and send me the bill."

So Jack did as his brother wished and sent Bob a bill for £100 which Bob paid immediately.

However, the following month, Bob received another bill for £100 and this happened each and every month. Eventually he managed to catch up with Jack and asked him what was going on.

"Well, you said do something nice for dad," protested Jack, "so I hired him a nice black three-piece suit."

Our Joan's so kind. She's always thinking of others. When she killed her husband, she used a knife rather than a gun so as not to wake the children!

Why is it that only 15% of men go to heaven?

If they all went, it would be hell.

After lying at death's door for more than six weeks, the man made a miraculous recovery. When the doctor told his long-suffering wife, she burst into tears.

"Oh no! What am I going to do now? I sold all his clothes and possessions to pay for the funeral."

"You know, June, I've been thinking, I'd like to be cremated."

"OK John, I'll just go and get the car."

Bernard only had minutes to live as he beckoned his wife to come closer.

"Doris, please do one last thing for me, please ride in the same car as my mother on the day of my funeral. Then I can die a happy man."

The wife paused for a moment and then replied,

"Well, all right then, but you know it will completely spoil my whole day."

As the congregation left the church on Sunday morning, the vicar spotted Mrs Jessop.

"Good morning, good morning," he boomed, "and how's your husband?"

"He passed away last week, vicar," she replied.

"Oh, no, how did it happen?"

"He was in the allotment, digging up some potatoes for lunch, when he collapsed and died," she replied.

The vicar looked suitably sombre. "What on earth did you do?" he asked.

"Oh, not to worry, I had a packet of oven chips in the freezer."

Did you hear about the ex-wife whose husband ran away with his secretary?

Two years later the ex-wife began ringing up her husband's office to be told over and over again that he no longer worked there because he had died.

After a while, the receptionist's curiosity got the better of her and she asked the ex-wife why she kept ringing.

"Oh, I just like to hear you say it," she said bitterly.

June was dying. She only had a few seconds to live and she called for her husband to come a little closer.

"Fred," she whispered, "when I die I want you to marry Josie from across the street."

"Oh, no," replied her husband shocked, "I don't want to marry anyone after you."

"I insist," she gasped.

"But why?"

"Because I've hated that tart for more than 20 years."

No woman has ever shot her husband while he's been hoovering.

An angry woman arrived home from her husband's funeral with his ashes in an urn. She tipped them out onto the table and began speaking to them.

"Here, Charles, look at this, it's a beautiful matching set of the finest leather handbag and shoes. Remember? You always promised you'd buy them for me but you never did."

Then she put a pearl necklace on the table.

"And this is the pearl necklace you always promised me – but then, you never kept your promises."

Suddenly she bent down and blew all his ashes on to the kitchen floor.

"Well Charles, you'll be pleased to know that's the blow job I always promised you!"

While his wife was still alive, the husband bought her a headstone engraved with the words "Here lies Doris, cold as usual."

The wife was so angry she immediately went out and got a headstone for him, with the words "In memory of Fred, stiff at last."

An old man was dying and his wife and family were standing around the bed. He had four tall and handsome blond sons and one small dark-haired boy. In the last few moments of life he beckoned to his wife and whispered,

"Patsy, my life is over, please tell me the truth. Is that small lad, that little one, is he mine?"

"Oh, yes, with my hand on my heart, I swear he is yours."

At that, the man died peacefully with a smile on his face.

"Phew," said the wife to herself, "thank goodness he didn't ask me about the other four."

An old man and a 20-year-old girl got married and for three weeks they were very happy, until one Sunday he collapsed and died.

Her mother arrived to console the unhappy girl.

"Oh, mum," she cried, "it was such a wonderful marriage. We were always so passionate, especially on Sunday when he would make love to the rhythm of the church bells."

The girl suddenly looked thoughtful. "Do you know, I'm sure he'd still be alive today if the fire engine hadn't gone past, clanging its bell so ferociously just minutes before he died."

It was a huge funeral. Hundreds of women walked solemnly behind Jack's coffin, while up front strode Hilda and her dog, Harvey. A woman from the next village asked someone in the procession what had happened.

"Old Hilda's dog savaged her husband to death," came the reply.

"Oh, really? Do you think it would be possible to borrow the dog?" she asked.

"I expect so, but you'll have to get to the back of the queue."

Poor old Jake was lying on his death bed with the dutiful family sitting round, when he suddenly roused himself on smelling his wife's cooking in the kitchen. When she saw him open his eyes, she whispered gently to him, "Jake, my poor man, do you have a last wish?"

"Oh, Mary, that I do," he croaked. "May I just have a small piece of that wonderful cake you're cooking in the kitchen?"

"Oh, no," said his wife, "that's for after the funeral."

Bob and Harold had just arrived on the 10th fairway when a funeral procession passed by. Harold stopped playing, put down his golf club and took his hat off.

"That was a nice gesture," remarked Bob.

"Well, it was the least I could do, after all she's been a good wife to me over the past forty years."

The day of the funeral was wet, windy and very stormy. As the mourners left the graveside, there was a tremendous flash of lightning and a deafening clap of thunder.

"Bloody hell!" cursed the new widow. "It didn't take him long to get up there and start pushing his weight around."

Said the doctor to the old man,

"I'm sorry, Mr Hodges, you've only got three minutes to live."

"Oh, no!" exclaimed the man. "Is there anything you can do for me?"

"Well, I could get the nurse to boil you an egg."

An old shop keeper was dying and the family had gathered around his bed. All of a sudden, the old man raised himself up and said:

"Is Jean here?"

"Yes, I am," she replied.

"Is Robert here?"

"Yes, I'm here."

"And is Leonard here?"

"I'm here too."

"Then who the bloody hell is looking after the shop?" he cried.

There's nothing wrong with my husband that a good funeral wouldn't cure.

Poor old George. Never out of the betting shop, he was the eternal optimist, believing that one day his boat would come in but it never did. His tips were never any good and he always lost his money. One day, however, his horse almost made third place and the excitement was too much. George dropped dead from a heart attack.

Later that day, Malcolm, an old friend, was asked to go down to the mortuary to identify the body. But when he got there, the attendant had muddled up the labels on the drawers and Malcolm was shown three bodies, not one of them being George.

"Oh dear," sighed Malcolm good naturedly. "Just like George, still unable to get into the first three."

A long-suffering wife rang up the doctor's one evening and said urgently,

"Hello, doctor, my husband's lying at death's door, could you possibly come round and pull him through?"

The funeral procession made its way down the road, six close members of the family carrying the coffin between them. On top of the coffin was a fishing line, a net and some bait. A passerby remarked, "He must have been a very keen fisherman."

"Oh, he still is," came the reply. "He's off to the river as soon as they've buried his wife."

DENTIST

"So, what's the verdict?" the man asked the dentist.

He replied, "Well your teeth are okay, but I'm going to have to take your gums out."

Bernard was really scared about going to the dentist but on this occasion he had no choice because of a raging toothache.

"Now come on Bernard," coaxed the dentist, "we'll have it out in no time."

Alas, the man kept his mouth firmly closed. So the dentist took the nurse aside and whispered something into her ear. Moments later she firmly gasped Bernard's balls and gave them a sudden twist.

"Arrrgh!" screamed Bernard, and as he opened his mouth, the dentist quickly yanked out the offending tooth.

"There!" said the dentist, "that wasn't so bad, was it?"

"No, I suppose not," agreed Bernard, "but the fucking roots went down a long way."

DOCTOR, DOCTOR

"Doctor, doctor, tell me how I can live to be 100."

"Well, you'll have to be very careful in what you eat – no more rich food, only plain uncooked vegetables. And you'll have to give up alcohol and cigarettes. And sex of course is right out…"

"Then will I live to be 100?"

"No, but it'll soon stop you wanting to."

"Doctor, doctor, I need help," said the distraught rugby referee.

"Every time the teams go into a scrum, I think they're talking about me."

"Doctor, doctor, please help me," said the distressed woman. "I've got a zit on my face and growing from it is a spreading chestnut tree and a picnic table and chairs."

"Now don't worry," said the doctor soothingly, "it's only a beauty spot."

An old lady went to the doctors complaining of a bad stomach. After examining her, he suggested she keep a note of everything she passed and come back and see him the following evening. When she saw him the next day, she was feeling a lot better.

"That's good," he replied, "Did you pass anything unusual?"

"No, not really," she said, "one dog, two bushes and a line of washing."

"Good gracious!" he exclaimed, "no wonder you're feeling better!"

"Doctor, doctor, my hair is falling out," said the worried man. "Can you give me anything for it?"

So the doctor gave him a box.

After examining the woman closely, the doctor recommended a course of the male hormone, testosterone. Three months later, she returned to the surgery to let him know how she was getting on.

"I feel a lot better," she reported, "the only drawback is that I'm growing hair where I never used to have it."

"Don't worry," said the doctor "that's just a small side effect of the drug. Where are you growing the hair?"

"On my balls," she replied.

"Doctor, doctor," said the simple farmer. "The wife's collapsed out in the field, I think our baby's coming."

As quickly as possible, he showed the doctor his wife laying on the ground moaning.

"I don't think there's time to move her," said the doctor, "we'll have to deliver the baby now. Quick, it's getting dark, shine the light over here."

Within minutes, the baby was born, a fit and healthy 7lb boy.

"Congratulations!" beamed the doctor. "Let's get them back to the house."

But all of a sudden, the wife began to moan again.

"Quick, bring the light back over," urged the doctor and a minute later another baby boy was born.

"So you have twins," said the doctor happily, "I think this calls for a double celebration."

But again the woman began to moan and again the doctor called for the light. Just in time for another baby boy."

"Well, well, well!" gasped the doctor, "I never expected this!"

The bewildered father picked up his three sons as the doctor helped the woman to her feet. But, alas, she fell to the ground in agony.

"Quick man, put the babies down, I think there's another baby coming. Get the light."

The farmer sighed,

"With all due respect doctor, don't you think it's this bloody light that's attracting them?"

A man went to the doctor complaining of bad headaches.

"Instead of giving you drugs, I'm going to prescribe a completely different treatment," said the doctor. "It works

because I've tried it myself. When I get a really bad headache I give my wife oral sex. As she reaches a climax, her legs squeeze my head tightly and it helps to release the tension. So you should do this every day for a month and then come back and see me."

"Thank you doctor, I certainly will," replied the man.

A month later, he returned to the surgery.

"Well, did it work?"

"Oh yes," replied the man. "I've never felt so good, it's a wonderful cure. By the way, your wife makes a lovely cup of tea as well."

The Lord of the Manor visited the doctor complaining of feeling unwell.

"Well, it could herpes or chicken pox," said the doctor. "We'll carry out a few tests and let you know the results tomorrow."

When Lord Farthing returned the next day he was told that the tests confirmed he had herpes.

"Well I could have told you that," replied the Lord scornfully. "Where on earth would I get chicken pox from?"

"Doctor, doctor, there's something terribly wrong with me. Every part of my body hurts. If I touch my head it hurts, if I touch my leg it hurts, my body, my arm – everything I touch hurts."

"Ah, I see the problem," said the doctor, "you've broken your finger."

One night, a woman opened her front door to find a huge cricket on her porch. Before she had time to react, it gave her a violent push and then ran off. The following night, the cricket appeared again and kicked her hard on the shins. On the third night, it bit her on the hand. By this time, the woman was so distressed that she went to see her doctor.

"Ah, yes," said the doctor, "I've heard there's a nasty bug going around."

★

"Doctor, doctor, my young son has swallowed a razor blade."

"Now calm down, I'll be over straight away. Have you done anything?"

"Yes, I've shaved with an electric razor."

"Doctor, doctor, call you help me please. My head hurts, I can't see properly, I feel claustrophobic and one of my legs feels shorter than the other."

"Hmm," said the doctor, "I can cure you. Just take your boot off your head and put it back on your foot and you should be fine."

"Doctor, doctor, I'm really worried about my wife," said the distraught husband. "She's posing in the nude."

"Well, that's nothing to get too concerned about," the doctor replied. "It's just her expression of freedom."

"Yes, but this was for her passport picture!"

"Martin, why do you always close your eyes when you drink your beer?" asked the curious barman.

"Doctor's orders," he replied, "he told me never to look at a pint again!"

The woman was so overweight that her health was suffering but she was unable to keep to a strict diet. Eventually, the doctor gave her the news that she would no longer be taking any food through her mouth. From now on she would take all nourishment through the rectum. Two months later, she returned to the surgery with the good news that she had lost three stones.

"Well done," congratulated the doctor, "keep on like this and we'll soon have you down to a reasonable size."

The woman smiled happily and walked towards the door.

"Just one thing," said the doctor noticing she was walking with a strange waddle, "Is there anything wrong with your legs?"

"Oh no doctor, they're fine."

"Then why are you walking in that strange way?"

"I'm only chewing some bubble gum, doctor," she replied.

"Doctor, doctor," says the worried man. "Something strange is happening to me. Every night when I go to bed, all I've got playing in my head is 'What's New Pussycat' and then when I wake up in the morning 'The Green Green Grass of Home' is going round and round in my brain. But that's not all. During the day I keep humming 'Delilah'. I think I must be going insane."

"No, you're not going insane," replies the doctor. "It's quite simple really. You've got Tom Jones Syndrome."

"Oh no!" despairs the man. "Is it a common complaint?"

"It's Not Unusual," replies the doctor.

A man went to the doctor's to find out if anything could be done for his baldness.

"Well, we could try some hair creams or a transplant," suggested the doctor, "but it's not 100% guaranteed."

"No, no," said the man in despair. "I've tried creams already and I can't afford a transplant."

"Hmm," the doctor thought for a moment and then said

"Okay, I do have one other cure, but I warn you, it's a bit unusual."

"Oh anything, anything," pleaded the man.

"Okay. You need to put some female secretions on the bald patch."

"Thank you," said the man. "I'll give it a try, but I can't help noticing that you have quite a bald patch yourself."

"That's true," agreed the doctor "but have you also noticed my wonderful moustache?"

"Doctor, doctor, please help me," said the worried man, "I think there's something dreadfully wrong with me."

"And what are the symptoms?" asked the doctor.

"I can't stop frying things. Everything I eat, I fry first. Even puddings! I fry rice pudding, jelly, trifle, absolutely everything. But it now seems to be spreading to other things. I fry the newspaper before I read it. I fry my shoes and all my clothes. Why! I even fried my bicycle."

"Well, that's quite simple to diagnose," said the doctor. "You're frittering your life away!"

A well-developed 14-year-old girl went to the doctors because she was worried about two bumps growing on her chest.

"That's nothing to worry about," said the doctor, "it just means you're becoming a woman."

Later the girl returned again to the doctor complaining about hair growing down below.

"That's quite normal," he told the anxious girl, "it means you're reaching puberty. Look, it happens to us all, " and he dropped his trousers to show her.

"Oh no!" she gasped in alarm, "when do I get one of those?"

"Hmm, I see you've been circumcised," remarked the doctor.

"Oh no," replied the young man, "just wear and tear."

The woman had to confess that the grazes on her knees and elbows were due to having sex doggy fashion in the outside yard.

"My goodness!" exclaimed the doctor, "why on earth don't you do it in a more conventional way?"

"Well, there's a bit of a problem," she replied, "my dog's quite ugly, and his breath stinks."

As the two doctors were taking lunch in the park, a man approached, shuffling long with his knees pressed together, fists clenched and doubled up.

"What do you reckon is wrong with him?" the first doctor asked his colleague.

"Severe arthritis, I would think. Do you agree?"

"No, I think its cerebral palsy," he replied.

All of a sudden the man came up to them and said through tight lips,

"Can you tell me where the Gents' is, please?"

A man went to the doctor's with a broken leg.

"How did this happen?" asked the doctor.

"Well, it started fifteen years ago…" began the man.

"No, no," interrupted the doctor. "I want to know how you broke your leg now, today."

"But I'm trying to explain," said the man. "Fifteen years ago I used to work on a farm and every evening, the farmer's daughter would come over and ask me if there was anything I wanted. She was very persistent, said she'd do anything for me, but I was quite happy, I didn't need anything. Then this morning, when I was tiling the roof, I suddenly realised what she'd meant all those years back and the shock made me fall off the roof."

★

A man went to the doctors complaining of feeling unwell. After a thorough external examination, the doctor asked him to bend over so he could examine his nether regions.

"Ah ha!" exclaimed the doctor, "there's some money stuck up your bum."

The doctor pulled out the cash and began to count it.

"There's £1,999 here," he said.

"Well that explains it," replied the man.

"I've not been feeling too grand!"

A couple are making out in the countryside when a bee comes along and flies up between the woman's legs, disappearing inside her.

"Help, do something!" she yells, so the man rushes her off to the local G.P.

"Hmm," says the doctor, looking at the young attractive woman. "There's only one thing for it," he continues, "it's a bit unorthodox but I think it will work."

The doctor goes on to explain that he will put a little bit of honey on the tip of his penis and insert it up the woman. When the bee detects the honey, he will withdraw and the bee will follow.

The man's not too happy about this but finally agrees, so the doctor proceeds. However, after a few moments of thrusting it in and out, the doctor gets carried away. He starts to moan and groan and fondle the woman's breasts.

"Hey!" says the man, "what's going on?"

"I've changed my mind," gasps the doctor. "I'm going to drown the bugger instead."

A man goes to the doctor complaining that his wife has lost all interest in him and she won't have sex. He pleads with the doctor for help so after a moment of deliberation the doctor gives him some tablets.

"Put one of these in her cocoa before going to bed," says the doctor, "but only one. Use one only, they're very powerful."

So the man returns home and that night he drops a pill in his wife's cocoa. Then he drops a second one in for 'good luck'. But moments later, the doctor's orders come back to haunt him – 'only one' he hears the doctor say, so to ease his conscience he puts one in his own cocoa as well. A little while later, they retire to bed. The wife strips off and the pill begins to work.

"Ooh!" she says. "I need a man."

"Me too!" replies the husband.

A man went to the doctors and handed him a note, which said, "I've lost my voice, I cannot speak."

"We'll soon put that right," said the doctor. "Take your willy out and put it on the table here." The man did as he was instructed and the doctor whacked it as hard as he could with a baseball bat.

"Aaaah!" screamed the man in agony. "Good, good!" said the doctor. "Tomorrow we'll try B."

A voluptuous young woman walked into the doctor's with a baby in her arms.

"I'm worried about the baby," she told him "he doesn't seem to be gaining any weight."

"Hmm," mused the doctor, "is it breast fed or bottle fed?"

"Breast fed," she replied.

"In that case, I'd better examine you. Would you kindly strip to the waist."

The woman did as she was asked, revealing the most perfect pair of breasts. He fondled them in his hands and tweaked her nipples.

"Well that's the problem," he said, "you're not producing any milk."

"I know," she replied. "I'm the baby's aunt. But never mind, it was nice to meet you."

"Doctor, doctor, I keep thinking I'm a pair of curtains!"

"Piss off out of my surgery now before I stamp on your fucking head."

Dear Dr. Ruth,

I am writing to tell you my problem. It seems I have married a sex maniac. For the past 12 years he makes love to me regardless of what I am doing... I can be ironing, cooking, cleaning, sweeping, cleaning the cat box, or writing letters. He just comes right at me and won't be

dissuaded for any reason. I would like to know if there is anything that ucnn hlp m wth   f

unothel   gothsl ehj fpslth3/   o,,   fjsl; (o ------   .

 lp sld mpskdlli

 dlks, a;ld:;' . . . . .

DRUNK

The policeman said to the drunk on the street corner,

"Come on mate, time to go home, you've been standing here ages."

"Ah ha," replied the drunk. "I've heard the world goes round every 24 hours so I'm waiting for my house to appear... Oh look, it won't be long now, there's my next door neighbour."

Every night of the week, Jack would stagger home after the pubs closed and every night of the week his wife would be waiting on the doorstep, ranting and raving.

"Oh Doris," she confided in her friend, the next day. "I'm so fed up with this, it doesn't seem to matter what I say, he just goes on getting drunk."

"Well maybe you're reacting in the wrong way," replied Doris, "why don't you try being nice to him and see what happens?"

So the following evening Jack arrived back, drunk as usual, but this time his wife remained calm.

"Come and sit yourself down," she said, giving him a kiss, "and I'll make you a nice cup of tea." After he'd drunk it, she whispered seductively,

"Shall we go up to bed now?"

"Might as well," he replied. "I'll be in trouble anyway when I get home."

Two men had been drinking in the bar all afternoon and were sozzled.

"I'll never forget the day I turned to the bottle as a substitute for women," said one.

"Why?" asked the other.

"Because I got my dick stuck in it."

A drunk staggers out of a bar and makes his way over to the car park where he begins to rub the roof of every car. The car park attendant watches him in amazement and finally goes over to speak to him.

"Hey mate, why do you rub the roof of every vehicle?"

"I'm looking for my car," he slurs, "and I know it's got two blue lights and a siren on the top."

A man popped into a bar for a drink but one led to another until an hour later he was very drunk.

"Oh bugger," he said to the barman. "I've just remembered, I left my girlfriend outside in the car."

"Don't worry," replied the barman. "I'll pop out to see if she's okay."

So the barman disappeared outside, located the car and peeped through the window to find the man's girlfriend making out with the man's best friend in the back seat. He went back inside and said to the drunk,

"Listen mate, I'd go out and check your girlfriend if I was you."

The drunk staggered to his feet and went off to the car. Moments later, he returned laughing.

"What a joke!" he said. "My mate's so drunk he thinks he's me!"

It was 11.30 at night when Jack finally got home from the pub, much the worse for wear.

"Oh Jack!" exclaimed his wife in dismay

"What a smell! Your head's covered in cow dung. Where have you been?"

"Sorry love," he said, burping. "Decided to cut across Farmer Giles' field on the way home and my cap flew off. I must have tried on half a dozen before I found the right one."

Two drunks were staggering along the pier when one tripped and fell into the sea.

"Help!" he cried, "help me please, I can't swim. Help, help, I can't swim!"

The other drunk replied, "Well neither can I, but I don't go around making such a bloody fuss about it."

A man was doing press-ups in the park when a drunk staggered past. Moments later the drunk returned, doubled over in laughter.

"What's so funny?" said the man gasping.

"I've got some bad news for you mate," grinned the drunk, "your girlfriend's gone home."

Every morning when the nurse came to change the old man's bed she would find shit all over the sheets. Finally, her patience snapped and she turned on him angrily.

"Right, that's it," she said, "if you do this once more, you can change your own sheets."

However, the next morning he woke up to find he'd done it again. He jumped out of bed, bundled up the sheets and threw them out of the window. As it happened, a drunk was staggering by at the time and the sheets landed on his head.

"Arrgh!" he screamed, punching wildly at the sheets until he finally wrestled free. He high-tailed it off to the nearest bar where he asked for a double scotch "and make it quick!" he gasped.

"Why, what's wrong?" asked the bartender.

"You'll never believe this," said the drunk, "but I've just beaten the crap out of a ghost."

"Good evening Sir," said the policeman, "did you realise you were doing 60mph in a 30mph zone?"

"Yeah, officer, I did!" replied the man. "But I'm so drunk, I have to get home quickly before I cause an accident!"

A drunk staggers up to the bar and don't bother with this one asks for a pint of beer. As he takes his first sip, he sees three darts on the table in front of him and asks the landlord why they are there.

"Well Sir, if any of my customers can get all 3 darts in the bull's eye, then they win a prize."

"That sounds good," slurs the drunk are you still reading this? who immediately picks up the darts and starts to aim but he's so drunk, other customers in the bar have to point him in the right direction before he can even begin. However, much to everyone's astonishment, he gets all 3 darts in the bull's eye even though he's so unsteady on his feet that, he twice falls to the ground.

"Bloody hell!" says the landlord I'm serious just skip this one, "no-one's managed that before, what the hell shall I give him." He looks frantically around the room and his eyes rest on the old tortoise, which is in a box next to the fire you've been warned.

"Here," he says, picking up the tortoise and giving it to the drunk, "this is your prize."

Smiling in delight, the drunk staggers out of the door and disappears.

The incident is soon forgotten and the pub carries on as normal, until 6 weeks later, the drunk re-appears. Once again he staggers up to the bar and orders a pint. Suddenly, he sees the very unfunny joke darts and remembering what happened before, he picks them up and throws them at the board. This time his hair is covering his eyes and his hands are shaking uncontrollably, yet he gets all three darts in the bull's eye.

"I don't fucking believe it!" exclaims the landlord, "how does he do it!"

"Okay, what do you want for a prize?" he asks.

"Same as last time," what did I tell you? grins the drunk, "that beef in a crusty roll was great!"

Two drunks were staggering through the graveyard on their way home. Suddenly Mac turned to his mate and said, "Hey, Martin, let's go and pay our respects to our old mate, Billy. He's buried in here somewhere."

For a while, they stumbled around and then Mac called out in triumph, "Here Martin, Billy's here, look."

Martin staggered over and saw a very ornate grave with a sculptured angel watching over it.

"Yesh, this is it," said Mac and he read out the inscription: "Here lies Billy White, much loved by friends and family and sadly missed."

Martin looked hazily up at the figure above. "Whoever done it, didn't know him very well," he remarked, "it doesn't look a bit like Billy."

A drunk staggered into a bar and asked for a drink.

"I'm sorry," replied the barman, "I think you've had enough. Go home and sleep it off."

The drunk left but came back a few minutes later and asked for a drink.

"No," said the barman firmly. "I'm not serving you."

Again the drunk left the bar only to reappear 5 minutes later.

"Look," said the barman impatiently, "I'm not serving you any more beer, you're too drunk."

"Okay," said the drunk, "I guess you must be right. That's what they said in the last two pubs as well."

"My problem is I love women too much," said the drunk sitting at the bar. "In fact it was a woman who drove me to drink and I feel really bad about it. I never wrote and said thank you."

"Now listen carefully," said the doctor to the drunk, hoping to scare him into doing something about his drinking. "If you carry on hitting the bottle, you'll begin to shrink and eventually turn into a mouse."

The drunk stumbled home, deep in thought. When he entered the house, he called to his wife, "Carol, do me a favour. If you see me getting smaller, for fuck's sake, kill the cat."

It was 2 o'clock in the morning and very cold when a couple were woken up by a loud knocking at the door.

"Go on John," nudged his wife, "you'd better find out who it is because it might be important."

Poor John had to get out of his nice warm bed and go downstairs. When he opened the door, he was confronted by a very drunk man who said, "Can you give me a push?"

"What!" exclaimed John, "how dare you disturb me at this time of the morning, now bugger off."

"Who was that?" asked his wife when he got back into bed.

"Some drunk idiot wanting me to give him a push," he replied. "I soon saw him off!"

"Oh John, how could you!" admonished his wife. "Don't you remember how we once broke down in the middle of nowhere and if it hadn't been for that kind man that stopped to help us, we'd still be there."

"Alright, alright," grumbled John, as he got out of bed a second time and went downstairs. He put on his coat, opened the front door and called out

"Hello, do you still want a push?"

"Yes please," came the reply.

"Where are you?" asked John.

"I'm over here."

John looked around, but couldn't see anyone. "Where are you exactly?" he called

"Over here!" shouted the drunk, "On the swing."

Having trekked through the jungle for nearly 3 months, the intrepid group of hunters were enjoying their last night together by roasting some wild game and supping large quantities of scotch. Late into the night, Jack wandered off to have a slash and when he staggered back to the campfire he'd failed to do up his flies.

"Watch out Jack," warned his mate, "I think you've just sat on something. I'm sure I saw a snake. Let me kill the bugger."

He picked up an empty bottle and brought it crashing down.

"Arrrgh!" screamed Jack, "quick do it again, the bastard's just bit me."

"Excuse me Sir," said the traffic cop flagging down a car that had just jumped a red light, "I believe you may have been drinking."

"Oh yes Officer," came the reply, "indeed I have."

"It started this morning when I had Buck's Fizz to celebrate my birthday, then I had four pints at lunchtime with the lads, a couple of bottles of wine tonight at the local Chinese and then a couple of double brandies at the Club afterwards."

"In that case Sir, would you mind stepping out of the car so that I can breathalyse you?"

"Why?" replied the motorist, "don't you believe me?"

A drunk was staggering through the park scattering bits of paper as he went along.

"Excuse me Sir," said the park keeper, "you're throwing litter everywhere, what's going on?"

"Well, you see," said the drunk, looking furtively around, "I'm keeping the lions away?"

"Lions! But we don't have any lions here."

"No," smiled the drunk, "it works really well, doesn't it?"

A guy walks into a bar and says to the bartender, "I want you to give me 12-year scotch, and don't try to fool me because I can tell the difference."

The bartender is sceptical and decides to try to trick the man with 5-year scotch. The man takes a sip, scowls and says, "Bartender, this crap is 5-year scotch. I told you I want 12-year scotch." The bartender tries once more with 8-year scotch. The man takes a sip, grimaces and says, "Bartender, I don't want 8-year scotch like this filth. Give me 12-year scotch!"

Impressed, the bartender gets the 12-year scotch, the man takes a sip and sighs, "Ah, now that's the real thing." A disgusting, grimy, stinking drunk has been watching all this with great interest. He stumbles over and sets a glass down in front of the man and says, "Hey, I think that's really far out what you can do. Try this one."

The man takes a sip and immediately spits out the liquid and cries, "Yechhh! This stuff tastes like piss!"

"It is!" says the drunk. "Now how old am I?"

"Waiter!" called the woman, "I'm feeling a little tipsy, can you bring something to sober me up?"

"Certainly Madam," he replied. "I'll bring the bill."

A drunk was on his hands and knees under a lamp post obviously searching for something on the ground. A kindly passer-by stopped to help him but after 10 minutes they'd failed to find his missing tooth.

"How did it happen?" asked the searcher.

"I tripped over the pavement at the bottom of this street and knocked my tooth out on the wall" said the drunk.

"So why are you looking for it here, if the accident happened at the bottom of the street?" asked the puzzled man.

"The light's better here," he replied.

A drunk staggered into the foyer of the cinema and bought a ticket for the film. He disappeared inside but returned a moment later and bought another ticket. Yet again he emerged some minutes later requesting a third ticket. The ticket seller looked extremely surprised and commented on his reappearance.

"This is the third ticket I've sold you in as many minutes. What's the matter?"

"It's like this," replied the drunk. "Every time I go through the door to find my seat, this big man comes up to me, snatches my ticket and tears it in two. And let me tell you, he's too big to argue with!"

"I demand another room immediately," said the drunk, staggering up to hotel reception.

"But I don't understand," replied the receptionist, puzzled, "all the rooms are exactly the same."

"I'm not going to argue," insisted the drunk. "Just change my room now."

"Of course Sir," said the receptionist. "I'll give you the key to room 85. But if you don't mind me asking, what's wrong with the room you have now?"

"It's on fire," he replied.

E

EDUCATION

The human biology course took place on a Monday afternoon and this week the subject was the male genitalia. The professor delighted in embarrassing his female students and began a story about a tribe of natives whose todgers were so long… At this point, one of the girls had had enough. She stood up and walked to the door only to have him remark loudly,

"You needn't be in such a hurry my dear. The next plane for Africa doesn't leave until tomorrow."

The professor is discussing human reproduction with his students.

"Bob, once the baby is born can you name three advantages for using mother's milk?" he asks one of his students.

Bob replies,

"Well… it gives the baby better protection from germs, it's full of vitamins and minerals and erm…" but Bob couldn't think of a third reason.

The professor turns to the student next to him.

"Darren, can you think of a third advantage?"

"Yes sir," he replies, "it comes in such attractive packaging."

Finding one of her students making faces at others on the playground, Ms. Smith stopped to gently reprove the child.

Smiling sweetly, the Sunday School teacher said, "Johnny, when I was a child, I was told that if I made ugly faces, it would freeze and I would stay like that." Johnny looked up and replied, "Well, Ms Smith, you can't say you weren't warned."

"Good morning children," said the new teacher, "my name is Miss Prussy. Now if you find that difficult to remember, think of a pussy and just add an 'r'."

The following day, the teacher came into the classroom and said,

"Good morning children, I hope you've all remembered my name."

"Oh yes Miss," said a voice from the back, "it's Miss Crunt."

"Alice, you're late," said the teacher crossly.

"Sorry Miss, I had to walk to school today."

"Alright, just sit down and get your geography book out, we're looking at the British Isles. Now, can anyone tell me where the Scottish border is?"

"Yes Miss," said Alice. "He's in bed with my mum. That's why I had to walk to school today!"

The professor's voice boomed out across the lecture theatre,

"Today, we will study the human body in closer detail," he told his class of first year medical students.

"Here in front of me is the dead body of a male aged 46. I shall remove parts of his anatomy. Here is the heart, here is the liver, these are the kidneys."

At that moment, a latecomer arrived and whispered to the student sitting next to him.

"Hey, what's he doing?"

"He's giving an organ recital," came the reply.

Mother complained, "You'll have to speak to our Colin, Ted. It's the third time this week he's not come straight home from school. Seems to think he can turn up when he likes."

So Ted spoke to his son.

"Sorry Dad, I'm late home because I have sex with the teacher," he said.

"Aye, well, sowing your wild oats is all part of growing up. I suppose. Just don't go upsetting your mum all the time. Now off you go. I know, why don't you take your bike out?"

"I can't, Dad," he replied, "my arse is still sore."

"Bobby," said the teacher, "can you give me another word for intercourse? Here's a clue. It's a four letter word ending in k."

Bobby jumped to his feet in anger.

"I know you don't like me, Miss," he said, "but you're not going to trick me into saying a bad word, just so that you can cane me!"

"Bobby, Bobby," she replied calmly. "I have no idea what you're talking about. The word 'talk' is not a bad word!"

At the beginning of the English lesson, the teacher announced to the class that they all had to think of a sentence using the word 'marvellous'.

"Last night I went to the theatre and saw a marvellous show," said Bethany.

"I had a marvellous time on my holiday!" said Matthew.

Then Martin put his hand up. "Please miss, I've got a sentence. Last night my sister told my parents she was pregnant and my dad said 'Well that's marvellous, bloody marvellous'!"

The teacher addressed her class.

"Today, children, we're going to concentrate on English and I'm going to ask you all to think of a story which has a moral attached to it. What about you, Mary?"

"Well Miss. It was a very hot day and a little girl called Carol was walking along the river bank looking at the cool, clear water flowing by. As time went on, she felt so tired ad sticky that she decided to go for a swim.

She ran behind a tree, changed into her swimming costume and without checking the riverbank she ran up to the edge and jumped in. Unfortunately, she'd jumped in just where a pile of rocks was jutting out of the water and badly grazed her legs. The moral of the story is 'look before you leap'."

"Not bad," commented the teacher. "Now you have a go, Peter."

"Bobby was a lazy boy and when he was told to collect the eggs from the hen house, he only took one small basket with him because he couldn't be bothered to look

for another. Of course, the basket was soon filled but instead of making a second journey, he balanced the remaining eggs on top. Alas, on the way home, the handle broke and all the eggs fell to the ground and were smashed. So the moral of the story is 'don't put all your eggs in one basket'!"

"Well done, we'll just hear one more before the break. David, have you got a story?"

"Yes Miss. Uncle Harry was sent to France in the Second World War and on one occasion, he got left on his own. He ended up in a deserted village and while checking for enemies he found an old wine cellar. At that point, there wasn't much he could do so he drank a few bottles and stowed away a few more before carrying on. Then a short distance outside the village, he spotted a group of six Germans who had parked their tank at the side of the road. Quick as a flash, Uncle Harry killed three of them with a hand grenade and shot the rest with his machine gun. Then he smashed up the tank's controls so it couldn't be used again."

"And what's the moral of the story?" asked the teacher looking puzzled.

"Well miss, it's 'don't mess with Uncle Harry when he's pissed'."

"Let's have some quiet, children, please," says the teacher.

"Today, we're going to talk about what you'd like to be when you grow up. But first, let's find out what your parents do."

"Jane, what does your father do?"

"He's a doctor miss."

"Very good. Now Matthew, how about your mum?"

"She's a bank manager."

"Good. And you, Jack, what does your dad do?"

"He serves drinks in a brothel, miss."

The teacher is shocked and quickly changes the subject, but later she goes to see Jack's father to tell him what has occurred. "Well you see, I'm really a lawyer," explains the father, "but you can't tell that to a nine-year-old kid."

The next day, the teacher continues her lesson on what the children's parents do for a living.

"My dad's a builder, miss," says Carol.

"That's good," replies the teacher, "your turn, Stephen."

"My mum's an airline stewardess," he replies proudly.

"Well, that's an exciting job, travelling all over the world."

The teacher looks around the classroom and notices Jake sitting very quietly in the back row.

"Come on Jake, tell everyone what your father does."

"He eats light bulbs miss," says Jake hesitantly.

"I'm sorry Jake, I think I misheard. Can you repeat what you said?"

"He eats light bulbs miss."

"Light bulbs! What makes you think that?"

"Well, last night when I went past my parent's bedroom, I heard dad say,

"Hurry up and turn the light off and I'll eat it."

"Children," said the class teacher, "tomorrow we're going to learn about the facts of life so for tonight's homework I want you all to find out what a penis is."

Young Charlie returned home and asked his dad, who immediately pulled down his trousers and pointed proudly to his manhood.

"My son, that is a perfect penis."

The next day at school, Charlie's best friend came running up to him in a panic.

"I forgot to find out what a penis was, what shall I do?"

"No problem," said Charlie, "Look I'll show you."

They went behind a tree and Charlie pulled down his trousers.

"There," he said, "that's a penis and if it was a bit smaller, it would be a perfect penis."

The teacher of class 3 was leaving to get married so on her final day, many of the children brought in going-away presents. They were all beautifully wrapped. Little Johnny, whose father was a jeweller, gave her a tiny wrapped box.

"I think I can guess this is a ring," she said, smiling.

"Yes Miss," Johnny replied.

Then Mary, whose father was a baker, gave her a light square box.

"Ooh," she said delighted. "I think this is a cake, is that right?"

"Yes Miss," said Mary.

Then Colin gave the teacher his present. His father was a wine seller and the parcel was quite long and thin.

"Well Colin," said the teacher, "what can this be? Did you wrap it yourself?"

"Yes Miss," he replied.

As the teacher picked it up, it leaked slightly, so she put her finger on it and then licked it.

"Hmm," she mused, "is it a bottle of wine?"

"No Miss."

She tasted it again. "Is it a bottle of brandy?"

"No Miss".

After trying another couple of times, she gave up.

"I don't know," she said, "what is it Colin?"

The little boy tore the paper off triumphantly.

"Look Miss, it's a hamster."

"Right, now listen everyone," said the teacher. "Tomorrow is your most important exam. You must be there. No excuses will be accepted unless it's severe illness or family bereavement. Do you understand?"

"Yes," they chorused.

"What about sexual exhaustion?" called a voice from the back.

As everyone laughed, the teacher replied,

"Not to worry, you can use your other hand to write."

The medical students were listening to a lecture on the importance of observation, given by Professor Hoodwink.

"It is very important to look at everything very carefully, to taste, to smell, to touch," he said.

Then he picked up a glass of urine.

"Look at this," he continued. "I see it's yellow, I smell it and I taste it."

The students gasped as he dipped his finger in the liquid and put it in his mouth.

"Now you try," he said.

The students were horrified but the professor was a famous man and if he could do it, then so could they. In turn, each of them dripped their finger in the liquid and put it to their mouth.

"Now that is very interesting," said the professor. "We are talking about the importance of observation yet none of you noticed I dipped my second finger into the urine, but put my third finger into my mouth!"

The class teacher was asking the children what sort of jobs their parents had. One said his mother was a doctor, another said his father was an engineer. Young Martin said his mum was a whore. The teacher was outraged and sent Martin straight off to see the headmaster. Some time later, he returned and the teacher asked him what had happened.

"Please Miss," said Martin, "the headmaster gave me an apple and asked for my phone number."

Alison Parker has been appointed as the new college counsellor, eager to advise any of the students that need help. One afternoon, she's strolling around the grounds when she sees a girl standing on her own, watching a group of students having fun playing football.

"Are you alright?" she asks the girl.

"Fine thanks," comes the reply.

The girl continues to stand there on her own and Alison speaks again.

"Are you sure everything's alright? Listen, would you like me to be your friend?"

The girl looks at her warily. "I'm fine," she says again, "Now please leave me alone."

"But you look so lonely standing there while everyone else is playing together" persists Alison.

"That's because I'm the bloody goalkeeper," replies the girl angrily. "Now shove off."

The schoolteacher had just completed his lecture on time and efficiency and was talking to his colleague.

"Do you practice what you preach?" asked his colleague "are you efficient?"

"Oh yes," replied the teacher. "Take breakfast for instance. It used to take my wife 20 minutes every morning to prepare. She would make endless trips to the cupboard and the fridge bringing back one item at a time. Eventually, I pointed this out to her and told her how to become more efficient…"

"Yes," interrupted his colleague, "so what happened?"

"Well now it only takes me 7 minutes to prepare breakfast!"

Wee Jimmy McDougall left his beloved Isles to go to a University in England. After he'd been there a couple of months, his family came to visit.

"So bonny lad, how's it going?"

"Fine, fine," replied Jimmy, "though I've got some awful strange neighbours."

"Yeah?"

"The one in the room on my right keeps banging his head against the wall all the time, and the one on the left keeps screaming."

"So how d'you cope with that?" they asked.

"Oh I take no notice," he replied. "I just keep on playing my bagpipes."

"Miss, miss," said the young boy. "I've just been circumcised and my willy's sore."

The teacher suggested he go ring his mother and tell her, so the boy did this and then returned to class.

Some time later, the teacher passed his desk and was shocked to see his willy hanging out of his trousers.

"What's going on?" she demanded.

The boy explained. "I told mum how I felt and she told me to stick it out till lunchtime and then she'd come and get me."

Tommy arrives home from school and sees his mum in the kitchen.

"What's this?" she asks, looking at the clock. "Why are you so early?"

"I was the only one to answer the teacher's question," he replies.

"Well done," she says, "and what was the question?"

"Who threw the rubber at me?"

ELECTRIC CHAIR

Moments away from pulling the switch of the electric chair, the prisoner got a sudden attack of the hiccups.

"Do you have a last wish?" asked the officer.

"Yes," replied the man, "can you do something to scare me?"

At the beginning of the last century, trams had become a very common sight on the streets of San Francisco. This particular tram was trundling its way down Main Street when suddenly the conductor grabbed a lady with her shopping and shoved her off the tram. She was hit by a car, and died on the spot. The police were called, and arrested the conductor, who had nothing to say in his defence. Well, the whole tramful of people were witnesses in court to what had happened, so he was quickly found guilty and sentenced to death. Appeals being shorter in those days, a few months later the conductor found himself in the electric chair. The warden pulled the switch, and thousands of volts coursed through the prisoner. When the doctor went in to check for life signs, however, he found to his amazement that the conductor was still alive.

THE MASSIVE ADULT JOKE BOOK

"It's an act of God!" said all the witnesses, and the conductor was allowed to go free. Soon after his release, he was rehired by the tram company. All seemed to be going well until one day, as the tram was trundling its way down Main Street. The conductor grabbed hold of an old man, and threw him out of the back of the tram. He died on the spot, and the conductor was soon arrested, charged, convicted, and found himself back in the electric chair. Now technology had improved since the last time, so this time the warden was confident that the prisoner would not escape. The switch was thrown, and just to be on the safe side, the current was left on for ten minutes. The doctor went to check for life signs, and sure enough, the prisoner was still alive, if a bit crackly.

"It's a miracle!" said all the witnesses, and once again, the conductor was allowed free, to be rehired by the tram company once again. Well, the tram was trundling its way up Main Street once more, when the conductor suddenly snatched a small child from its seat, and hurled it out the back of the tram. To cut a long story short, passenger outrage, cops arrive, due process of law, conductor back in the electric chair. Again.

"Okay, smart guy!" thought the warden to himself, "this time you're gonna fry." The electric chair had been hooked up to the U.S National Grid, and the entire power supply for California was diverted into the prisoner as the warden pulled the switch. The lights went out all over the state, power generators went into overdrive, and the sky above the prison crackled with blue light. Half an hour passed, and the warden knew that this time, nobody could have survived. The doctor went in to check, and guess what? The prisoner was sitting in the chair, looking quite perky.

"Well, that's it," said the warden, "we've tried three times to execute you, and we've failed every time. There's nothing more we can do; according to the Constitution, you're free to go and kill whoever you like."

"Great!" said the prisoner, "although I think I've learnt my lesson now, and I don't think I'll be killing anyone else for quite some time to come."

"Well, that's good," said the warden, "but tell me one thing; I have to know, how the hell did you survive all that electricity? It's against all the laws of physics; nobody has ever done it before."

"Well," said the prisoner, "I've always been a very poor conductor!"

F

FARMS & FARMERS

It was a very busy time on the farm so the elderly farmer took on a Frenchman to help him castrate the sheep.

As the Frenchman picked up the bits to throw away he was stopped by the farmer who said,

"No, don't do that. Give them to the wife and she'll fry them up for supper. They're very good for you, we call them sheep fries."

So for the next two nights they had sheep fries for supper.

However, on the following day, the farmer came home for lunch complaining that his assistant had not turned up for work.

"Mmm," replied his wife, "he seemed a bit odd this morning. As he was leaving to meet you, he asked what we were having for supper and when I said 'hamburgers and French fries', he went pale and ran off."

The farmer was sitting reading his weekly magazine when he said to his wife,

"Listen to this. It says here that it's only in humans where the female achieves an orgasm."

"Really!" she sneered, "prove it."

The farmer disappeared and arrived back an hour later.

"Well it doesn't happen in sheep and cows," he said, "but I couldn't be sure with pigs, they always make so much noise squealing."

An old farmer didn't often get the urge, but when he did, he had to act upon it immediately.

One day he was ploughing down in the bottom field, when he felt a mighty erection coming on.

"Bloody hell!" he shouted, running madly for the house and waving his arms frantically to get the wife's attention. He rushed through the door to find her scrubbing the kitchen floor.

"Quick, quick!" he panted, "get upstairs and strip off while I've still got the urge." Sadly, by the time she did as he wished, the moment had passed and he was unable to perform.

"Now Martha!" he said forcefully, "don't hang around next time. When you see me rushing home, get upstairs immediately."

A few weeks passed and one afternoon, as the wife looked out of the window, she caught sight of her husband rushing towards the house waving frantically. Straight away she ran upstairs, stripped off and got into bed.

"Martha, Martha!" he called "where are you?"

"I'm up here," she replied, "waiting for you."

"Well get down here!" he yelled, "the bloody barn's on fire!"

"I have to go to market," said the farmer to his foreman "So I'll leave you in charge. Old Bernie Jenkins is coming over to see the bull, tell him its £100 a go if he wants his herd serviced and £200 if he wants the ram as well."

Later on in the morning, a car drew up outside and an angry man stormed across the farmyard.

"Where's Chivers!" he roared, "that bloody son of his has got my daughter pregnant."

"Well he's not here at the moment," replied the foreman, "and he didn't tell me how much he charges for that!"

The local radio station was doing a feature about life on isolated farms. They interviewed one such farmer and asked him whether it was true that people like him shagged cattle, sheep, goats and chickens.

"What!" roared the outraged farmer, "chickens!?!"

Farmer Giles was looking forward to the County Show and exhibiting his prize bull. However disaster struck just two days before the event when the bull suddenly went cross-eyed. The vet was summoned immediately and he assured the farmer that it could be put right very easily. He took a length of hosepipe from his van, stuck one end up the bull's backside and blew as hard as he could in the other end. Miraculously the bull's eyesight returned to normal.

"If it happens again, just repeat the process," he said to the farmer before departing. The morning of the show dawned bright and sunny but the farmer's expectant mood changed to one of despair when he saw the bull had gone cross-eyed again.

"Oh hell!" he cursed, running out to get the hosepipe. He stuck one end up the bull's backside and blew forcefully down the other. But nothing changed. In a blind panic he rang the vet's and begged him to come out as soon as possible.

"And you did exactly as I showed you" said the vet when he arrived.

"Yes, yes," said the farmer impatiently. "I'll show you."

The vet watched as nothing happened. Then he took the hosepipe out, turned it round and stuck the other end up the bull's backside. Then he blew fiercely and the animal's eyesight returned to normal.

"What did I do wrong?" asked the farmer. "Did I have the pipe the wrong way round?"

"Oh no," said the vet. "It doesn't matter which way round you have it."

"Then why did you change it round?"

"You don't think I'm going to put that end in my mouth after you've been sucking on it?"

One morning, the farmer's wife woke up, looked out of the window and saw their only cow lying dead in the field.

"Oh no!" she wailed, "now we have no animals left, what can I do, how can I feed us?" and she was so distraught, she hanged herself.

When the farmer woke up, he discovered his dead wife and was so overcome with grief, he shot himself. So three sons were left on their own. The first son went walking along the seashore and met a mermaid.

"Don't look so sad," she said. "If you have sex with me five times, I will bring your family back to life and restore your farm to its former glory."

So the boy gladly took up the offer, but by the fourth time he was struggling and was unable to perform at all on the fifth attempt. Bitterly disappointed, he walked into the sea and drowned himself. Some time later, the second son came by and bumped into the mermaid.

"Do not despair," she said. "If you can make love to me ten times, I have the power to bring back your family and make the farm successful."

Eagerly the boy agreed and began with determination. Alas, he failed after number seven and was so ashamed he walked into the sea as well.

So there was only the youngest son left. He went looking for his brothers and was met by the mermaid. She told him what had happened but assured him that all could be put right if he made love to her twenty-five times. The boy thought for a moment and replied warily,

"Yeah, but how can I be sure it won't kill you like it did the cow?"

FATHERS

A little girl wandered into the bathroom while her father was taking a shower.

"Daddy, daddy, what's that?" she asked, pointing at his tackle.

"Well... erm... It's a hedgehog," he replied.

"Gosh!" she exclaimed, "it's got a hell of a big dick."

FISHING

A man went down to the lake to fish but it was so cold that he had to cut away the ice first. After two hours he hadn't caught anything but a bad cold and he was feeling very miserable.

Just then, another bloke appeared, cut himself a hole in the ice and began fishing. Within the next 30 minutes, he'd caught half a dozen fish.

"How come I've been here for more than 2 hours and caught nothing while you've caught six already?" he complained.

"Ron raf roo reep ru rooms rorm," came the reply.

"What?"

"Row raf roo reep ru rooms rorm."

"I'm sorry, I don't understand," said the discontented fisherman.

The other bloke took a load of wriggling slime from his mouth and said,

"You have to keep the worms warm."

A keen country lad applied for a salesman's job at a city department store. In fact it was the biggest store in the world – you could get anything there. The boss asked him, "Have you ever been a salesman before?"

Yes, I was a salesman in the country," said the lad. The boss liked the cut of his jib and said, "You can start tomorrow and I'll come and see you when we close up."

The day was long and arduous for the young man, but finally 5 o'clock came around. The boss duly fronted up and asked, "How many sales did you make today?"

"One," said the young salesman.

"Only one?" blurted the boss, "most of my staff make 20 or 30 sales a day. How much was the sale worth?"

"Three hundred thousand dollars," said the young man.

"How did you manage that?" asked the flabbergasted boss.

"Well," said the salesman, "this man came in and I sold him a small fish hook, then a medium hook and finally a really large hook. Then I sold him a small fishing line, a medium one and a huge big one. I asked him where he was going fishing and he said down the coast.

I said he would probably need a boat, so I took him down to the boat department and sold him that twenty-foot schooner with the twin engines. Then he said his Volkswagen probably wouldn't be able to pull it, so I took him to the car department and sold him the new Deluxe Cruiser."

The boss took two steps back and asked in astonishment, "You sold all that to a guy who came in for a fish hook?"

"No," answered the salesman "He came in to buy a box of Tampons for his wife and I said to him, 'Your weekend's shot, you may as well go fishing.'"

FLIRTING

A handsome but naive boy was discovered by police walking around town with just his shoes on.

"Hey Malcolm, how come you're walking around naked?" they asked.

"Well it's like this," replied the boy. "I was on the river bank fishing when Mandy came along, sat down and started kissing me. Then she took all her clothes off and told me to do the same. So I did. I took all my clothes off except my shoes. Then she opened her legs and said,

"Go on Malcolm, go to town, so here I am."

A woman was walking down the street when she stumbled, causing her glass eye to fly out. Fortunately, a man was coming the other way and he managed to catch it.

"Oh thank you so much," she said. "Please let me treat you to lunch."

A few minutes later, they were seated in a bistro ordering food. As the waiter left, the man remarked, "Do you often treat men to lunch?"

"Oh no," she replied. "You just happened to catch my eye."

"Hello Sharon," greeted the arrogant man. "Tonight I'm going to buy you lots of drinks…"

"Oh no you're not!" she replied.

"Then I'm going to take you to dinner and buy you lots more drinks…

"Oh no you're not."

"And I'm going to take you clubbing…"

"Oh no you're not."

"And then back to my flat…"

"Oh no you're not."

"And I'm not going to wear a condom either."

"Oh yes you are."

FRIENDS

Two countrywomen were harvesting potatoes in a field. One of them picked up a couple of potatoes and said to her friend,

"These remind me of my husband's testicles."

"What! Are they that big?" exclaimed her friend.

"No, that dirty," came the reply.

Why did the Lone Ranger kill Tonto?

He found out what Kemo Sabe meant.

Within a couple of months of each other, two friends were involved in nasty divorces so they decided to stay away from women forever. One of them suggested taking a cabin for the winter, high up in the mountains, and the other readily agreed. They closed their businesses and set off, stopping first at a supplies store to stock up on fuel and food.

The storekeeper also gave them each a board lined with fur with a hole cut in it.

"You'll also be wanting this," he said, "you'll find it mighty lonely without a woman up there."

The men said farewell and departed.

The following year, one of the men returned to the store to pick up more supplies.

"Where's your mate?" asked the storekeeper.

"I had to shoot him," came the reply. "I found him in bed with my board!"

Two men talking in a pub.

"You know Don, every night my wife plasters her face in cold cream and puts curlers in her hair."

"Does it do any good?"

"No, not really. I can still tell it's her."

Three old women were sitting in the garden sipping tea and moaning about old age.

"It's getting to the point where I'll be in bed and I won't remember whether I'm going to sleep or just about to get up," remarked the first woman.

"Oh I understand," said the second woman nodding her head. "My memory is so bad, sometimes I'll feed the cat ten times a day and at other times he doesn't get anything."

"Oh dear," sympathised the third woman, "thank goodness I don't get problems like that, touch wood," she said, knocking her hand on the table... "Oh! I'll just get the door."

The Lone Ranger and Tonto were riding through a canyon when they heard the sound of many horses coming up behind them. Sure enough, 200 Navaho Indians in full war paint were bearing down on them. Suddenly, in front of them, came the sound of much yelling and 300 Apache Indians came riding into view.

The Lone Ranger turned to his trusted friend and said,

"Well Tonto, it looks like we're really in trouble this time."

Tonto replied, "What do you mean 'we', white man?"

Two women chatting over a cup of tea.

"Oh Flo, I was so depressed last week, I tried to kill myself by taking 500 pain killers."

"Oh no," gasped her friend. "What happened?"

"Well after two, I felt a lot better."

G

GAY TIMES

It so happened that three gay guys, who'd lost their partners, all had the funerals on the same day. Each of them walked out with their ashes and the first man said,

"I'm going to scatter his ashes in the sky because he loved flying."

The second man said,

"I'm going to scatter his ashes on the sea because he loved sailing."

And the third man said,

"I'm going to scatter his ashes in a hot bowl of chilli, just so he can tear my ass one more time."

One prisoner said to the other,

"I think my cell mate's gay."

"How can you tell?"

"He closes his eyes when I kiss him goodnight."

A woman falls pregnant by another man and is so frightened of what her jealous husband might do, she pleads for help from her doctor. Now the doctor is quite sweet on the woman himself, so he agrees to help. When the baby is born, the doctor gives the newborn to a priest in the next ward who has just undergone an exploratory operation.

"We'll tell the priest that a miracle has happened and he's the one who has given birth," the doctor tells the grateful woman. So the astonished priest is told the news of the miracle and devotes the next 16 years to bringing up his son as best as he can. But as each year passes, so the priest feels more and more guilt at what has happened. On the boy's 16th birthday, he breaks down and confesses all.

"I'm sorry son, I'm not your father."

"What do you mean?" demands the son.

"I'm afraid I'm your mother, your father is the Bishop."

Two gay men are driving along a country road when a lorry hurtles round the corner from the opposite direction and crashes straight into them.

"Oh, Jules," cries out one of the men, "get out and tell him we'll sue for everything he's got."

So Jules goes up to the cab and says to the huge 6'5" tattooed lorry driver.

"This is all your fault, we're going to sue you."

"Oh yeah," sneers the man, climbing down from his cab. "You can kiss my arse!"

Jules goes back to the car, puts his head through the window and says to Ainsley, "It's all right, he wants to settle out of court."

A patrolling police car discovered a couple of men in the bushes outside a pub. One of the men had his trousers round his ankles while the other had a finger up his mate's bum.

"Hey, what's going on here?" demanded the policeman.

"Oh hello officer, my friend's had too much to drink so I'm trying to make him sick," came the reply.

"Well you don't put your finger up there," replied the policeman. "You put it down his throat."

"Yeah, I'm just about to do that."

A convicted killer escaped from jail after 15 years and broke into a house to get provisions. He tied up the young couple as he went on the rampage from room to room.

"Karen," whispered her husband. "This doesn't look good. He'll stop at nothing to get what he wants so don't struggle. Just lay back and remember you may be saving our lives."

"Well, I'm glad you said that darling," she replied, "He did mention what a cute arse you have."

Have you heard about the new lesbian sneakers called Alldykes?

Sales dropped dramatically when customers found the tongues weren't long enough.

An elderly man is put in an old people's home by his son.

"Don't worry dad, it's only on a trial basis and if you don't like it then we'll find somewhere else," he tells him, "and I'll ring every day to find out how it's going."

The following morning, the old man wakes up with a hard on and the nurse who brings in his breakfast gives him a wonderful blow job.

"How's it going dad?" asks his son when he rings later in the day.

"Wonderful, wonderful," enthuses the old man "why this morning I had a hard on and a pretty nurse gave me a blow job. It was just perfect."

"Well that's good Dad, I'm glad everything's going well."

However, later in the day, as he's walking down the corridor, he drops his glasses and bending down to pick them up he gets molested. A male orderly whips out his todger and takes him from behind, giving him a right good seeing to. On the phone that night, he starts sobbing.

"Son, I can't stay here, it's a nightmare. I dropped my glasses today and got fucked up the backside by this huge male orderly. Come and get me please."

The son tries to calm him down.

"Now wait a minute dad, don't forget about that pretty nurse. Isn't it worth staying there just for that?"

"No, no, you don't understand," says the old man in an anguished voice. "I only get a hard on once every two weeks, but I drop things at least half a dozen times a day!"

Two men get talking in a bar and after a couple of drinks one says to the other,

"Listen Karl, if you woke up in the morning with a sore arse, would you tell anyone about it?"

"No," replies Karl.

"How do you fancy going camping with me this weekend?"

GENIES

Monica Lewinsky was walking in the countryside when she spotted an old lamp in the undergrowth. It was covered in mud but as she began to rub the dirt off, a genie appeared in a puff of smoke.

"I am the genie of the lamp," it pronounced, "and I grant you one wish."

Monica thought for a few moments. She was famous and wealthy so what could she ask for? Then an idea came to her.

"I know," she said. "Could you make these love handles of mine disappear?"

"Of course!" replied the genie. And whoosh! And her ears fell off.

"Gerald, look at this," said his mate excitedly. "It's a magic pair of sandals. When you put them on, it makes you irresistible to women. Look, I'll show you."

His friend put on the sandals and sure enough, as he walked down the street he was continually mobbed by beautiful women.

"Bloody hell!" exclaimed Gerald, "let me have a go!"

Gerald put on the sandals and headed off down the street but instead of being embraced by hoards of women, he found himself pursued by gay men at every turn.

"I don't understand," he said desperately. "What's happened?"

"You've got them on the wrong feet, you fool!" said his mate.

A man was walking along the beach when he discovered an old lamp that had been washed up onto the rocks. Picking it up, he was just in the process of rubbing off the dirt when a genie popped out of the spout.

"You have one wish," said the genie. "What do you want?"

The man thought for a moment and replied.

"I would like to be rich, dark and irresistible to women."

So the genie turned him into a box of Black Magic.

A rabbit was being chased through the woods by a great macho grizzly bear when they bumped into a genie.

You have two wishes each," said the genie, once he had picked himself up. So the bear said, "Well this is great! I would like to have such amazing sex appeal that it makes me irresistible... And... erm... for my second wish I would like all the other bears in the forest to be female."

"Shazam!" exclaimed the genie. "Your two wishes have been granted."

Then the genie looked at the rabbit.

"Ok, it's your turn," he said, "What would you like?"

Now the rabbit had been listening closely to the conversation between the bear and the genie, so he answered immediately.

"For my first wish I would like to get as far away from here as possible and secondly I wish for the bear to be gay!"

GOOD NEWS/BAD NEWS

The lawyer looked at his client and said,

"I've got good news and bad news. Your wife has found a picture worth £1 million."

"Well that's amazing!" exclaimed the client, "but what's the bad news?"

"It's a picture of you and your secretary."

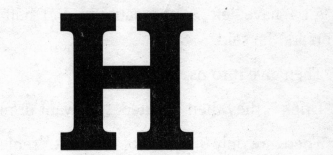

HAGS

An isolated part of the country was being terrorised by a gang of ruthless bandits and people were fleeing their homes. In one village, all that remained was a young boy and his toothless, 85 year old Grandma.

One morning, they were woken by a tremendous noise as the gang rode into town.

"We want food," they demanded of the young boy.

"All I have left is one sausage and half a loaf of bread," he said.

"Then give it to us. War is war."

"Drink," they then shouted, "we want drink."

"There are only 3 bottles of beer left," replied the boy.

"Good. Let's have them now. War is war."

"Women. Bring us women," they yelled later.

"There is only my grandma," he said, pointing to the old hag who was smiling at them.

"Well… er… perhaps we'll forget about the women," one of them said, looking at the horrible sight.

"What do you mean?" said the old woman crossly. "War is war."

HEAVENLY MATTERS

Said God to the archangel, "I've just arranged for 12 hours of darkness to be followed by 12 hours of light – and this I'll alternate down on earth."

"So what are you going to do now?" asked the archangel.

"Oh, I think I'll call it a day," came the reply.

Three married couples arrived at the Pearly Gates at the same time and were met by St. Peter.

He said to the first couple, "May I have your names please?"

"Yes, of course," replied the husband. "I'm Bob Crossley and this is my wife Sherry."

"Oh I'm sorry," said St. Peter, "I can't let you in. I can't have anyone in here with a name related to drinking."

So the first couple walked away sadly.

St. Peter turned to the second couple. "Names please."

"I'm Martin Parker and this is my wife Penny."

"Oh dear," St. Peter said shaking his head. "No one can come in here if their name is related to money."

So the second couple departed.

Then before St. Peter could ask the third couple any questions, the husband took his wife by the arm and led her away.

"Come on Fanny, let's go," he said.

Three men all line up outside the Pearly Gates where St. Peter says to them

"Listen fellas, we're quite busy here at the moment. I'll tell you what I'll do. You can go back down to earth and carry on your lives as long as you give up your bad habits. Otherwise, it'll be back up here and standing in line for the next few months until I have a chance to deal with you."

The three men are overjoyed. The fat man promises to stop being greedy, the gambler promises to stop yearning after money and the superstar promises to stop being so promiscuous.

For two weeks, the men keep to their pledges but then one lunchtime the fat man is walking past a 5-star hotel when the smell of food is more than he can bear. He goes in and finds a sumptuous carvery laid out, the best he's ever seen. Rushing up to the table he takes not one, but two plates and fills them to overflowing but just as he's about to take the first forkful, 'WHOOSH' he disappears. Meanwhile, not far away the gambler and the superstar are just saying their goodbyes after having lunch together. As the gambler walks off down the street he sees a young woman drop a £10 note. Instead of calling to her, he waits till she has gone and then bends down to pick it up – WHOOSH… both the gambler and the superstar disappear.

A nun dies and finds herself standing outside the Pearly Gates.

St. Peter says, "I know you have led a truly unblemished life Sister, but I must ask you one question before you come in. What did Eve first say to Adam?"

"Gosh, that's a hard one," she replies.

"Well done," says St. Peter and opens the gates.

It's a nice day so Jesus and St. Paul decide to have a round of golf. They reach the 10th fairway and Jesus asks St. Paul for his advice.

"What should I use for this shot?"

"I'd use a 5 iron," St. Paul replies.

Jesus thinks for a moment. "I don't know," he replies, "I think Jack Nicklaus would use a 6 iron."

"No, no," said St. Paul "You've got to make sure you get over the lake and miss the bunkers on the right."

"No, I'm going with a 6 iron."

Jesus takes his shot and the ball plunges straight into the lake.

"Never mind," he says, and with that he walks across the water to retrieve the ball. Just at that moment, another golfer walks by and sees Jesus walking on the water.

He turns to St. Paul and says

"Who does he think he is? Jesus Christ."

"Oh no," replies St. Paul, "he thinks he's Jack Nicklaus."

God and the archangel Gabriel went out to play a round of golf. On the first tee, the archangel hit a tremendous shot right down the middle of the fairway. Then it was God's turn. He hooked the ball badly and it went flying towards a deep bunker. However, at the last moment, a bird flew over, caught the ball in its beak and headed towards the first green where it dropped it safely into the hole. The archangel turned to God angrily and said,

"Listen, are we going to play golf or just fuck about?"

Two men arrive at the Pearly Gates and as St. Peter signs them in, he shakes his head in disappointment.

"Oh dear, oh dear," he sighs. "I see from your records that both of you cheated on paying taxes back on earth, I'm afraid you'll have to pay a penalty for that."

So the two men enter heaven but are paired up with a couple of old hags who will be with them for eternity. Some months later, they bump into an old friend of theirs. On his arm is the most beautiful woman they've ever seen. The two men take him aside. "Wow! Bert, you've done alright for yourself," they say.

"Oh yes," he enthused. "Isn't she gorgeous? You want to see her in bed – talk about heaven! What puzzles me, though, is after we've made love, she always turns over and mutters 'bloody income tax'."

When Einstein died and arrived at the gates of heaven, St. Peter wouldn't let him in until he proved his identity.

Einstein scribbled out a couple of his equations, and was admitted into paradise.

And when Picasso died, St. Peter asked, "How do I know you're Picasso?"

Picasso sketched out a couple of his masterpieces. St. Peter was convinced and let him in.

When George W. Bush died, he went to heaven and met the man at the gates. "How can you prove to me you're George W. Bush?" Saint Peter said.

Bush replied, "Well heck, I don't know."

St. Peter says, "Well, Albert Einstein showed me his equations and Picasso drew his famous pictures. What can you do to prove you're George W. Bush?"

Bush replies, "Who are Albert Einstein and Picasso?"

St. Peter says, "C'mon on in, George."

HONEYMOONS

A young couple get married and on their honeymoon night they retire to the hotel bedroom to consummate the marriage. The man takes off his shirt and the woman notices that his back is covered in small scars.

"How did you get those?" she asks.

"When I was eight years old I had the pneesles," he says.

Then the man takes off his trousers and she notices that he has a withered leg.

"What's wrong with your leg?" she asks.

"I had rolio when I was 10," he replies.

Then the man takes his Y-fronts off and she says scornfully, "Let me guess, smallcox!"

The newly married couple arranged to spend the night at the bride's parent's house before setting off on their honeymoon the following day. However, when they hadn't put in an appearance two hours before leaving for the airport, the bride's mother began to get worried.

"Has anyone seen June and Malcolm since yesterday?" she asked the rest of the family.

"I did," said the young son of 7. "Last night when I went to the bathroom, Malcolm asked me if I had any Vaseline. I wasn't sure what that was, so I gave him some of my modelling glue instead."

The honeymooners arrive at the 4-star hotel, covered in confetti.

"Aha!" said the receptionist, "you'll be wanting the bridal."

"Oh no," blushed the new bride, "I'll just hang onto his ears until I get used to it."

Three daughters all got married on the same day and spent their honeymoon night in their parent's palatial mansion. The couples retired to bed early and some time later, the parents turned off the lights and went upstairs as well. Now the parent's bedroom was in the west wing and to get there, they had to pass their daughters' rooms. As they walked past the first door, they heard their daughter laughing. Behind the second door, they heard their daughter crying, but behind the third door there was no sound at all. The following morning, the parents took their daughters aside and questioned them about the night before.

The first daughter said, "Well, you always told me it was polite to laugh if someone told you a joke."

And the second daughter said, "You always told me to cry if I was hurt."

Finally, the third daughter said, "And you told me never to speak with my mouth full."

Jake had only been away one day on his honeymoon before he returned home alone to his small village.

"Why Jake, what brings you back so soon?" asked his mother.

"It's Jessica," he replied. "I found out she is still a virgin so I left her."

"Good for you son," replied the mother. "If she's not good enough for the rest of her family, she's not good enough for you."

It's the honeymoon night and the new bride is breathless with anticipation. She gets into bed and waits for her husband to come out of the bathroom, but what a shock when he does! He gets into bed wearing a woolly vest and thick underpants, turns over and goes straight to sleep. The bride is devastated but doesn't say anything, hoping it will be better the following night.

However, it's worse. The bride gets into bed wearing a very short and sexy negligee but this time her husband crawls under the duvet fully clothed and goes straight to sleep. The bride is overcome with sadness.

On the third night, she's lying there totally naked but this time her husband gets into bed, not only fully clothed but wearing a woolly hat, thick gloves, an overcoat and furry boots.

Her sadness turns to anger.

"Gerald!" she exclaims, "What's going on? Don't you know there's a hole between my legs?"

"So that's where the bloody draft is coming from," he replies.

A man married a Japanese woman who had been brought up to please her husband as much as she could. On their honeymoon night, they spent many hours making mad passionate love and in the morning, when the woman got out of bed, she farted.

"OK 'scuse me," she said, "front hole so happy, back hole whistle."

The vicar and his new wife were preparing for bed on the honeymoon night. But first the vicar said, "My darling, let's kneel down and pray together for strength and guidance."

She replied "Just pray for strength, Maurice, I'll do the guiding."

A mother's three daughters were married on the same day and each went abroad for their honeymoon. Before leaving, mother asked the daughters to send her a postcard letting her know what kind of husband each of them had married.

"But write to me in code," she said. "So as not to embarrass your men."

A couple of weeks later, mother received three postcards. The first daughter had written

"Duzwell Coffee – satisfaction to the last drop."

Mother smiled and nodded with approval. Then she read the second postcard. "Best lay Mattress – Full size, king size". Again mother smiled to herself with satisfaction.

Finally, she read the third postcard which said,

"BA – three times a day, seven days a week, both ways."

On the morning of the wedding, the bride-to-be asked her friend to buy a black sexy negligee and pack it in her going-away bag.

"I don't have time to do it myself," she explained, "and I do so want to look my best for tonight."

So the friend popped down to the shops but couldn't find a black sexy negligee anywhere. In the end she chose a short pink one and stuffed it quickly in the top of the bag. So the wedding took place and after much celebration the newlyweds left for their hide-away hotel. They retired to the bedroom and it was then that the bridegroom had last minute nerves.

"Look Tracy," he said blushing madly, "I'm a bit shy, would you mind leaving me while I take my clothes off."

"Of course not darling," she replied. "I'll change in the bathroom."

So the bride took her bag into the bathroom, opened it and discovered the negligee.

"Oh no!" she said aloud "it's short, pink and wrinkled."

"Hey!" came a voice from the other room. "You promised you wouldn't peek!"

A 25-year-old gold digger met a 75-year-old millionaire and decided she was going to get her hands on his money 'come hell or high water'.

"With any luck, he'll drop dead on our wedding night," she thought.

Three months later, her plan was working.

They had a fabulous wedding and then flew off to the Caribbean for a month's honeymoon.

On the first night, she got into bed hoping to 'love him to death' but gasped in astonishment when he emerged from the bathroom. He was naked except for a rubber on his 12" penis, and a pair of earplugs and nose plugs in his hands.

"What are those for?" she asked warily.

"Well, if there are two things I can't stand, it's women screaming and the smell of burning rubber," he replied.

HOSPITALS

A man had been so badly injured that he could only be fed rectally through a tube. When his wife arrived at the hospital to find out how he was, the nurse replied, "Oh much better, we're really pleased with his progress. It was good to see his arse snap at a bowl of cornflakes this morning."

As the man wakes up from a routine operation to have his tonsils removed, he sees a group of doctors standing around the bed.

"What's wrong?" he asks nervously, looking at their solemn faces.

"I'm afraid there's been a mix-up in taking your tonsils out, we've given you a sex change operation instead. We've taken away your penis and given you a vagina."

"Oh no!" wails the man, "this is dreadful. It means I'll never experience another erection."

"Now hold on a minute," replies the surgeon, "that's not necessarily true. You can experience another erection. It just won't be yours."

A man went into hospital to have an appendectomy but unfortunately the surgeon sneezed half way through and his knife slipped and cut off one of the man's testicles. In a panic, the surgeon replaced it with an onion. A few weeks later, the man returned for a check up.

"How's it going?" asked the surgeon.

"Oh fine," said the man, "apart from some odd side effects."

"Really!" said the surgeon with a sinking heart, "and what are those?"

"Well, every time I go for a piss, my eyes water. When my wife gives me a blow job, she gets indigestion and when I smell hamburgers, I get an erection."

The rugby player was rushed to hospital with a dislocated shoulder. As the doctor manoeuvred it back into place, he groaned and yelled out in pain.

"Stop acting like a baby," remarked the doctor, "a big rugby player like yourself should show a bit more courage. Now there's a woman next door who's having a baby and she's not making a fuss like you."

"Maybe not," replied the rugby player through gritted teeth, "but then in her case no one's trying to push anything back in."

Margaret loved doing good deeds and was a regular visitor to the local hospital, chatting to patients left on their own and boring the pants off them. As she was about to leave one morning, she bumped into the Ward Sister of men's surgical.

"Well I think I've cheered them all up," she said naively, "although I did have trouble with the man at the end. He's Russian isn't he?"

The Ward Sister looked puzzled.

"Russian? No we haven't anyone here from Russia."

"Well that's strange, I popped over to see him, told him I was there to cheer him up and asked what his name was. I'm sure he mumbled 'Opitchabitch."

A Scotsman, an Englishman and an Indian are pacing the waiting room of the local maternity hospital. All three are expecting their first babies and the tension is mounting. As luck would have it, all the babies are born within a few minutes of each other and the nurse appears some time later with some disturbing news.

"We've got the babies mixed up," she says, "so we hope you might be able to identify the one that is yours."

The Scotsman is first through the door and into the nursery.

"I'll have that one," he says quickly.

"Hold on," says the Englishman, "that's the brown baby, you must know that can't be yours."

"I know," replies the Scotsman, "but this way I know I haven't picked the English one!"

A pretty nurse went along to the psychiatrist.

"I've got an awful problem," she said, "every new doctor I meet, I end up in bed with him. But afterwards I feel so guilty and depressed."

"So you want me to stop your urges to jump into bed with all these doctors?" asked the psychiatrist.

"Well, no," she replied, "I want you to stop me feeling so guilty and depressed."

A man and a woman are sitting in a hospital corridor waiting to be called. They strike up a conversation.

"I'm here to give blood," she says, "it's £5 a pint, what about you?"

"I'm here to donate sperm" he answers, "its £30 each time."

"Oh really," she says, looking thoughtful. Some weeks later, the same two people meet again at the hospital.

"Have you come to give some more blood?" asks the man.

"Uh, Uh," she says, shaking her head and keeping her mouth closed.

HUNTING

Two men thought up a great idea for hunting down a grizzly rogue bear who had been terrorising the local neighbourhood. They dressed up in a female bear costume hoping to lure the grizzly close enough to shoot him. All went according to plan and in the middle of a forest clearing they heard the mighty roar of the bear as it strode into view.

"Quick, Fred," whispered the man at the front of the costume, "let's get out and shoot him."

"We can't," came the muffled voice at the back, "the zip's stuck. What shall we do?"

"Well I'm going to start stripping bark," said the voice at the front, "but you'd better brace yourself."

HUSBANDS

Two deaf men go out for a night on the town and return home very late and very drunk. When they meet the following day, the first man signs that his wife was asleep when he got in so he was able to slip into bed without waking her. The second man shakes his head sadly and signs 'no such bloody luck'. The wife was awake and started giving me hell."

"So what did you do?" signs the first man.

"I turned the light off," he signs back.

A man walked up to an attractive girl and said,

"I've lost my wife, do you mind if I talk to you."

"Why?" she asked.

"Because every time I talk to a pretty girl, my wife always appears out of the blue!"

"I demand to see the burglar who broke into our house last night," demanded the irate man to the duty officer.

"Now, now Sir," came the reply. "You'll have to wait until he appears in court later this morning."

"But I only want to ask him one question," said the man. "I want to know how he managed to get into the house without waking my wife up… I've been trying for years and I've never managed it."

The lights of the patrol car picked out a man staggering along the street at 2.30 in the morning. They pulled up beside him and one of the officers got out.

"Where are you going?" he asked.

"A lecture" replied the man.

"What! At this time of night? Who's giving it?"

"My wife," he replied.

I was waiting in the queue at the bank when this woman starts talking about marrying her 4th husband. It turns out her 1st hubby was a gynaecologist, and all he liked to do was look at 'it'. Her 2nd husband was a psychiatrist and all he liked to do was talk about 'it'. And her 3rd husband was a stamp collector, and GOD! How she misses him!

"Doctor, I have a problem, I can't get sexually aroused for my wife," said the distraught husband.

"Now don't worry too much," replied the doctor, "just bring your wife in tomorrow and I'll see what can be done."

The following day, the man's wife came to the surgery with him.

"Hello Mrs Plainly, would you mind taking all your clothes off and sitting on the bed with your legs in the air... That's fine, thank you. Now you can get dressed."

The doctor took the man aside and said confidentially to him. "Don't worry, it's not your fault. Your wife does nothing for me either."

A man sat at the bar looking at a centrefold.

"Hey, John," he called to the barman. "What's this?" he asked, holding up the picture.

"It's a girl," came the reply.

"But it can't be. That's what I married and she doesn't look anything like this!"

"Hello darling," said the man to his wife as she walked into the pub. "What can I get you to drink sweetheart?"

The order was given and the man went up to the bar.

"You old romantic!" remarked the barman. "You always call your wife by such lovely names."

"Well to be honest," replied the husband, "I forgot her real name about five years ago!"

I

INFIDELITY

A woman discovered her husband had been cheating on her, so the next time he went off to the oil rig she plotted her revenge. One morning a parcel arrived for the husband, containing a batch of home made cookies and a video of his favourite TV programmes.

"Oh great!" he said, and invited his friends to come round and watch it with him that night after their shift had finished. They settled down, watched the video and munched away at the cookies. However, an hour and a half into the recording, it suddenly went blank and then a picture of his wife appeared giving his next-door neighbour a blow job. As he watched in horror, she spat the contents of her mouth into the cookie mixture, turned to the camera and hissed, "I want a divorce!"

Late at night, there was a knock at the door and when the wife answered, a man demanded, "Do you know how to have sex?"

The woman closed the door in alarm and the man went away. But for the next three nights he returned, shouting at her through the letterbox. "Do you know how to have sex?" he kept repeating.

Now her husband had been away on business for the week, but when he returned on Friday he could see she was very upset. It didn't take long for him to find out what had been

happening so he advised her to open the door and he'd be waiting behind it to deal with the pest.

Sure enough, later that night, the man returned banging on the door. The wife opened it as he shouted, "Do you know how to have sex?"

"Yes, I do," she replied.

"Then give it to your husband," he said angrily, "and tell him to leave my wife alone."

After a good romp in the back seat, the man turned to his date and said,

"Do you tell your mother everything?"

"Oh, she's not interested," came the reply. "It's my bloody husband who's so nosy."

Instead of going home after work, the man took his secretary for a drink, then dinner, then back to her place for a session of wild sex. A few hours later, he realised he ought to be getting home so he dressed quickly, combed his hair and looked aghast at the love bite on his neck. How was he going to talk his way out of this one!

Later, as he opened the front door, the dog bounded up and greeted him wildly. Immediately the man had a great idea. He fell to the floor and allowed the dog to jump on top of him, just as his wife appeared in the hall.

"Look at this!" he said feigning anger. "Look what the dog's done to my neck."

"Well, that's nothing," she replied, ripping off her blouse. "Look what he did to my tits."

The couple's marriage was on the rocks so the wife decided to go and see a psychiatrist. After 30 minutes of general chat, the subject turned to sex and it soon became apparent that the problem lay in this area.

"When you make love, do you ever watch your husband's face?" asked the psychiatrist.

"Well, I did once," she replied.

"Once!" he exclaimed, "and how did he look?"

"Very angry," she replied.

"Well, this is most extraordinary," he remarked. "Not only is it very unusual to have only seen your husband's face once, but I'm amazed to hear that he looked so angry. Can you give me some idea of what was happening at the time?"

"Yes, he was watching me through the kitchen window!"

A man was walking through Piccadilly Circus on his way home when he passed a novelty stand and there on the counter were lots of funny certificates. One said,

"The holder of this certificate is authorised to have 3 hours of sex every day, wherever she likes."

The man thought this was a great joke and bought it to take home to his wife as a silly present.

"I'm home darling!" he called as he went into the house, "and I've bought you a present."

The wife appeared from the kitchen, read the certificate and smiled broadly.

"Oh John, that's wonderful," she said, grabbing her coat. "Dinner's in the oven, I'll see you in 3 hours."

"Eileen, there's something I must ask you," said her husband. "Now that our five children have all grown up and left home, there's something that's always bothered me. It's Charlie. He doesn't look anything like the other four. Has he got a different father? Come on Eileen, just tell me. It's all in the past so I won't get angry."

The wife looked sadly at her husband and nodded her head.

"Yes Jack. You're right, Charlie does have a different father from the other four."

"I knew it," muttered Jack, sitting down in the chair. "Who is the father, Eileen?" he asked apprehensively.

She looked at him cautiously and replied,

"You are, Jack."

★

Two neighbours met up in the street. One said to the other,

"You filthy pig, you're lowering the tone of the whole street. When I walked past your window last night I could see your wife giving you a blow job."

"Well you were wrong!" snarled the other. "You'd better go and get some glasses because I wasn't even home last night!"

A man happened to pass an old antique shop and on the spur of the moment popped inside to have a look around. On one of the top shelves, he saw an old pair of glasses and as he reached up to take them, the owner approached.

"Ah, I see you're interested in the spectacles," he remarked. "In fact they're very special glasses because when you look through them, you see everyone naked."

"Get away!" laughed the man, "that's hard to believe."

"Try them on Sir, and you will see for yourself."

So the man did, and gasped with amazement. There was the owner standing there completely naked and as he looked out of the window all the passers-by were naked as well.

"I'll have them!" he said, "no matter what the cost."

So, having purchased the unique spectacles, the man decided to go home and show his wife what he had bought, before going back to work. He arrived home, entered the house, put on the glasses and walked into the front room. Sitting on the sofa was his wife and Mr. Brown from next door, both of them completely naked.

"Hello, it's me!" he said, taking off the glasses.

But the couple on the sofa remained naked.

"Oh no!" complained the man. "£500 I paid for these, and they're knackered already!"

"Darling, we've been married nearly 60 years and I'm still very happy. But in all that time have you ever been unfaithful?" he asked.

His wife looked at him in surprise.

"Well, if you must know, I was unfaithful just three times."

"Really! When?"

"The first time was when you put in for promotion to become the youngest general manager in the company and it all depended on the vote of Malcolm Havelot."

"So being unfaithful that one time has helped me work my way up to being one of the most successful men in our industry. Thank you, darling. When was the second time?"

"That was fifteen years ago when there was a threat of a by-pass being built at the bottom of our land. If you remember, there were two options and the final decision rested with the Planning Officer and the Environmental Surveyor."

"So you saved our house, how wonderful," he said in gratitude. "Even if you did sleep with two men at the same time. And the third time?"

"Okay, yes. You remember that time you wanted to restructure the company and you were 84 votes short…"

After spending two months abroad on business, a man came home to the loving embrace of his wife and son. They spent a delightful evening together, catching up on all the gossip and it wasn't until the next morning, that he noticed his son playing on an expensive games console.

"Where did you get that from son?" he asked.

"From hiking," replied the son.

"Hiking! Come off it," said dad, "you don't get money hiking. Now where did it come from?"

"Honest dad, it's true. While you were away, Mr. Miles from the council would come round to see Mum, and he'd always say to me, "here lad, have this £10 and take a hike."

A man came home from the pub earlier than usual to discover his best friend was in bed with his wife.

"Oh Jack!" he exclaimed, sadly shaking his head, "I have to. But you?"

Five minutes after leaving the house for work, the man realises he's forgotten some important papers. He turns round, gets home and walks into the kitchen to see his wife standing over the sink. Quick as lightning he goes up to her and grabs her tits from behind saying jokingly, "Now what can I do you for today?"

"Just six eggs and a pint of cream please," she replies.

A man came home early from work to find his wife in bed with another man.

"What the hell are you doing?" he screamed.

"I'm listening to the music," said the stranger who had his head between the wife's breasts.

"Get off," said the husband, "let me have a go… Well I can't hear anything."

"Of course you can't," replied the stranger. "You're not plugged in."

A man walked into the bedroom to find his wife in bed with a midget.

"Not again!" he roared. "Last month it was an all-in wrestler, last week a filing clerk and now, today, a midget!"

"Well look at it like this," she answered, "at least I'm cutting back."

Instead of going home, the man took his new young secretary out to dinner where they drank a lot and then went back to her place for coffee and bed. Alas, no matter how much he tried, he could not get an erection so eventually he went home, very embarrassed. He slid very quietly into bed, next to his fat snoring wife and as their bodies touched he finally got the erection he'd been trying for all night. Cursing under his breath, he got out of bed again looked down at his wondrous organ and said,

"No one wonder they call you a fucking plonker!"

Two men were talking over their pints of beer.

"You know Jack, yesterday I was reading in the paper that the world has too many people. We're running out of space."

"So?"

"Well its true. When I went home last night, I found a man in our wardrobe."

A distraught wife raged at her husband.

"A mistress? You have a mistress, but why? What's she got that I haven't?"

So the husband told her.

"She's so wonderful in bed, she moans and groans all the time. Not like you, you're so unresponsive."

The following evening, the wife decided to show her husband just how good she could be. She turned to him in bed, roused his manhood and when he started making love to her, she began.

"Well, what a day I've had. First the car ran out of petrol and I had to walk 2 miles to the nearest garage, then it started to rain, our daughter was sick all over the carpet, the cat peed all over the kitchen floor..."

INSECTS

Professor Blenkinsop had made the study of spiders his life work. Now, after fifty years, he was revealing to the world, the results of his painstaking research.

He placed a spider on the table and told it to walk ten paces forward. The spider did exactly that. Then he told the spider to walk ten paces backwards and again the spider obeyed. The gasps of astonishment and applause from the audience were tumultuous.

Professor Blenkinsop put his hands up to quieten the crowd. Then he picked up the spider and pulled off all its legs.

"Walk ten paces forward," he commanded the spider. But it didn't move.

"Okay," he said, "walk ten paces backwards."

But still it didn't move.

The Professor turned to the audience and in his most solemn voice he declared,

"Ladies and gentlemen I have just proved without a doubt that if you pull the legs off a spider, it can no longer hear."

"Daddy, daddy," said the little girl, "what are those two insects doing?"

"Well my darling, they're doing what comes naturally. I've told you about the birds and the bees."

"And daddy, what are those two insects called?" she continued.

"Daddy long-legs."

"But daddy, one must be a mummy long-legs," she persisted.

"No, my little sugar plum, they're both daddy long-legs."

"Ugh!" she squealed, went up to the insects and squashed them underfoot.

"What did you do that for?" asked daddy, surprised.

"Well I'm not having anything like that going on in our garden!" she replied angrily.

"Three double whiskeys," said the flea, hopping up to the bar. He drank them one after another and then went rushing out of the door, jumped high into the air and landed with a crash on the ground.

"Bugger!" he cursed, "someone's gone off with my dog!"

J

JEWISH

A Jewish man stared sadly into his pint of beer and his sad demeanour attracted the attention of the barman.

"What's up?" he asked.

The man sighed deeply and said,

"Three weeks ago my father died and left me £250,000 in his will."

"I'm sorry to hear that," said the barman. "It's always hard to lose a parent."

"And then two weeks ago," continued the man, "my wife died and her million pound estate came to me."

"Why that's awful!" exclaimed the barman. "Your poor wife."

"And only last week, my great aunt died leaving me £100,000."

"God Almighty!" said the astonished barman. "Three deaths in three weeks. No wonder you're looking miserable."

"So what happens this week?" said the Jewish man, holding out his hands and shaking his head, "Nothing, absolutely nothing."

A Jewish man is reading his newspaper when suddenly he exclaims loudly,

"Lynn, Lynn vot is syphilis, it says you can die from it, but vot is it? Many people get de syphilis."

"Now, now," says his wife. "I'll look it up in the medical encyclopaedia, don't panic."

Moments later, the wife returns with the book and smiles at him.

"Nothing to worry about old man, it says it only affects de gentiles."

A Jewish girl goes away on holiday and on returning, rings her mother from the airport.

"Hi mum, I've got some wonderful news. I met this gorgeous bloke and it was love at first sight. We've got engaged and I'm bringing him home to meet you. One thing though, he's not Jewish."

"Well, okay," replies Mum, "but I expect he's got a good job?"

"No he hasn't. He's unemployed. He doesn't want a nine to five job. He hopes to play in a rock band."

"Well, okay. Where will you live once you are married."

"If it's alright, mum, we'd like to stay with you until we save up some money."

"Well, okay. Your dad can sleep downstairs and you can have our room."

"But what about you, mum? Where will you sleep."

"Me! Don't worry about me. As soon as you put the phone down, I'm going to drop dead!"

A man who had performed circumcisions in his community for more than 50 years decided to retire because of failing eyesight. Throughout those 50 years, he had taken home the foreskin from each circumcision and stored it in a big trunk in his basement. He decided to take this trunk to his good friend, the leather designer, and ask him to make something with them to commemorate his career. The leather designer agreed to the strange request and told the man to return in two weeks time.

"Come in, come in," said the leather designer two weeks later, "it is all done, I think you will be pleased." With that, he opened a small cupboard and handed the man a beautiful wallet. The man couldn't hide his disappointment.

"You don't like it?" asked the leather designer, looking crestfallen.

"No, no, it's not that," said the man "it's superb. It just doesn't seem a lot for all those years of work."

"Ah, my friend, you don't understand. This is a unique wallet. When you rub it, it turns into a suitcase!"

Two children were playing on the beach with their dog when a freak wave carried the poor animal out to sea. Luckily, a passing rabbi saw the plight of the dog so he dived in and dragged it from the water, laid it on the sand and gave it mouth-to-mouth resuscitation.

"Are you a vet?" asked the children.

"Am I a vet?" replied the rabbi. "I'm soaking."

Two Jewish businessmen travel up to London every day on the 8.15 to Waterloo. Then one morning Morrie turns to his companion and says,

"You know, it's amazing; after all these years of travelling together you never asked me how my business is doing."

"I'm sorry," replies his companion, "how is business?"

"Oh," says Morrie, "don't ask."

KIDS

As Little Tommy walked into his father's bedroom, he saw him putting a condom on the end of his dick. Dad immediately bent over the bed to hide his erection, hoping the young child had not seen it. So when Tommy asked him what he was doing, he replied quickly, "I'm looking for a rat."

"What!" exclaimed the boy, "Are you going to fuck him then?"

While Dad was away on business there was a terrible storm one night and the kids were so frightened, they crept into Mum's bed. When he returned, they told him all about it saying they wished he'd been there to look after them.

A few weeks later, Dad was away again and on his return, the kids met him at the railway station.

"Daddy, Daddy!" they called, pushing their way through the crowds,

"It's alright, no one slept with Mum this time."

A little boy wakes up in the middle of the night needing to have a pee. On the way back from the toilet, he hears a noise from his parent's bedroom, he peeks round the door and sees them in the throes of lovemaking.

Quietly, the boy creeps back to his own bedroom and wakes up his young sister.

"Come with me," he whispers and takes her along to see their parents.

"Look at that," he says, "and we get smacked just for sucking our thumbs!"

Late one night, the doctor was called out to the house of a woman expecting a baby. Unfortunately, the weather was very stormy and by the time he got there, the electricity had failed. He realised he would have to deliver the baby by candlelight so he was forced to ask for the help of the woman's young 5 year-old son.

Thirty minutes later, the baby was born and all was well, thanks in part to the young boy holding the candle. The doctor examined the new arrival and gave it a tap on the bottom to make it cry. At that point, the young son said forcefully,

"I'd smack him harder than that, he shouldn't have been up there in the first place."

"Mummy, Mummy, can I go and watch the builders next door please?" said the young six-year-old boy.

"Alright," replied mum, just don't get in their way."

So the little boy spent all day watching the workmen and when he came back for tea, Mum asked him if he'd enjoyed his day.

"Oh yes," he said enthusiastically, "it was great."

"Well, tell me about it," she said.

"I watched the plumber. He put the fucking pipe under the sink but the frigging seal was broken so he had to start the bloody thing again. It was a right bastard."

"Tommy!" gasped his shocked mother. "Wait till you father gets home, I'll let him deal with you."

So when Dad arrived home, he listened to what his son had to say and was so angry, he shouted loudly,

"Tommy, you need to be taught a lesson. Go out and get me a switch."

But Tommy replied,

"Go fuck yourself, that's the electrician's job."

"Hello, Mrs Smith, have I ever mentioned my children?"

"No," replied Mrs Smith, "and I'm eternally grateful for it."

"Sophie, what are you doing with my toothbrush?" asked Dad.

"I'm cleaning the dog's teeth," she replied. "But don't worry, I'll put it back when I've finished, like I always do."

The family sat down to lunch and young Emma looked expectantly at her Grandma.

"What is it?" asked Grandma.

"I'm waiting for you to get your nosebag out" she replied.

"Nosebag? I don't understand," said Grandma.

"Well I heard Mummy and Daddy say you ate like a horse."

"Tomorrow we will discuss human reproduction so I'd like you to go home tonight and find out as much as you can about the subject," said the class teacher.

Young Tommy went home and found his mother in the kitchen.

"Mummy, where did I come from?" he asked. Too busy to sit down and tell him the truth, she replied,

"A stork brought you darling and put you under the rose bush."

Tommy went into the dining room where his grandma was watching TV.

"Where did my mum come from?" he asked her.

Now Grandma didn't discuss such things so she replied,

"A stork left her under a bush in the garden."

Finally, Tommy sought out his great grandmother who was upstairs in the bedroom.

"Great Grandma," he said softly "where did my grandma come from?"

"Not now darling," she replied, "I'm a bit tired, but you must have heard of the stork?"

The next day in school, the teacher asked the children what they had learned.

"Please miss," said Tommy putting up his hand, "as far as I can see, our family hasn't had sexual relations for three generations."

"Children! What are you doing down there?"

"We're making love."

"Well that's nice, dears, as long as you're not fighting."

Marjorie and her 20-year-old niece were in the drawing room when Charles walked in and tripped over the dog.

"Fuck me!" he said angrily.

"Charles!" exclaimed his wife, "do watch your language in front of our niece."

Charles glanced at his niece and replied knowingly, "I'm sure you've heard that expression before, my dear?"

"Oh yes," she said winking, "but not usually in that tone of voice."

"Daddy, Daddy, what are those two dogs doing?" asks the little boy.

"Well son, they're making puppies," replies Dad.

Some time later, the boy passes his parents bedroom and peeps in to find them making love.

"Daddy, Daddy what are you doing?" he asks.

"We're making a baby," Dad replies.

The boy thinks for a moment and then says,

"Dad, can you turn Mum over 'cos I'd rather have a puppy."

"Mummy, Mummy, why is Daddy running zigzag across the garden?"

"Shut up and reload."

★

The twins' 8th birthday was close at hand and their mother was worried about buying them presents. She consulted a child psychiatrist.

"My daughter is a very happy child," she said, "always seeing the best in everything. But my son sees nothing but doom and gloom, no matter what I do. Can you help me?" she asked.

"Hmm," mused the psychiatrist. "You have got to try and break into your son's dark mood. I suggest you buy him some wonderful presents, things that you know he really wants. As for your daughter, well she'll be happy with anything – even a sack of manure!"

So the morning of their birthdays arrived and the little boy opened 3 huge parcels. One contained a bike, the second contained a Playstation™ and the third was a pair of very expensive trainers.

"How do you like them?" asked Mum.

"Okay, I suppose," he replied, "but I'll probably fall off my bike and break an arm and a leg so I won't be able to use the Playstation™ or wear my new shoes."

Mum was devastated at the failure to cheer up her son. She turned to her daughter whose arms were thrashing wildly around in the manure.

"What about you Susie?" she asked, "What did you get?"

"I think it's a pony," she replied, "I just can't seem to find him at the moment."

Mum sat her young son on her lap and said,

"I have a big surprise for you sweetheart. You're going to have a baby sister. The stork is bringing her in a few days time."

"Golly, Mum," said the boy, "Dad says there's going to be a baby left under the rose bush and grandma says the hospital is going to give us one. We're going to have bloody kids everywhere!"

"Mummy," said the little boy. "I think daddy's got a bicycle."

"And why do you think that?" asked Mum.

"I found a tiny inner tube in his pocket," he replied.

A woman was given some deer steaks which she cooked and served for dinner that evening.

"What's this Mum?" asked the young daughter.

"Why don't you try and guess?" replied Mum.

"Is it beef?"

"No"

"Is it lamb?" asked the son.

"No, try harder."

"I'll give you a clue," said Dad. "It's what your mum sometimes calls me."

"Arrrgh!" screamed the son, spitting out the food. "Don't eat it, sis, it's arsehole."

The young daughter was passing her parents' bedroom one night when she saw them engaged in some passionate lovemaking. The following morning she asked her father what they had been doing.

"Oh nothing to worry about," replied Dad. "Your mum was having a fit and I was holding her down."

The following week, when Dad came home from work the little girl ran to him and said

"Oh Daddy, I'm so glad you're back. Mummy had another one of those fits today and the next door neighbour had to hold her down."

Once upon a time a son was born and it was just a head. Even though there was no body, he was loved dearly by his parents and had a very happy childhood. Then on his 18th birthday, his father took him to the pub for a drink and as he supped his first pint, all of a sudden his body appeared. As he drank a second pint, an arm appeared and so forth. Each time he had another pint, more of his body appeared until he was a whole man. It was a miracle. At closing time, father and son left the pub but the son, having drunk so many pints, was very unsteady on his feet. He accidentally staggered into the middle of the road and was hit by a car. He died instantly.

"Oh dear," said the barman. "He should have quit while he was a head."

"Mummy, mummy, can I lick the bowl, please?"

"No, dear, pull the chain like everyone else."

L

LITTLE RED RIDING HOOD

Little Red Riding Hood is walking through the forest on the way to meet her Grandma when she spots someone moving.

"Mr. Wolf, Mr. Wolf," she trills, "I can see you! Come out from behind that tree."

"Bugger off," he replies angrily and disappears deeper into the forest.

Moments later, Red Riding Hood spots him again.

"Mr. Wolf, Mr. Wolf!" she calls. "I can see you behind the bush."

The wolf glowers at her and runs off. A short while later she sees him hiding behind a big rock.

"I can see you, I can see you," she says, pointing her finger at him.

"Now look here," says the wolf, "who the hell are you and what are you doing in the forest?"

"I'm Little Red Riding Hood and I'm on my way to see Grandma," she replies.

"Then fuck off and do it," yelled the wolf, "and let me have a crap in peace."

Little Red Riding Hood was walking through the forest one day, when she ran into the Three Little Pigs.

"Little Red Riding Hood, beware! The Big Bad Wolf is waiting for you!" they said. "He's gonna pull up your little red dress, pull down your little red panties, and ride your little red socks off!" Little Red Riding Hood nods her head and says, "That's okay," and continues on her way.

A little while later Smokey the Bear comes up to her and says, "Little Red Riding Hood, beware! The Big Bad Wolf is waiting for you! He's gonna pull up your little red dress, pull down your little red panties, and ride your little red socks off!"

Again she nods her head and says, "I'm not worried." and continues on her way. Well she walk on a bit further, and soon the Big Bad Wolf jumps out and says, "Little Red Riding Hood, beware! I've been waiting for you. Now I'm gonna pull up your little red dress, pull down your little red panties, and ride your little red socks off!"

Very calmly Little Red Riding Hood goes into her basket and pulls out a .357 Magnum. Points it straight between the wolf's eyes and says, "No you're not! You're gonna pull up my little red dress, pull down my little red panties, and eat me like the story says!"

LUCK

One morning, a bored suburban man wakes up to hear a voice in his head saying,

"Give up this awful life. Sell everything, tell your boss to bugger off and take all your money to Monte Carlo."

The man thinks nothing more of it and goes to work as usual. But the voice keeps coming back.

"Go on, sell up, gamble all your money at Monte Carlo."

No matter what he does, the voice keeps pounding away in his head until he finally breaks. He quits work, sells everything he has and flies out to Monte Carlo where he takes all his money to the gambling casinos. When he arrives, the voice says,

"Go to the roulette table, fifth on the right."

He goes to the fifth table.

"Now put all your money on Black 25."

He puts all his money on Black 25 and the croupier spins the wheel. The ball stops on Red 32.

"Oh fuck," says the voice.

Little Tommy went to his mother one day and asked her where he came from. His mother stripped off and showed him. The following day the boy went to school and told all his mates that from now on he wanted to be known as Lucky Tommy.

"Why?" they asked. "Why do you want to be called Lucky Tommy?"

Tommy held up two fingers an inch apart and replied, "Because I was that close to being a turd."

A little girl was up a ladder washing windows. As an old man passed, he noticed she wasn't wearing any knickers and gasped in horror.

"Hey, little girl," he called "here's £10, go and buy yourself some underwear." The little girl ran back inside and told her mother what had happened.

"Really!" exclaimed mum, thinking fast.

"I'll finish the windows," she said, and the next moment she went up the ladder, having removed her knickers first. Lo and behold, the old man passed the woman on the way back from the shops and of course, noticed her lack of underwear.

"Hey, old woman," he called, "here's a quid, go and buy yourself a razor."

The local Mayoress is visiting the amputee ward of the General Hospital, and it's quite gruelling. She goes up to the first bed and meets a man who's had one leg amputated and when she asks how he's getting on he answers bravely,

"Not so bad, your Worship, they're looking after me very well.

She visits a second man who has lost both legs but he smiles politely at her and tells her that he's going to train for the Paralympics when he gets out. In the third bed is a man with no legs or arms.

"I'm alright," he replies in answer to her question. "There are many people worse off than me."

Finally, she gets to the bed at the end of the ward where there's just a head lying on the pillow. Attached to it are many different tubes keeping it alive.

"Hello," she says gently. "I've just come to see how you are."

"Fuck off," comes the reply.

The Mayoress retreats, looking very upset.

"He told me to fuck off," she tells the Ward Sister.

"Oh don't let it upset you, ma'am," she replies, "he's having a bad day. They're taking all his teeth out later."

★

The phone rang.

"Colonel Fanshaw," said the voice at the other end of the line.

"Your new second-in-command is on his way over to see you. Good chap, but has a weakness for gambling. See what you can do."

Moments later, there was a knock on the door and Lieutenant Hill entered, saluted smartly and waited for his orders. As they were talking, the Colonel was taken aback when the Lieutenant asked him if he was suffering from testiculitis.

"No, no I'm not," he replied.

But the Lieutenant was adamant there was something wrong. He said he could detect it in the way the Colonel sat and he would bet £100 he was right.

Thinking this might cure the Lieutenant of squandering his money, the Colonel agreed to the bet. He then dropped his trousers and revealed all. The Lieutenant examined the Colonel closely, feeling for any signs of something amiss, and admitted defeat.

"You're quite right Sir", he said, handing over £100. "There's nothing wrong with you."

Later that day the Colonel spoke to the Adjutant and told him what had happened.

"I'm sure it was a good lesson to learn," he said, "he'll think twice before gambling away so much money again."

However there was a loud groan at the other end of the line.

"Oh no," came the reply, "the sod's done it again! He bet us £500 he'd have you by the balls within an hour of meeting you."

The door opened and a huge 6'5" man walked into the pub and up to the bar. He was almost as wide as he was tall with a neck the size of a tree trunk. But, he had a tiny head.

Now the innkeeper was unable to hide his curiosity and addressed the stranger.

"Look, I'm sorry about this but I have to ask. You're such a big man, yet you have such a tiny head. How come?"

The man shook his tiny head in dismay.

"You'll never believe this," he replied "I was walking along the beach last Sunday and I found a magic lamp."

"Why, what happened?" asked the innkeeper, agog.

"Well, I rubbed the lamp and this beautiful genie appeared. She asked me what I wanted and I said I'd like us to have a shag. Well, you would, wouldn't you?" said the big man, confidentially.

"Yeah, yeah," gasped the innkeeper, "so what happened then?"

"She said genies didn't shag so was there anything else, and I said, okay then, how about a little head?"

Two friends from San Francisco visit Las Vegas and on the last night they win the million-dollar jackpot.

"I can't believe it!" gasps one man, "it's fantastic! Can't wait to get home tomorrow and see my wife's face when I tell her."

"Well let's go now," replies his friend. "Bugger the plane. We'll take a limo."

"No, no," says the first man, caught up in the excitement, "Let's take a taxi."

So they flag down a cab and tell the driver to take them back to San Francisco.

But just as they're getting in, one man says to the other, "Hold on, whereabouts in San Francisco do you live?"

"Just outside, in Oakland," he replies.

"Yeah, I thought so. I'd better get in first because I'm a couple of miles further on."

M

MADNESS

The doctor was on his daily round of the mental asylum and had just entered the room of two of his long-term patients. One was sawing imaginary wood into hundreds of little pieces and the other was hanging upside down from the ceiling.

"What are you doing?" the doctor asked the first man.

"I'm sawing wood," he said, "isn't that obvious?"

"Well what's your friend doing?"

"Oh don't mind him, he thinks he's a light bulb."

"Don't you think you should help him down before all the blood rushes to his head?" continued the doctor.

"What!" exclaimed the man, "and work in the dark!"

The ward sister was doing her rounds in the lunatic asylum when she noticed that one man was racing around the room with his arms spread out making zooming noises.

"Hello Colin," she said, "What are you doing?"

"I'm flying to America," he replied.

Two days later she saw him lying on the ground with his arms still spread out, but making no noise.

"What's happened now?" she asked.

"I've just landed in America," he replied.

So the ward sister moved on and spotted Gerald sitting down behind his bed, masturbating furiously.

"Now, Gerald, what's going on here?" she said sternly.

"I'm shagging Colin's wife while he's in America," replied Gerald.

MARRIAGE

On his way home from work, a man broke down on the M62 between Leeds and Huddersfield. He decided to walk to the nearest telephone to get help when an Alfa Romeo drew up beside him and a sexy voice said,

"Can I help. Do you want a lift?"

He looked down to see a beautiful young blonde, wearing the skimpiest low cut dress, smiling up at him.

When he had explained what had happened, she suggested he come back to her place and ring the garage from there.

The man couldn't believe his luck. When they got back to her place, they wined and dined... and ended the evening in bed, so it was the early hours of the morning before the car was repaired and he arrived home.

"Where the hell have you been?" yelled his wife, "it's nearly 2 o'clock in the morning!"

The man explained about his car breaking down and how a kind blonde in a sports car had offered him dinner while he waited for his car to be repaired.

"Why you lying bastard!" she screeched. "So you expect me to believe a story like that. I know exactly where you've been, out with the lads losing your money at cards again."

A wife came home from work to discover her husband crying inconsolably.

"What's wrong?" she asked.

"Do you remember 12 years ago when I got you pregnant and your father threatened to have me put in jail if I didn't marry you?"

"Yes".

"Well today, I would have got out!"

A couple were going through a very rocky time with their marriage so the wife suggested they go and see a marriage counsellor. The man listened intently while the wife told him all the grievances she had towards her husband, particularly the fact that he had lost all interest in her. The counsellor nodded his head in understanding. Certainly the husband had shown no reaction to what was being said.

So the counsellor decided on some radical treatment. He went over to the wife, took her in his arms and gave her a long lingering kiss.

"There," he said to the bored husband. "Your wife needs that at least three times a week.

"Okay," he replied. "I'll bring her in Mondays, Wednesdays and Fridays."

"Hello John, you look a bit thoughtful this morning. What's up?"

"Oh nothing really. It's just that the wife made toad in the hole for dinner last night."

"So?"

"So she made it with real toads."

"Well just be grateful she didn't decide to make spotted dick!"

The newly married couple returned home from honeymoon and travelled down to the husband's country mansion.

"We'll take the pony and trap, darling," he said, "and then you can get a better view of our land."

However they'd only travelled a mile when the pony began to get awkward and refused to cross over a small stream.

"Come on you bugger!" stormed the man and he hit the pony a severe blow. The animal moved on slowly.

"Right, that's one," said the man.

Ten minutes later, the pony stopped again. The man got down and hit the animal with a piece of wood.

"Now get moving," he yelled. "That's two."

But just as they came in sight of the house, the pony was startled by a flock of pigeons and refused to move. No matter how hard he was hit, he remained still.

"Right!" screamed the man, enraged, "that's three." And he took his hunting rifle from the back of the trap and shot the pony dead.

"Good heavens!" exclaimed the new bride. "How on earth could you be so cruel? I feel as if I'm married to a monster!"

"Right. That's one," replied the husband.

"What would you do if you came home early from work one day and found me in bed with another man?" asked the wife.

"I'd beat him over the head with his white stick," he replied.

"Hello Cyril, what's up?"

"It's the wife. She says she'll leave me if I keep going to all the football matches."

"Oh dear, that's a shame."

"Yes, I shall really miss her."

A middle-aged couple were visiting the local May Day country show and while he went off to the beer tent, she wandered around the livestock area. In the bottom pen stood a mighty bull and a notice on the gate informed the reader that the bull had been out to stud more than 200 times in one year. As she looked up, she caught the owner's eye and recognised him from the local farm.

"Hello Harry, this is a fine beast! You must be very proud. Do me a favour please. If you see my husband tell him about the bull and about him going to stud more than 200 times."

Later on, Harry bumped into the husband and gave him the message from his wife.

"I see," said the husband, "and was this with the same cow every time?"

"Oh no," replied Harry, "two hundred different cows."

"Good. Let my wife know that when you see her, will you?"

An elderly couple were driving home late one night when they were stopped by the police.

"Excuse me, madam," said the officer, "this is just to warn you that your brake light isn't working. You need to get it fixed tomorrow."

The old woman cupped her hand over her ear and said

"What did you say?"

The old man shouted in her ear

"He said the brake light's not working."

"Can I see your driving licence?" continued the officer.

"What?" she asked.

"He wants to see your driving licence," shouted the old man.

As the officer looked at the licence he remarked,

"Oh, I see you come from Bolton. I went there once, met a woman, had the worst sex ever."

"What did he say?" the old woman asked her husband.

"He said he thinks he knows you," came the reply.

The man booked into the 4 star hotel and went up to his room. After having a couple of drinks in the bar and a meal in the restaurant, he returned to his room and rang down to reception.

"Room 205. I'd like a woman up here immediately," he demanded.

"I'm sorry Sir, it's not that kind of hotel," came the reply.

"Oh come on," said the man. "I've paid a lot of money to stay here, and I've been a regular customer for years. Tonight, though, I'm really missing my wife, and I just need someone to take her place for a few hours. What's so bad about that?"

Well, the receptionist was moved by this, so he relented, and got on the phone to a girl he knew would be interested.

An hour or so later there was a knock on the door and the girl entered the room.

The guest looked at her for a moment then said,

"Good, that's fine. Right, get undressed and into bed".

The girl did as he asked and the man did the same.

"Okay," he said, "turn your back to me, tell me you've got a headache and start whingeing."

A couple were so bored with their marriage that they decided to liven it up by competing against each other. But as the weeks went by, the husband became very depressed because his wife was always the winner of any game they played. One night in the pub, his mate took pity on him and suggested a new game.

"You can't fail with this, Steve. It's who can piss up the wall the highest. The bloke's bound to win."

The husband thought this was a great idea and rushed home to tell his wife. She agreed and they went out into the back yard to begin the competition. The wife dropped her knickers, lifted her leg and peed 2' up the wall.

Confidently, the man undid his zip, took out his dick and was just about to start when his wife said,

"Hold on, stop right there, no hands allowed!"

A woman sat in the waiting room while the doctor examined her husband. Afterwards, he came out to speak to her.

"I'm afraid to say your husband is quite seriously ill. He must be cared for at all times. He must have only the best food, plenty of rest and a spotless house. It'll be quite hard for you to cope because you'll now have to do everything yourself – all the heavy chores and the gardening. But I know you'll think it's worthwhile."

As they drove home later, the husband asked his wife,

"So Doris, what did the doctor have to say?"

"He said you're going to die," she replied.

★

An elderly couple had met in an old people's home and after a few months the man got down on his knees and asked for the woman's hand in marriage. She gladly accepted.

However, the next morning when the old man woke up, he couldn't remember what the woman's answer had been. Feeling extremely embarrassed, there was no way round it but to ring her up and find out.

"Hello Gloria, it's Cyril," he said. "I feel awfully silly about this but I wondered whether you'd tell me again what your answer was to my marriage proposal. I'm afraid I can't remember!"

"Oh Cyril," she replied happily, "I'm so glad you phoned. I knew I'd said 'yes' to someone but I couldn't remember who it was!"

"You're going to be really sorry," screamed the wife to her husband. "I'm going to leave you."

He replied "Well make up your mind, which one's it going to be?"

A newly married couple arrived home from the honeymoon and no sooner had they unpacked, he started laying down some rules.

"Just so you understand," he said, "I'll go out with my mates, when I want and where I want. I don't need permission from you. I also expect clean clothes everyday, a clean and tidy house, and dinner on the table at 6.00 p.m. sharp, whether I'm here or not."

"Okay," she said calmly. "But just let me say this. There'll be sex here every night at 7.30 whether you're here or not!"

"Oh Sharon," said her husband, "I've invited Derek round for supper tonight."

"Tonight!" she shrieked, "but the house is in a terrible mess, the kitchen needs a good clean and the dirty washing's piling up."

"Perfect," he said, "the fool's thinking of getting married."

The young couple arrived home from an idyllic honeymoon and took up married life. But within two days the new bride went round to her parent's house in tears.

"Oh Mum," she sobbed, "he was so wonderful on holiday, but now we've returned home he keeps using four letter words!"

"Oh you poor darling," sympathised Mum. "What's he saying?"

"Dust, cook, wash, iron…!"

After 10 years of being divorced, the couple met again at a party.

The ex husband had been drinking quite heavily and he suggested they go to bed 'for old time sake.'

"Over my dead body!" she retorted.

"Well I see you haven't changed," he replied.

A woman went for an eye test and after the examination she was told she had perfect vision.

"Rubbish!" she exclaimed.

"But it's absolutely true" protested the optician. "I can show you the results."

"I do not have perfect vision and I can prove it," she said again. "I can show you my husband,"

Said the bitter man to his wife,

"You know, Beryl, you should go braless."

"Really!" she said. "Is that because my breasts are still young and firm, even after all these years?"

"No, it's because they might pull the wrinkles out of your face," he replied.

The small community had been warned for days that the river was swollen and could break its banks at anytime. It happened on a Sunday afternoon and within hours the area was under 6' of water. Doris and Ida were sitting on the roof of Ida's bungalow waiting for the waters to recede when suddenly Doris spotted a hat on top of the water. As she watched, the hat would move slowly one way and then come back the other way, over and over again.

"Well, that's odd," she said, pointing the hat out to her friend. "It seems to be moving up and down."

"Oh that's just my Jack," replied Ida, dismissively. "I told him he had to get that lawn mowed today come hell or high water!"

A woman walks into the bedroom to discover her husband packing his bags.

"Where are you going?" she asks.

"To Florida," he replies.

"Why?"

"Somebody told me that every time you make love there, they give you £10."

Immediately, the woman starts packing her bags as well.

"What are you doing?" demands the husband.

"I'm going to Florida."

"Why?"

"I've got to see how you're going to live on just £20 a year," she replies scornfully.

Said the husband to his mate.

"The problem with reading girlie magazines is that it gets boring looking at all those naked girls... and my wife also says..."

The man leaned over and whispered into his bride's ear, "I love you terribly."

"I know," she replied, "but we've got a lifetime to work on it."

MEN

Why do bankers make the best lovers?

They know the penalties for an early withdrawal.

Said the bitter woman to her friend, "When the only thing that's stiff is his socks, then it's time to take the money and run."

A husband and wife were having a flaming argument about their money problems.

"If it wasn't for my money, that Porsche and that swimming pool wouldn't be here."

She retorted, "If it wasn't for your money, I wouldn't be here!"

"Hello Josie, you look preoccupied this morning," remarked her friend.

"I am a bit," she replied. "This morning my boyfriend lost all his money on the stock market."

"How awful! You must feel so sorry for him."

"I am. I'm just wondering how he will cope without me."

A bloke walked into a butcher's shop and picked up a chicken. He examined it closely, sniffing under the wings and looking up the rear end. After a couple of minutes he turned to the man behind the counter and said accusingly, "This chicken's not fresh."

"Excuse me, sir," replied the offended butcher, "could you pass the same test?"

A man was set upon by muggers as he walked down the dark street. Although there were four of them, the victim put up a good fight but was eventually battered to the ground with broken ribs and a broken nose.

One of the muggers went through his pockets and to his amazement found 54p.

"Hey, why did you put up such a fight for a measly 54p?" asked the mugger.

The poor man gasped in pain, "I didn't know that's all you were after," he moaned. "I thought it was the £200 I had in my shoe."

Every wife likes her husband to have something tender about him, especially legal tender.

A man buys a packet of salted nuts and gives one to his wife. Five minutes later she asks for another one.

"Why do you want another one?" he replies. "They all taste the same."

A rich young man was involved in a very bad car crash, and his Porsche was a write-off. As he lay stunned at the side of the road, he moaned quietly to himself, "Oh, my car, my poor car".

A paramedic overheard his words and knelt down beside him.

"Excuse me, sir," he said gently, "I think you should be more concerned about your arm."

The young man looked down to where his arm should have been and started to cry in anguish, "Oh my Rolex, my Rolex!"

Lady Highbrow was sitting in her bedroom when her butler walked into the room. "Marlow, how many times do I have to tell you, don't walk into my room without knocking first. There could be times when it would be very embarrassing," she said.

"Nothing to worry about, ma'am," he replied. "I always check first by looking through the keyhole."

On another occasion, Lady Highbrow was forced to sack her cook.

"It's no good, Dorothy, you are unable to maintain the standards I expect. Your cooking is boring and the state of the kitchen is a disgrace."

"Well, good riddance to this flaming job," retorted the cook. "Not everyone in this house thinks I'm bad. Your husband says I do a great coq au vin and what's more, I'm better in bed than you are."

"What!" roared Lady Highbrow. "Who told you that? My husband?"

"No, the gardener, so there!!"

What's your idea of a perfect husband?

A man with a £1 million life insurance who dies on his wedding night.

A woman rushed into the lounge to find her husband asleep on the sofa.

"Quick, Jack, get up. I've just won the £20 million jackpot. Get packing and ring the bus station."

Jack jumped up. "What shall I ask for? What's the destination?"

"I don't care," she replied, "just as long as you're out of here before lunch-time."

What do a man and the tax office have in common?

They're both impossible to get through to when you want to talk.

"George, I'm going shopping. Can I have some money?" asked the wife.

"Money, money, money, that's all you ever ask me for. Sometimes I think you need more brains than more money."

"Maybe, darling," she replied calmly, "but then again I thought I'd only ask you for what you had most of!"

Any girl can live on love – if he's wealthy.

A man was talking to his mate in the pub about his financial problems.

"It's no good Tony, I'm going to sit down with my wife tonight and tell her a few home truths. She has no idea about money."

The next day they met up again and Tony asked how it went.

"Oh great," he replied, "we've sorted things out. I'm going to give up beer and football."

A very insecure man was anxious to know how much his wife loved him.

"Darling, if I was horribly injured in a car crash and had to spend the rest of my days in a wheelchair, would you still love me?"

"Of course I would, sweetheart," she replied, "I'll always love you."

He continued, "And if I became impotent and could no longer make love to you, would you still love me?"

"Don't be silly, I'll always love you," she replied.

"And if I lost all my money on the stock market, would you still love me?"

She looked at him for a moment and then said, "Sweetheart, I've told you, I will always love you...and I'll miss you terribly."

On the eve of his marriage a man was having last-minute doubts.

"Oh Julie, you're not just marrying me because I've inherited £1 million from my late uncle?"

"Of course not," she replied, "I'd marry you no matter who left you the money."

Lady Challerton called for her manservant.

"Jeeves," she said, "take off my shoes, take off my coat, take off my dress, take off my stockings and take off my bra and lacy knickers. Now Jeeves, one more thing, I don't ever want to see you wearing them again."

A despicable young man heard that his elderly aunt only had six months to live. Now his aunt was very rich and doted on her two Siamese cats. So the young man decided to curry favour with his aunt, hoping that she would be generous to him in her will.

Every week he would travel to her house and make a big fuss of the cats, feeding them, grooming them and even taking them for walks.

Six months went by and the old lady died. Sure enough she remembered him in her will. She left him her cats!

Two tight-fisted men, Graham and Robert, were on a mountaineering holiday in Scotland when Graham slipped badly and ended up hanging by his fingertips over a crevasse.

"Quick, Bob," he screamed, "get down to the village and buy a rope. I don't know how long I can hang on here."

Bob raced off, leaving Graham hanging there and after 20 minutes his grip was beginning to weaken. Then to his relief, he heard Bob returning.

"Hurry up, help me quick," he yelled, "have you got the rope?"

"No," said Bob, "those greedy buggers in the village wanted £10 for it."

A famous Hollywood star was standing naked at the bedroom window doing his exercises. Suddenly his wife came into the room, rushed over to the window and pulled the curtains.

"You idiot," she hissed, "if people see you, they'll think I only married you for your money."

Harry, the old skinflint, was sitting by his wife's bed. She was desperately ill and had very little time to live.

"Martha," whispered Harry, "I've got to get down to the post office to collect my pension. If you feel yourself going before I get back, will you turn the light off."

When do you care for a man's company?

When he owns it.

A young man was keen to buy his girlfriend a very special present but, unsure of what to get, he took her sister along to help him choose. A little later, they decided to buy her some gloves – something not too personal but at the same time something that she would wear often and think of him.

As he gave the gloves to the assistant to be wrapped, the sister had also been buying for herself and handed in a pair of knickers. However, unknown to the two buyers, the assistant muddled up the packages and they both got each other's purchase.

Sadly, the boyfriend didn't check his package before sending it off. He simply wrote the following note to go with it.

My darling,

I hope you like the enclosed gift. I bought them because I notice you never wear any when we go out together and your sister thought the short ones were better than the longer ones because they're easier to remove. I hope you like the colour. I know they're a little light but the lady in the shop showed me the ones she's been wearing for the past month and there was hardly a mark on them. She also tried them on for me so that I could see what they'd look like. It's such a shame I won't be there to help you put them on for the first time. Others will see them before I do.

Just one little tip. When you take them off, blow in them as they will be slightly damp from wearing.

Looking forward to seeing you wear them on Saturday night, much love,

Ken xxxx.

The young man got down on his knees and said shyly, "Darling will you marry me?" as he offered her a glittering ring.

"Oh my!" she said, looking pleased. "Are they real diamonds?"

"They'd better be," he replied. "Otherwise I've been cheated out of £15."

A beggar went up to a well-dressed man and said, "I'm so hungry, I haven't eaten in three days."

"Well, force yourself," came the reply.

Little William walks past his parent's bedroom one night and spots them making love. The following morning he asks his dad why they were acting in that way.

"It's because your mother wants a baby," replies dad.

A couple of days later, he sees his mother performing oral sex and later asks his dad why she was doing that to him.

"Because she wants a Porsche," replies dad.

MISERS

Did you hear about the miser who was so mean, the only way he would take a bubble bath was to eat baked beans the day before?

Did you hear about the miser who lived in Appletree Avenue?

One day, his friend saw him scraping paint off the walls and putting it in a paper bag.

"Are you redecorating?" asked the friend.

"No, I'm moving," was the reply.

A millionaire was driving along in the countryside when he saw a man eating grass in a field.

"I say," he called, "why are you eating grass?"

"Because we're so poor, we don't have any money for food."

"I see," said the millionaire, "in that case, stay here and I'll get my man to pick you up in the jeep."

"But sir, I have a wife and four children," said the wretched man.

"That's alright, bring them all along."

The man was overcome with gratitude.

"Oh sir, what can I say, this is wonderful! To think we're going to have a new life!"

"No, no," replied the millionaire, "You're getting carried away. The grass on my estate is more than 3 feet tall and I can't get the mower to cut it."

A young man went to Las Vegas and won a million dollars on the jackpot. He arrived back in England and rang his parents to tell them the good news.

"And I'll be giving you and mum £100 each," he said.

On hearing this, the parents were very upset and the father, in a moment of rage, told him they were not really his parents.

"What!" exclaimed the man, "are you telling me I'm a bastard?"

"That's right, and a fucking mean one at that!" came the reply.

An old skinflint was out with his wife in the car and as she turned into a Mayfair Street, the brakes failed.

"John, what shall I do!" she screamed as the car ran out of control towards the parked cars.

"Hit the cheapest one, hit the cheapest one," he yelled.

An Englishman, Scotsman and a Jew met up in an hotel, and decided to go and have dinner together. They chose an expensive restaurant, and really went to town, with four courses each and the best champagne available. After the meal, the Englishman realised with a sinking heart that he would very likely be landed with the bill. He began to reach for his wallet, when suddenly the Scotsman piped up, "Don't worry about the bill, lads, this one's on me!"

"Thanks very much, very decent of you," replied the others.

They made their way back to the hotel, and the Englishman said goodnight to his companions in the hotel lobby, and went up to bed.

He was on his way into breakfast the following morning, when the newspaper headline caught his eye: "Famous Jewish ventriloquist kicked to death in hotel lobby".

MONEY

A couple parked in Lovers Lane and started necking. As they got more and more aroused, the man began to undo the girl's blouse.

"Wait a minute," she said. "I think I ought to tell you that I'm a prostitute and if you want sex it'll cost you £20."

Feeling angry but beyond the point of no return, he handed over £20 and they carried on.

Much later, once they'd got dressed again, they sat back in the front seats but he didn't start up the car.

"Hey, what's wrong?" she asked.

"Well, I think I ought to tell you that I'm a mini cab driver and until you pay me £25 for the fare, I'm not driving you back into town."

Sky high rates had left the Lord of the Manor badly in need of funds. He said to his wife,

"Cynthia, old dear, times are hard, we're going to have to cut back a bit. If only you'd learn to drive, we could get rid of the chauffeur."

"And if only you'd learn to fuck, we could get rid of the gardeners!" she replied.

A man lost his wallet on a train from Paddington to Penzance. He stood up in the carriage and addressed his fellow passengers.

"Excuse me ladies and gentlemen, may I have your attention please. I've lost my wallet containing £150. If anyone finds it, I will gladly give them £20 reward."

As he finished speaking a voice was heard to say,

"Anyone giving the wallet to me will get £40 as a reward."

"And I'll give £60 to anyone who gives it to me!" said another.

For three weeks a woman had been the main contestant on a national TV quiz show. Time after time, she had defeated every other contender and was only one question away from winning £1 million. On the eve of her big day, nerves were beginning to make her ill so her husband sneaked into the TV studio and found the jackpot question and answer.

"Doris," he said, "tomorrow's question is about the male anatomy and the answer is head, heart and penis."

For the rest of the evening and during the night he asked her the same question every 5 minutes. Alas, her nerves were so bad, she kept forgetting the answer. Ten minutes before the show, he was still instructing her.

"Come on Doris, don't forget, it's the head, heart and penis."

"Head, heart and penis," she kept muttering to herself, as the programme got closer.

"Ladies and gentlemen," announced the quizmaster, "please welcome back Mrs Doris Parsons who is one question away from £1 million."

"Doris, can you name the three main parts of the male anatomy. You have 12 seconds."

There wasn't a sound to be heard as the seconds started ticking away.

"The head," said Doris.

"That's right. 9 seconds left."

"Er… the heart," said Doris.

"Yes!" said the quizmaster, "5 seconds left."

"And... um... er... oh dear, my husband kept driving it into me last night... er... I had it on the tip of my tongue this morning."

The bell went for the end of time.

"Well that's good enough for me," said the quizmaster. "You've just won £1 million!"

A man walked into a bar and ordered four double shots of rum. As the bartender put the drinks in front of him, he would immediately down it in one go.

"Hey," remarked the bartender, "You're in a bit of a rush, aren't you?"

"Well you would be if you had what I've got," replied the man.

"What's that then?"

"One pound thirty-eight."

A frail old lady of 98 won £3.4m on the lottery. Her family were concerned that the news would shock her so much, it might lead to a heart attack, so they called in the doctor and explained the problem.

He smiled at them kindly and said reassuringly

"Don't worry about a thing. Although I say so myself, I'm very good at breaking news to people and the old lady's health will not be affected."

The doctor went to see the lady and over afternoon tea, they chatted about all kinds of things until he eventually brought the subject round to money.

"So Mrs Weaver," he said, "what would you do if you won millions of pounds on the lottery?"

"I'd give half to you," she promptly replied.

The doctor dropped dead with shock.

"Hello Mark, you look worried, what's wrong?"

"Oh hello Jack. Yes, I am a bit. I've got a house on the French Riviera, a chateau in Switzerland and a 200 acre spread in Surrey. And I've just bought a castle in Scotland."

"So what's the problem? It sounds good to me."

"But I only earn £150 per week!"

Her father went absolutely berserk when his daughter told him she was pregnant. He stormed off to get his shotgun, loudly proclaiming that he'd make sure the slimy bugger married her.

"But he can't, Dad," she wailed, "it's your boss and he's already married."

"Well he's not getting away with this scot free," roared the father. "Just wait until I get my hands on him."

Some time later, in the drawing room of his employer's mansion, the two came face to face.

"Now look here Morgan," said the boss. "I'm sure we can settle this amicably. I'll give you £5,000 if it's a boy and £4,000 if it's a girl."

"And what if it's twins?" asked the father.

"Then I'll give you £8,000."

Satisfied, the father started to leave when he stopped suddenly and said.

"But what happens if she has a miscarriage. Can she try again?"

The painter and decorator did a beautiful job on the outside of the house and the husband was so impressed, he gave him extra money.

"Here, take this," said the husband passing him another £50, "take the missus out to dinner."

Later that night, there was a knock on the door and the husband was surprised to see the painter standing there.

"Hello, did you forget something?"

"No," replied the painter. "I've come to take your missus out to dinner."

"Oh John," said his wife at breakfast. "I had a wonderful dream last night, I dreamt you bought me a diamond ring. What do you think it means?"

John replied confidently, "You'll know tonight."

Lo and behold, when John arrived home from work he gave her a book on the meaning of dreams!

A couple were faced with severe financial difficulties so the husband suggested that his wife take up prostitution.

"Charge them £80 if they go the whole way or £30 for a hand job," he said.

So the wife spent a week walking the streets and doing the business. Then one night a man approached her and asked about the price.

"I can't afford to go the whole way so I'll just have a hand job," he said, giving her £30, and dropping his trousers.

Oh my! When the woman saw how well endowed he was, she ran round to her husband who was waiting in the car and said,

"Derek, have you £50 I could borrow?"

A successful executive decides it's time to make a man of his son so he takes him down to the local brothel. The son disappears into a room with one of the girls while he waits outside – but he can't help listening through the door. Now the son is very well endowed and the girl gasps at the amazing sight. As they begin the business, he takes it very gently but the girl begs for more.

"Just put it in another inch," she says. A little later, she repeats her wish.

"Oh please put in another inch and I'll knock £5 off the price." So he does but still she begs for more.

"Another inch and I'll knock off £10," she informs him.

And so it goes on, the girl is so delighted with the man's performance that she promises to take off more and more money.

"Please, please," she moans till eventually she cries, "a little bit more and it's free, it's free."

Now all this time, the father has been listening outside the door and when he hears this, he bursts into the room and shouts,

"Move over son, leave this to me, it's time to make a profit."

A fair is being held in the grounds of a convent to raise funds for the orphan children. One of the attractions is a stall where people can play darts for prizes. Two men pass by and decide to have a wager between them.

"Come on Martin, I bet you £50 you can't get 180 with your next 3 darts."

Now Martin has a reputation for being quite good with the darts, so he readily agrees to the bet. His first dart hits treble twenty, but his second dart only hits a single.

"Ah ha," says his mate, "that's £50 you owe me, you won't get it now."

Martin throws the last dart at the board half-heartedly, it hits the wire and bounces right back hitting a nun in the eye. As she falls to the ground, he announces in triumph,

"Not so fast, I think you owe me. That's one nun dead and eighty!"

Three men visited a brothel and were told that the price they would pay, would be three times the length of their dick. Afterwards, the first man complained that he'd had to pay £38. The second man said he'd had to pay £30, but the third man smiled and said he'd only paid £6.

"How come?" they asked in astonishment.

"Ah well, you see, after thinking about it, I decided to pay on the way out!"

MOTHERS

It was Saturday night and three sisters were going out with their boyfriends.

"Bye mum," said the first sister, "I'm going out with Chas to listen to jazz."

Moments later the second sister came to say goodbye.

"I'm going out with Lance to dance."

Then the third sister walked in.

"Bye mum, I'm going out with Chuck."

"Oh no!" exclaimed the mother quickly. "You're not going anywhere."

A woman was walking along the street with her blouse undone and her breast hanging out. A passer-by stopped her and said,

"Excuse me Madam, did you realise your blouse is undone?"

"Oh no," she wailed, looking down. "I've left the baby on the train!"

Another woman was also taking her new baby for a walk in the pram when she met an old school chum.

"Oh yes, he's just like his father," said the old friend, "lying there on his back clutching a bottle!"

A woman is sitting in the park with her baby when she is pestered by a group of unruly kids. They start calling her names and one shouts out,

"Hey Missus, what an ugly baby! Cor, it's the ugliest baby I've ever seen."

The woman bursts into tears and the park attendant hears this, and comes over to see what is wrong. However the woman is too upset to tell him so the kindly man goes off and brings her back a soothing drink.

"Here you are love, here's a nice cup of tea for you, and a banana for your monkey."

Poor mum! She was tearing her hair out at the behaviour of her young son. Whenever he met anyone he would run up to them, kick them hard on the shins and pinch their backsides.

Eventually mum took him to see a child psychiatrist and as they entered the consulting room, the little boy ran up to the doctor, kicked him hard on the shins and pinched his backside.

Immediately the psychiatrist bent down and whispered in the boy's ear. It had a miraculous effect. The boy turned pale and ran back to his mother, cowering behind here.

"This is wonderful," she enthused, "he's cured! What did you say to him?"

"I told him that if he ever did that again I'd come and find him and smash his fucking face in."

Barbara was pushing her newborn son along the road when she met her old friend.

"Ooh, let's have a look," said her friend, "isn't he beautiful. He looks just like his father."

"Yes, he does, doesn't he?" replied Barbara sadly. "I only wish he looked a bit more like my husband."

A woman had just given birth to a baby boy and the nurse was cleaning him up.

"You do know your baby is black?" she asked.

"Is he?" replied the woman "well I did get friendly with a man at work who was black."

"He's also got blonde hair," remarked the nurse.

"Ah!" replied the woman. "Yes, I was quite friendly with a blonde haired man at the health club."

"And he's got slant eyes."

"Oh! Well I suppose I was quite friendly with a Chinese man living next door."

The nurse handed the baby to its mother and as she cuddled him in her arms, it began to cry.

"Oh thank goodness for that!" she said, looking relieved. "For a moment I thought it was going to start neighing."

MOTHERS-IN-LAW

A man had been out all night on a stag do. They'd ended up watching blue movies so by the time he crawled home about 5 o'clock in the morning, he was as randy as hell. He tore his clothes off, ran upstairs and slid quietly into bed where he roused his wife and spent the next 45 minutes in wild sex.

Later, just before falling asleep he went back downstairs to get a glass of water and noticed someone asleep on the sofa.

"Arrgh!" he wailed, looking down to see his wife. "What are you doing here?"

"Oh hello Jim," she mumbled. "Mother had a headache so I said she could sleep in our bed."

Relations between the man and his mother-in-law were so bad that it was affecting the man's marriage. To make amends, he decided to get the old bat a present when he next travelled abroad and he found just the thing in a tourist market in Hong Kong. It was a jade jewellery box with Chinese writing on the inside of the lid.

Well the present did the trick and both husband and mother-in-law began to tolerate each other a lot better. However some months later, the hinge on the box became loose so she took it to a jeweller in China Town for repairs. "Isn't it lovely!" she enthused. "My son-in-law gave it to me. Can you translate the writing inside?"

"Certainly," said the jeweller obligingly. "It says 'Licensed by Yin Tang area of China. Property of Mai Ling, prostitute of brothel 568'!"

The phone rang.

"Mr. Jones, I'm afraid I have some bad news," said the voice at the other end. Your mother-in-law has died while on holiday in America. Do you know if she wished to be cremated, embalmed or buried?"

"Better safe than sorry," came the reply. "Let's go for all three."

A woman's face was disfigured in a bad car crash so her devoted husband volunteered to have skin grafted from his backside onto the scars. It was a great success and his wife was as beautiful as ever.

Some months later, he was recounting the incident to a mate in the pub.

"Bloody hell! That must have hurt," exclaimed his mate.

"Yeah, but it was worth it," replied the husband, "because every time I see my mother-in-law kiss my wife, I know she's kissing my arse!"

As the man walked into his office, one of his colleagues remarked.

"You've had an argument with your mother-in-law, haven't you?"

"Yes," he replied astonished, "but how the hell did you know that?"

"You've still got an axe stuck in your head."

The man ran into work 5 minutes late and immediately bumped straight into his boss.

"Sorry I'm late Sir," he panted, "it's the mother-in-law. She's been staying with us and this morning when she went into the kitchen, she slipped, knocked her head and slumped unconscious over the breakfast table."

"Oh my God!" exclaimed his boss. "What did you do?"

"I had to finish my breakfast in the lounge."

"I hate my mother-in-law," said the angry man.

"Oh come on," replied his mate, "if it hadn't been for her, you'd never have met your wife."

"That's what I mean!" he replied with feeling.

Did you hear about the man who saw a sign that read, 'Keep Britain Beautiful!'?
He went home and shot the mother-in-law.

MEN

God made Eve and for a while she was very happy in the Garden of Eden, then one day she went to him and said,

"I'm lonely, I'd like a companion."

"Okay," said God. "I'll make you a man and we'll call him Adam. But I must warn you, he'll be flawed. He'll be nasty and aggressive, he'll only pretend to listen to you, he won't see your point of view and he'll pick fights. However, on the good side, he'll have strong muscles, be a competent hunter and be quite good in bed. But I'll only do this on one condition," said God.

"What's that?" asked Eve.

"That you let him believe he was made first."

Late one night, long after the couple had gone to bed, an intruder forced his way into the house. The couple woke to find him standing over them with a gun in his hand.

"I'm going to kill you!" he snarled, "but first, I want to know your names."

The woman said her name was Margaret.

"Margaret," he said dreamily, "why that was my mother's name. I couldn't kill anyone called Margaret."

Then he turned menacingly to the quivering man, "And what's your name?"

"Jack," he replied, "but my friends call me Margaret."

The pregnancy class had just finished and the couples were preparing to leave.

"Just one more thing before you go," said the organiser, "exercise is very important. I'd like to see all the mums-to-be taking daily walks… and I'd like to see their husbands walk with them for encouragement."

For a moment there was silence, then one man asked,

"Is it alright if she carries a golf bag as she walks?"

A man got a terrible illness that meant he couldn't stop crapping. Hour after hour he sat on the loo, crapping all the time. It got so bad, he eventually crapped his brain out.

And that was when he put down the toilet seat for the first time!

Three men were sitting on the commuter train going home.

"When I get in, I'm going to pour myself a double whisky, put my feet up and relax" said the first man.

"Well I'm going to strip off, get into the sauna and sweat out all the tension of the day," said the second man.

"And when I get in, I'm going to take the wife's knickers off," said the third man.

The other two looked at him and winked.

"You're a randy old devil," they said laughing.

"No, they're just too tight for me," he replied.

Two motorists are driving towards each other on a narrow country lane. As they slow down to pass each other, the woman sticks her head out of the car and shouts 'pig'.

So the man immediately puts his head through his open window and yells 'bitch'. The incident is over in a second and each continue on their way, except that as the man drives around the next bend he crashes straight into a pig walking in the middle of the road.

How do you impress a woman?

Flatter her, protect her, help her, listen to her hopes and dreams, buy her presents, take her out and wine and dine her, support her and love her.

How do you impress a man?

Turn up naked, bring beer.

What is a perfect man?

One who makes love for hours and then turns into an Indian takeaway.

When a man says 'Relax and let me give you a massage' he means 'let me grope you.'

What are the three lies most told by men?

"I love you."

"I'll give you a call."

"I promise I won't come in your mouth."

Women will never be equal to men until they can walk down the street with a huge beer gut, a builder's bum and still think they're fanciable!

When a man says he's hungry he really means 'make me something to eat'.

N

NEIGHBOURS

A woman popped round to see her new next-door neighbour and found her standing in the hall naked.

"My goodness!" she exclaimed. "What's going on?"

The neighbour explained that she was waiting for her husband to arrive home and she was wearing her love dress.

The woman went home intrigued by what she had seen. She decided to do the same. At 6 o'clock that night, she stripped off and stood in the kitchen waiting for her husband.

"I'm home!" he called out a few minutes later and then gasped in astonishment when he saw his naked wife.

"Carol, what are you doing?" he demanded.

"This is my love dress," she replied sexily.

"Well you could have ironed it first," he replied.

Three neighbours were chatting over the garden wall. They got on to the subject of their husbands.

"I call my husband 'the dentist'," said the first woman, "because of his mighty drill."

"I call my husband 'miner'," said the second woman, "because of his impressive shaft."

"Well I call my husband 'the postman'," said the third woman, "because he delivers late and often in the wrong box!"

Jack's best friend's wife has died so he pops round to his house to see how Bob's coping. No one answers the door so Jack just walks in to find his mate, having sex with the next door neighbour on the living room carpet.

"Bob, man, what are you doing? Your wife only died yesterday."

"I know," says Bob, looking up, "but with all this grief, I don't know what I'm doing."

As Carol was hanging out her washing, she spotted her next door neighbour in the garden. She called over.

"Hey, Betty, can I have a quick word?"

"Yeah, sure."

"Do you like men with fat, spreading arses?"

"No, of course not," Betty replied.

"Well do you like men with beer guts that hang over their trousers?"

"No, I don't."

"And how about fat men with saggy tits?"

"Course not. Look what's all this about?"

"I'll tell you," said Carol. "If you don't like men with fat arses, floppy beer guts and saggy tits, how come you're sneaking round here after my husband every time I go out?"

★

Three women were chatting over mid morning coffee and complaining about the weather.

"It's hopeless," said the first one. "More often than not, I put my washing out and in 5 minutes it starts to rain."

"I agree," said the second. "This morning when I put out my washing, the sun was shining. Now look at it!"

The two women glanced over at their companion who had not said a word.

"Now I come to think about it, you're always lucky when you put washing out. What's the secret?" they asked.

"Well it's quite simple," she replied. "When I wake up in the morning I look at my husband and if his penis is hanging to the left then I know it's going to rain. If it's hanging to the right then I know it's going to be a bright and sunny day."

"Ah ha," interrupted the second woman, "but what if he's got an erection?"

"Well, on a day like that I don't do the laundry."

It just so happened the two men who lived next door to each other, and didn't see eye to eye, were having their hair cut at the barbers.

"Would Sir like a little hairspray?" said the barber to the first man.

"Good gracious, no," he replied, "if my wife smelled that, she would think I'd been in a brothel."

Overhearing this, the other man said loudly,

"You can put some of that on my hair, my wife's never been in a brothel."

NUDIST COLONY

A bloke joined a nudist colony and after a couple of days, he decided to explore the gardens. He came across a notice that said 'Beware of gays'. Thinking nothing much of this, he walked on, and came across a similar notice pinned to a tree. Looking nervously around, he continued his walk and spotted some words chiselled into a bench. As he bent down to look more closely, it read 'Sorry, you've been warned twice.'

Unbeknown to his family a man joined a nudist colony. A few months later he received a letter from his mother who wrote that she hadn't seen him for a while and would he send her a recent photograph. Unfortunately all the photos of himself were in the nude so he cut one of the pictures in two and sent her the top half.

A couple of days later another letter arrived from his mother, thanking him for the photo and asking him to send one to his ageing Grandmother! The poor old dear's nearly blind, he thought to himself, I'll just send the other half of that photo, she'll never know the difference!

Some time passed and one morning, a letter arrived from his grandmother.

"Dear Ernest," it read, "thank you for the photo, though I must say that your new hairstyle makes your nose look much longer."

O

OFFICIAL BUSINESS

"F131," said the voice at the end of the line.

"Good," responded the caller. "I think you ought to know that Martin Carucci of 32 Orchard Garden is growing dope in his woodshed."

Two hours later, the woodshed was raided and all the logs were cut into small pieces in the search for the illegal weed. The next day, Martin received a phone call.

"How did it go?" asked the caller. "Did you get your wood cut?"

"Oh yes," replied Martin. "It's saved me a lot of time."

"Well don't forget, it's your turn to make a phone call next. I'm desperate to get the garden dug over."

There was such a long queue at the ticket office that people were having to wait more than an hour before reaching the counter. Half way down queue D a man suddenly began massaging the shoulders of a bloke standing in front of him.

"What the hell are you doing?" asked the bloke, turning round angrily.

"Well I'm a masseur," explained the man, "and I could see you were very tense so I thought I'd relieve the pressure."

"Well fuck off," replied the bloke. "I'm a tax man, but you don't see me screwing the person in front of me."

The man sat down after giving his after dinner speech when an old lady tapped him on the shoulder.

"Mr. Duncan, I have to tell you that your speech reminded me of a little terrier I have at home."

"Oh really. How sweet! Like a little terrier at home! What kind of terrier?"

"Bull," came the reply.

"Why is our toilet always blocked?" the man asked the plumber.

"How many are in your family?" replied the plumber.

"Well, there's nine of us."

"Ah ha, well that explains it," said the plumber nodding his head. "You see plumbing's a bit like a game of poker. You can't have a full house and a straight flush at the same time."

The county officials had not known a fire like it for as long as they could remember. The whole paint factory was burning out of control and fire engines from more than 50 miles away had been called to the scene. But still the fire blazed uncontrollably.

Then suddenly, from out of the blue, an old tattered engine arrived from the furthest part of the county. Rarely used, it had stood idle for more than a year but here it was now, heading straight for the blaze. Not for a moment did it ease up, but ploughed on into the heart of the fire and disappeared inside the factory.

Gasps of astonishment were heard from the onlookers, but within minutes it became obvious that by fighting the fire from the centre, the blaze was now under control and within an hour, it was extinguished.

The county officials greeted the fire heroes with smiling faces.

"Men, tonight you showed great courage above and beyond the call of duty. Is there any way we can thank you?"

The driver of the truck wiped the soot from his face and replied angrily,

"Yes, you can get the fucking brakes on this thing fixed."

Is it true that air hostesses are a little deaf?

When they go up to a man and ask him if there's anything they can do, they never seem to hear his first request!

An old woman rang up the ambulance service in great distress.

"Oh please help me," she whimpered. "I think I've broken my leg and I can't move."

"Okay, now just stay calm," came the reply. "Now can you tell me where you live?"

"It's… oh no! I can't remember, I'm too distressed to think properly."

"Well how do you expect us to get there?" he said.

"What do you mean?" she replied in surprise, "Haven't you got one of those shiny white vans?"

"Ladies and gentlemen, we apologise for the delay in flight 101 taking off," said the stewardess. "The pilot wouldn't take off due to a peculiar knocking sound in one of the engines, so it's taken us some time to find a replacement for him."

OLD AGE

A 92-year old man visited the doctor for his six monthly check up. The following week, the doctor bumped into the man walking along the High Street with a flashy woman on his arm.

"I did as you suggested," laughed the man. "Get a hot mamma and be cheerful."

"No, no," said the doctor horrified. "I said you've got a heart murmur. Be careful."

A man stepped into a lift and was taken aback by the awful smell. The only other occupant was a little old lady, and he spoke to her.

"Excuse me, are you suffering from wind?"

"Of course I am," she replied. "You don't think I stink like this all the time?"

Three old men were chatting over a game of dominoes.

"These days I've got such shaky hands," said the first man, "it's causing me a lot of problems. I went out to prune the roses and cut off all the flowers."

"Oh I know what you mean," nodded the second man. "When I tried to shave this morning, I cut my face to ribbons. See?"

The third man looked at his companions and smiled sympathetically.

"Well just look at the way my hands shake," he said. "Last time I went for a piss, I came three times!"

Two old ladies were sitting on the veranda enjoying the last few minutes of daylight before retiring to bed. One of the ladies turned to her friend and said,

"Nancy, do you still get horny?"

"Oh yes," she replied.

"So what do you do?"

"I suck a lifesaver," she said.

After a few moments silence came the question.

"But who drives you to the beach?"

Three old men were sitting talking and smoking.

"Can you still blow smoke rings, Bert?" asked the first man.

"Oh yes," replied Bert "what about you? You used to blow smoke through your eyes."

"A little," he replied, then turned to the third man and said, "and you Jack, you blew smoke out of your bum?"

"What makes you think that?" said Jack puzzled.

"I've seen the tobacco stains on your underpants," came the reply.

The doctor had an appointment at the local old people's home to check on three women and test them for dementia.

"Okay Mrs Brownley, can you tell me what four plus four equals?" he asked gently.

"940," she replied.

So he asked the second woman the same question.

"March," came the reply.

The doctor sighed and turned to the third woman.

"Hello Doris, can you tell me what four plus four equals?"

"Yes," she replied immediately, "it's eight."

"Correct" said the doctor, happily, "well done Doris."

"Oh it was easy," she replied. "I just added 940 to March."

Two old people became friendly at the social club and in time their feelings blossomed until one night they decided to go back to his place for a little bit of passion. Being old and arthritic, they found the easiest way was to do it doggy style and as they got into the rhythm, the bloke began talking.

"It was a great day when the war ended, wasn't it?"

"Yeah," panted the old girl.

"I remember celebrating in Trafalgar Square," he continued.

"Oh yeah?" she replied.

"Yeah, a few of us had landed back in Blighty just a couple of days before. We really enjoyed ourselves."

They continued their lovemaking and later when it was all over, she turned to him and said,

"How come you started to talk about the end of the war just now?"

"I read about the celebrations on the piece of newspaper stuck to your backside" he said, "and it brought back all the memories."

The old man said to the doctor,

"Do you think I'll live another ten years?"

"Do you drink?" asked the doctor.

"No."

"Do you smoke?"

"No."

"Do you have sex?"

"No."

"Then what the hell do you want to live another ten years for?"

An old couple had retired to bed and the woman was feeling a bit frisky.

"Oh Harold," she said. "Sometimes it feels just like yesterday that you would put your arm around me as we lay in bed. Where's all that romance gone?"

So the old man, to keep her happy, put his arm around her.

"And then, you used to kiss me," she continued.

The old man sighed, turned over and kissed her.

"And then, do you remember," she said excitedly, "you used to nibble my ears?"

At that, the old man got out of bed and walked to the door.

"Harold!" she called, sitting up in alarm, "where are you going?"

"Just to the bathroom, dear," he replied, "to get my teeth."

Two old men were sitting in the park watching all the pretty girls go by in their skimpy clothes.

"Phwooarr! God, just looking at them makes me want to sit them on my knee and kiss and cuddle them," said the first man drooling.

"Mmm," agreed the other, nodding, "but wasn't there something else we used to do as well?"

Judge Martha Peters had retired from the bench after 30 years of service and was moving to a new house a couple of streets away from where she presently lived.

"Now don't forget dear," said her ageing husband. "Today's the big move so when you come back from your retirement party, don't come here. You know what your memory's like."

"Oh John, really!" she exclaimed, "I'm hardly likely to forget something like that."

However, that evening Martha found herself walking down the familiar road when suddenly she stopped with dismay.

"Oh no!" she muttered to herself "I shouldn't be here … but where should I be?"

After wandering around for a few minutes, she spotted a young woman coming towards her.

"Excuse me, dear, I'm Judge Martha Peters, you wouldn't happen to know where I've moved to?"

"Of course, Mum," said the woman, "it's this way."

An old woman turns to her elderly husband and says,

"Ooh Albert, I could just do with some sweets, a packet of those pick 'n' mix from Myrtle Street. Be a dear and pop out for me, will you? My legs aren't as good as they used to be."

"Right you are Doris, what would you like?"

"Well, I'd like some chocolate éclairs, not the ones in gold paper but in brown… and um… some fruit drops but no orange ones… mints, get me the soft white round ones and some toffees but make sure they're not too hard."

Albert puts on his hat and coat and disappears out of the front door. Doris falls asleep and it's almost two hours later before he returns.

"Here you are love," he says, putting a bag of fish and chips on her lap. Doris looks inside the bag and turns to him disappointed.

"Oh Albert, you've forgotten the vinegar!"

An old man was watching television in his hotel room when a beautiful young girl walked in.

"Oh dear!" she exclaimed blushing, "I'm so sorry, I think I'm in the wrong room."

The old man shook his head sadly and replied,

"No, no my dear, you're in the right room – you're just forty years too late!"

An old woman of 70 had a baby and when she arrived home, she was greeted by lots of friends and relations, eager to see the new arrival.

"When can we see it?" they asked.

"Soon," she replied.

"Can we see it now?" they asked again, 30 minutes later.

"Very soon," she replied.

However another 30 minutes passed and everyone was getting very impatient.

"When can we see the baby?" they said irritably.

"When it cries," she replied.

"But why? Why do we have to wait until it cries?"

"Because I can't remember where I put it," she replied.

An eighty-two year old man started attending a senior citizen's social club in town. After several weeks of visiting, he formed a friendship with an old woman called Ivy and a couple of months later, they ended up in bed.

A week later, the man noticed he was dripping so he went to the doctors for an examination.

"Have you had sex recently?" asked the doctor.

"Yes," he replied.

"And are you still in contact with this woman?"

"Yes. Why?"

"Well, if I was you, I'd pop round to see her because I think you're about to come."

An old man was driving down the M1 when his car phone rang.

"Oh Charles, dear," said his wife on the other end of the line, "there's just been a traffic item on the news. They say a car is travelling the wrong way down the motorway, please be careful."

"Hell Louise, it's not just one car, it's hundreds of them!" he replied.

What's 8 feet long and smells of piss?

A line dance at an old peoples home.

You know you're getting old when you have a party and the neighbours don't even realise it.

"I'm at that cereal age," said one old man to the other.

"I feel my corns more than my oats!"

P

PARENTS

Mum was tidying up her son's bedroom when she discovered an S&M magazine under his bed.

"Oh Ron," she said, showing it to her husband. "What shall we do?"

"Well I don't think spanking him would be a good idea," he replied.

A family of storks had taken up residence on the roof of the town hall. One day, little stork asked dad where his mother was.

"She won't be long" he replied, "She's just making some "happy deliveries."

The following day, dad was away and when little stork asked where he was, mum replied that he was taking good news to some grateful couples. A few months passed and little stork went missing all night.

"What happened to you?" asked his parents the next morning.

"Oh I just popped down to the campus and scared the shit out of some college kids," he replied.

Mum walked into the kitchen wearing her beautiful new fur coat.

"Isn't it fabulous?" she said to her daughter. "What do you think?"

"Oh Mum," replied the girl, "some poor dumb beast suffered so you could have that."

"Dorothy!" exclaimed her mum. "Don't talk about your father like that."

A beautiful baby boy was born to a joyous couple. He was perfect in every way except he didn't cry or make any noise at all. Although this concerned the parents, the doctors assured them that there was nothing wrong with his vocal chords. For some reason, he just didn't want to speak. And so it continued throughout his early life. He grew up normally but just never spoke.

Then, at the age of seven, he was sitting in the kitchen having tea when his mother passed him a glass of juice.

"I haven't tried this flavour before," she said. "I hope you like it."

The boy took a sip and replied, "Ugh, it's horrible, I prefer the other sort."

"Oh my goodness!" exclaimed the mother, looking at him open-mouthed, "you spoke. Why have you never spoken before?"

He replied, "Well up to now, everything's been fine."

"Sharon," said her mum angrily, "I found a condom under your bed. Are you sexually active?

"No," replied her daughter. "I just lie there."

"Mum, it's me," said the voice at the end of the line. "How are you?"

"I'm fine son, just fine," she replied, "though I haven't eaten for 10 days."

"Ten days!" he exclaimed "but why?"

"I didn't want my mouth to be full of food in case you rang!" came the reply.

The leader of the Hells Angels and his equally tough girlfriend had a baby son. A few months after the birth, the father rushed out looking for his girlfriend.

"Hey, honey, guess what?" he said proudly. "Our son's just spoken his first half-word. He said mother."

"Hi dad, it's Martin," said the voice at the end of the line. "I had to stay at Tim's last night because I missed the last bus home but by then it was too late to ring you because I knew you'd be in bed. I hope you're not too angry."

At this point the listener realised the caller had got the wrong number so he said, "I'm sorry, I don't know anyone called Tim."

"Bloody hell dad," came the reply, "I didn't think you'd be that mad!"

"Another two pints," said Jack, as he went back to his mate. "You know, Steve, I've got so many problems at the moment. Take the kids, for instance, they're out every night till 1.30 in the morning."

"What? Clubbing?" replied Steve, taking a sip of his beer.

"No, no," replied Jack, "looking for me."

"Please dad, can you help me with my maths homework?" pleaded the young boy.

"I'd like to son," came the reply, "but it wouldn't be right."

"I know," replied the boy, "but at least have a go."

Over the years, Louise had taken many men home to meet her parents but they had all failed to pass the test. Her latest boyfriend was Ernie and she was determined that nothing should go wrong, no matter what it took.

"So where do you live?" asked her father.

"I've got a flat near the park," Ernie replied.

"A flat near the park!" snorted Louise in disbelief.

"Dad, he has a penthouse overlooking half of London."

"Do you have a good job?" asked her mum.

"Well, it's quite interesting," said Ernie. "I work in a bank."

"Work in a bank!" laughed Louise, "he's only the top man in their investments department.

At that moment, Ernie started to cough.

"Oh dear, have you got a bad chest?" asked mum.

"Bad chest? No way!" said Louise hysterically, "he's got pleurisy."

"Oh no!" gasped the mother as her daughter told her she was pregnant.

"You silly girl, I thought you knew better!"

"But Mum," she protested, "he told me it was quite safe because the stork flies south for the winter."

A young boy needs to go and have a wee but he'll only go with his grandma.

"Dad, can you tell grandma I need the toilet please?" he says.

"I'll take you," says dad, "we don't have to bother your grandma."

But the little boy is adamant. He doesn't want anyone else taking him.

"But why son? Why does it have to be Grandma?" asks dad.

"Because her hand shakes," he replies.

Mother and Father were entertaining some important new clients when their six-year-old son came dashing into the room shouting

"Mummy, mummy, I want to poo poo."

Mummy took him to one side and said,

"Sweetheart, in future if you want to poo, just say you want a quiet word, OK?"

The little boy agreed.

A couple of nights later, at 3am, the little boy crept into his parent's bedroom and whispered to his mum

"I want a quiet word, mummy, please."

But mummy was too tired to think properly.

She replied,

"Not now dear, go and have a quiet word in your dad's ear."

The phone rang and Matthew picked it up.

"Son, it's your father here. I'm afraid I'm divorcing your mother."

"What! Dad, you can't! You've been together 40 years!" exclaimed the shocked son.

"It's no good, I'm going to see a solicitor tomorrow," said dad.

"But let me speak to mum," wailed the boy.

"No, not now. She can't come to the phone."

"Listen, dad, don't do anything till I see you, please. I'll drive up tomorrow."

"Well… alright, but will you tell your sister, this is all too painful."

With that, Matthew's father rang off.

Half an hour later, the phone rang and dad picked it up.

"Dad, it's me," said Matthew. "I've spoken to Claire and she's coming with me so we'll be with you at tea time."

Dad put down the phone and turned to his wife.

"Well it's worked. They're both coming tomorrow, though I don't know what we'll do next year to get them to visit."

PARTIES

A woman went to the Fancy Dress Ball dressed all in red – red stockings and suspender belt, red panties and red bra.

"How shall I announce you?" asked the doorman.

"I'm Dying Embers," she replied, "and if I don't get a poke soon, I'm going out."

The 'human emotion' fancy dress party of the year was in full swing as more and more guests arrived. A group of four pulled up in a taxi and got out. The first man was painted green all over and had a big N&V written on his chest.

"I'm going as envy," he said.

Next to get out was a woman dressed all in pink with pink feathers covering her private parts.

"I'm tickled pink," she explained.

Then the other two men got out. Both were naked – one had his dick in a pear, the other had his dick in a bowl of custard.

"So what are you two?" they were asked.

"I'm dicspear and I'm fucking discustard," came the replies.

Early one Saturday night the local vicar called round to see one of his parishioners only to find a party in full swing. As he walked into the front room, he was astonished to find a circle of naked men and a group of blindfolded women moving amongst them, feeling their todgers. The host explained that the women had to guess the name of the man by feeling his genitals.

The vicar blushed and replied,

"Oh dear, I really don't think I ought to be here."

"Nonsense Vicar!" replied the host, "your name has been mentioned twice already."

A pair of Siamese twins joined at the shoulders, lived at the bottom of the street, one loved singing and the other loved shagging. One morning the music twin exclaimed, "A world famous baritone is going to be singing here next month. Let's get tickets, I'd just love to see him!"

So on the night of the concert, the Siamese twins took their seats in the front row. The singer twin sat there enthralled as she listened to his voice while the other twin spent her time pouting at him seductively. Now this didn't go unnoticed by the baritone who invited them round to his dressing room after the show. While the singing twin serenaded them, the other two shagged all over the room in every conceivable position. So, a year went by and posters began to appear, advertising a return visit by the world famous baritone.

"Let's go again and get invited round for another party," said the sex mad twin.

"No, I don't think so," said the singing twin, "I doubt he'd even remember us."

Maurice had picked an awful after-dinner speaker. After 20 minutes of the most boring prattle, he could sense the audience becoming very restless.

"Bloody hell, I wish I could get the old bugger to shut up," whispered Maurice to the man sitting on his right.

"I've got an idea," came the reply. "Leave it to me."

The man wrote something on a napkin and passed it to the speaker. Within moments he sat down.

"That was incredible," said Maurice, impressed. "How did you manage that?"

"Easy. I just wrote 'your flies are undone' on the napkin," said the man grinning.

As Penelope stood gazing at the party-goers, a hand suddenly tweaked her backside and then embraced her. She turned round angrily and came face to face with a very drunk man.

"Oh Shorry," he slurred, "I thought you were my wife."

"How dare you!" she exclaimed, "go away this instant, you smell like a brewery and you look like something the cat's dragged in."

The man grinned and exclaimed, "I don't believe it! Not only do you look like my wife, you even act like her ash well."

An elephant and an ant fell in love at first sight and spent a night together in the throes of passion. Sadly, when the ant woke up the next morning the elephant had died.

"Oh no!" exclaimed the ant. "One night of passion and I spend the rest of my life digging a grave!"

PEEPING TOM

The clock strikes 11 o'clock. Snow White yawns and tells the seven dwarfs that she's off to bed. As soon as she goes upstairs, the dwarfs run outside, get on each other's shoulders until the one at the top is able to see through her bedroom window. This night it happens to be Bashful.

"She's just taking her blouse off," he whispers to the dwarf below him.

"She's taking her blouse off," the second says to the third and so the message is relayed down the line.

"Now she's taking her bra off," whispers Bashful.

"She's taking her bra off, she's taking her..." and so the message goes down the line.

"She's taking her skirt off..."

"She's taking her knickers off..."

"She's absolutely naked... Naked... Naked..."

Suddenly, Happy hears someone moving about in the bushes.

"Someone's coming!" he whispers.

"And me... And me... And me... And me..."

PENIS

A man has been a priest for more than 20 years and decides just once that he must experience sex to find out what he's given up. He goes to the red light district of a large town and enters a brothel where he's told to go to room 7. There, on the bed, is a naked girl waiting for him but when he strips off and she sees the huge size of his manhood, she sits up in alarm.

"No way mister," she says, shaking her head, "something like that could do a girl some serious harm."

So the priest goes off and finds another brothel. He enters room 5 where a girl is waiting, strips off and heads towards the bed. Alas, the girl gets an eyeful of his massive tackle and says quickly,

"Whoa, there, big boy. No way are you coming near me with something as big as that."

Undaunted, the priest finds a third brothel but this time he tells the girl he's a bit shy so would she mind if he strips off in the dark. The girl agrees, the man strips off and the action begins.

"I've never done it with a priest before," she remarks. "In fact when I first saw the dog collar I thought you wanted to talk to me about JEEEEEEEEEEES CHRIIIIIIIST!"

A man was riding through the desert when he saw an Indian lying naked on the ground with his penis sticking up in the air.

"What are you doing?" he asked.

"Me telling time," the Indian replied and sure enough his willy acted like a sundial, casting a shadow across his body. "It's 4 o'clock," he said. A little further on, he saw another Indian lying naked on the ground, with his penis sticking up in the air.

"Me tell time," said the Indian as the man rode by. "It's 6 o'clock," he said. Then 5 minutes later, he saw a third Indian lying naked on the ground but this one was masturbating. To hide his embarrassment, the rider remarked,

"Telling the time are you?"

"No, winding watch," came the reply.

A woman walked into the ladies toilet to find a man standing there.

"Hey!" she exclaimed, "This is just for women".

"So is this," he said, turning round.

A man is reading the evening paper when his eye catches an advertisement for the biggest John Thomas competition, to be held at his local pub.

"I think I'll have a go at that," he says to his wife.

"Oh no, Terry, don't."

"Why not? I could win £250."

"But I couldn't stand anyone seeing yours it would be so embarrassing."

Nothing more is said but a few days later the wife catches her husband counting out a wad of notes.

"Oh Terry!" she exclaims, "you did go in for that competition. You took it out for everyone to see."

"Oh come on love, don't be so upset. I only took enough out to win."

A man was sunbathing nude on a secluded beach when he saw three women walking towards him. In a panic, he grabbed his towel and put it over his face so as not to be recognised. As the women walked by, the first remarked,

"Well, it's certainly not my husband."

The second remarked,

"It's not my husband either."

The third woman exclaimed,

"Well girls, he certainly isn't from round here."

A woman was up a ladder mending some loose tiles on the roof of the house while her husband was sunbathing in the garden. Suddenly, the next door neighbour popped his head over the fence and said,

"Fancy letting your wife do that kind of work. You really are lazy. You should be damned well hung."

"But I am," he replied, "that's why she doesn't complain about doing jobs like these."

Three men walk into a pub in the rough quarter of the city and order 3 pints of beer. Watching them is a group of thugs in the corner.

"Come on," says one, "let's have some fun."

The leader of the thugs swaggers over to the newcomers and says in a loud voice,

"Hey, you three, this is our pub and we're a bit choosy about who drinks in here. So here's what we're going to do. If your three dicks add up to 22" between you then we'll pay for your pints… If not, then me and my mates are going to beat the shit out of you."

The three men at the bar get their dicks out and put them on the counter. The first man's measures 11", the second 10" and the third, 1".

Disgruntled, the thugs pay up and walk away.

"Phew," says the first man, "it's a good thing mine was 11" or we'd have been in trouble."

"Now wait a minute," complained the second, "My 10" was just as important."

"Lads, lads," says the third man, "I'm the one who got us out of trouble. If I hadn't had a hard on, we wouldn't be sipping these beers now."

A man went to the tattooist to have something special done for his wife.

"How about 'I love you' tattooed on your John Thomas," said the shop owner.

The man agreed and that night in bed he revealed all to his wife.

"How about this darling," he said proudly.

"What a surprise," she said scornfully, "trying to put words in my mouth again."

A woman went to the opticians for an eye test.

"Now Mrs Jones, can you tell me what this letter is?" said the optician pointing at the smallest line.

"No," she replied.

"Well, how about this?" he continued, pointing at a letter on a higher line.

"I don't know," she said.

"Try this one," he said, pointing at the largest letter.

"No, it's no good, I can't see it," she declared.

"Well can you see this?" he growled impatiently as he dropped his trousers and showed her his willy.

"Oh yes," she said, "I can see that."

"Just as I thought," he replied, "you're cock-eyed."

The doctor and his medical students were on their ward rounds when they came to Mr. Biggun's bed. On examining him, they discovered he had the biggest penis they'd ever seen.

"Goodness!" exclaimed one of the students "what's it like when it's reduced?"

"It's down now," replied the man.

"Then what on earth is it like when it's extended?"

"I don't know," replied the man sadly.

The group sympathised with him for being unable to get it up.

"No, no, you don't understand," he protested. "I mean I've never seen it when it's up. Every time I get a hard on, I pass out."

"Doctor, doctor," said the worried young man. "I'm hoping to get married soon but I'm embarrassed about my small penis."

"Oh, we can soon cure that," replied the doctor. "Just visit a farm everyday for the next month, dip your penis in milk and have a calf suck it off."

A few weeks later, the doctor bumped into the man in the street.

"Hello there, how's your marriage?"

"Oh I didn't get married in the end," replied the man. "I bought the calf instead."

A young man lost his penis in a car accident but thanks to the miracle of science, he was able to have an artificial one attached.

"You can have a rubber one for £50 or a metal one for £200," said the surgeon. So being out of work at the time, the young man was forced to buy a rubber one. Many years later, the man got married and had a son. On his seventh birthday, the son came home from school complaining that the kids in his class were calling him 'Bouncing Ben'.

"Take no notice," replied the man bitterly, "if I'd had a bit more money you'd have been 'Iron Man'."

A man went to the doctors complaining that there was something wrong with his penis.

"Oh dear, oh dear, oh dear," said the doctor shaking his head sadly. "I'm afraid it's bad news. This penis has just worn out. It's been over used and there is nothing I can do about it. So you'll only be able to have sex another 25 times."

When the man returned home, he told his wife the bad news. She was very kind and sympathetic to his plight.

"We'll certainly have to make the best use of these last 25 times," she said. "You'll have to have the best sex ever."

"I'm glad you said that," he replied, "because I made a list on the way home and I'm afraid there isn't room on it for you."

Little Tommy invited his friends round for his 8th birthday party. They went swimming in his father's pool, riding on his father's horses and then had a sumptuous bar-be-cue.

"When we changed for swimming, did you notice how small Tommy's willy was?" one friend said to the other.

"Yeah," he replied, "but I guess rich kids have lots of toys to play with."

A white man and a black man were sitting at the side of a pool. The white man put his dick in the water and remarked,

"The temperature of this water is 62°."

The black man put his dick in the water and added,

"Yes, and its two feet deep."

Every Thursday four men would meet at the sports centre for a game of squash. Afterwards three of them would shower and then go to the bar for a few drinks but the fourth always made some excuse and dashed away. Eventually one of the other three men took him aside and asked him why he never joined them.

"Well, to be honest," said the man blushing furiously, "I'm embarrassed about my willy. "It's so small."

"But does it work?" he was asked.

"Oh yes."

"Then how about swapping it for one that looks good in the shower?"

A man went into the public toilets and saw a bloke without any arms standing at the urinals.

"Do us a favour mate," he said, "can you get my pecker out for me?"

"Yeah, sure," said the man, so he unzipped the blokes flies and aimed his pecker at the porcelain. But as he looked down, he noticed it was red raw with horrible sores all over it and oozing puss. Afterwards, the man zipped up the other's flies but couldn't help remark,

"What's wrong with your willy, it doesn't look right to me."

"I don't know," replied the bloke, "but I wouldn't touch it myself," and he took his arms out of his shirt.

A woman was cleaning the public toilets when she discovered that someone had drawn a penis on the wall. She got a wet cloth and rubbed it off, only to discover the next day that a larger one had been drawn in its place. So, for a second time she rubbed the drawing off.

However on the third day, she discovered the drawing of the penis was now taking up most of the wall and underneath was written.

"Don't you know, the harder you rub it, the bigger it grows."

He picked her up at a nightclub and invited her back to his place. Nothing much was said on the way back so when they got there she remarked,

"You haven't got much to say for yourself."

"No. I do all my talking with this," he said dropping his trousers.

The girl walked forward and squinted,

"Bloody hell, don't tell me that's all you've got to say?"

Dave and Pete were lined up at the urinals and Dave couldn't help but notice how well endowed his mate was.

"Wow!" he exclaimed, "that's a remarkable piece of equipment you have there."

"Yeah," replied Pete, "It wasn't always like that. I wasn't happy with the one I had, so I went to this exclusive private clinic and had a transplant. It cost £1,500 but it was worth it."

Now Dave couldn't stop thinking about this so a few weeks later, he got the address from Pete and booked into the same clinic. The next time they met, he smiled at his mate and said,

"I think you were had, my new todger only cost £750."

"What!" exclaimed Pete. "Same place, same doctor? Let's have a look."

Dave showed off his new possession and Pete creased up with laughter.

"Oh that's alright," he said, "no wonder it didn't cost so much, it's my old one."

POLICE

A man was speeding through town when he saw a police car coming up behind him with the siren blaring. The motorist put his foot down immediately and the speedometer was touching 80 as he turned into the High Street.

'Oh shit,' he said to himself, 'this is no good' so he slowed down and pulled over.

The police car drew up behind the car and an officer got out to speak to him.

"Did you realise you were doing 80 miles an hour in a 30 mile an hour zone?" he asked.

The man replied,

"I'm sorry Officer, you see my wife ran off with a copper a few months ago and when I saw you chasing me, I thought you were trying to give her back."

A traffic copy flagged down the motorist and said,

"Excuse me, Sir, you may have slowed down but are you aware that it's an offence not to stop at that junction?"

"Stop, slow down, what's the difference," said the driver impatiently.

The cop got out his truncheon and began beating the man over the head with it.

"Shall I stop or slow down?" asked the cop.

"Stop, stop, please," cried the man.

"Now do you understand the difference?" he replied.

A man is driving along the road when suddenly he's pulled over by the police.

"Excuse me, Sir," says the officer, "have you been drinking?"

"No, officer," replies the man. "I'm sorry, was I driving erratically?"

"Not at all Sir, your driving was fine. My suspicions were aroused when I noticed that fat heffalump in the passenger seat."

"Hey, what's going on here?" demands the policeman when he catches a man throttling a young boy outside the concert hall.

"It's this little snotbag here," yells the man in frustration. "He just ran into the club and twiddled a peg on my violin."

"OK, OK, calm down. I think you've done enough now. Let the boy go."

"But you don't understand," gasps the man, close to tears, "the little bugger won't tell me which peg!"

Patrick Murphy went for an interview to be a policeman. The kindly sergeant decided to try and put the man at ease by asking him a simple question.

"Now, Mr. Murphy, can you tell me who killed Jesus Christ?" he asked.

Patrick started to sweat and looked worried. After a moment the sergeant continued,

"I can see this is a bit of an ordeal for you. Why don't you go and have a cup of tea and think it over. Pop back in 15 minutes."

Patrick went off to the canteen where he saw his friend Sean who greeted him warmly.

"So me old mate," he said, "how's it going?"

"Great," replied Patrick, "I'm on my first case already."

A woman broke down on the motorway and pulled onto the hard shoulder. She then opened the boot of the car and released two men in dirty raincoats who stood at the side of the car, exposing themselves to everyone who passed. Very soon, there was a 2-mile tailback as word got round about this strange behaviour.

Eventually a police car arrived and two angry officers confronted the woman.

"What the hell's going on here?" asked one, "can't you see the disruption you're causing."

The woman replied calmly,

"I'm sorry officer, but I broke down so I'm using my emergency flashers."

A young boy was skateboarding along the pavement when he was stopped by a policeman on horseback.

"Nice skateboard," remarked the officer ,"was it a present from Father Christmas."

"Yeah," replied the boy.

The officer continued,

"Well I have to tell you son, that next time I see you riding along here I'm going to take it away from you and speak to your parents. Okay?"

The boy nodded and the policeman was just about to ride away when he was called back.

"Hey mister," said the boy, "did you get that horse from Father Christmas?"

"Yes, I did," replied the officer humouring him.

"Well next time," said the boy, "get him to put the dick underneath the horse instead of on top."

"Book him, sarge, for drunk and disorderly behaviour," said the bobby on the beat.

"Are you sure he's drunk? It's not that obvious," asked the duty sergeant doubtfully.

"But he was having a very heated argument with someone at the bus stop, sarge."

"So?"

"There was no one else at the bus stop."

POLITICS

Speaker's Corner on a Sunday morning and a man was standing on his soap box encouraging people to think of the world as one big happy family.

"Let's not separate countries off," he said, "in my veins there runs the blood of English, Scottish, Italian, Chinese, Polish and French."

At that point, a voice was heard at the back of the crowd,

"Good gracious man, your mother must have been a good sport!"

A coach load of eminent politicians, travelling to an important convention, ran off the road and crashed into a tree. The wreckage was strewn over a large area. First on the scene was a local man who dug a large hole and buried all the bodies. Later, he went down to the police station to report the accident.

"So they were all dead?" asked the policeman.

The local man replied,

"Well, some of them said they weren't but since when could you ever believe what a politician had to say!"

PRATS

An arrogant young man was setting up a computer system for one of the pretty secretaries.

"Now you're going to need a password," he said, and hoping to embarrass her, he typed in the word PENIS.

However, she had the last laugh when the screen flashed back the message 'password rejected, not long enough.'

"Hey darling," said the prat, "do you want to play magic?"

"What's that mean?"

"You come to my house, we fuck and then you disappear."

As soon as the man woke up, he knew there was something special about the day. Of course! It was his birthday and he loved birthdays. However, as he went down to breakfast, nothing was said. His wife and his two daughters never mentioned anything and by the time he left the house, he was in deep despair.

"They've forgotten," he said to himself. "They just don't care."

The man arrived at work to be greeted with a smile from his secretary as she wished him Happy Birthday. He was overjoyed, at least someone had remembered.

That evening, as he was about to leave for home, his secretary suggested they go for a birthday drink. He readily agreed and for the next hour they really enjoyed themselves. For the first time, he realised how pretty she was, and how kind, so it wasn't surprising that when she invited him back for coffee, he quickly accepted.

"Make yourself at home," she said when they got back to her flat. "I'll just go and slip into something more comfortable."

"I'm alright here," he thought to himself and quickly stripped off, ready for her return.

All of a sudden, the bedroom door opened and out came his wife, daughters and friends singing,

"Happy Birthday to you…"

The arrogant man sidled up to the beautiful woman in the nightclub and said,

"Hey, gorgeous, the word tonight is 'legs'. How about coming back to my place to spread the word!"

On a busy Friday night when everyone was out partying, a lone man shopped in a late night supermarket. In his basket he placed one individual pie, half a pint of milk, 1 doughnut, 12 apples and one helping of vegetables. At the check out, the girl behind the till looked at him sympathetically and remarked,

"You're single aren't you?"

"Why, yes," he replied somewhat surprised, "how can you tell?"

"Oh come on!" she exclaimed, "with a face like that!"

Five minutes out of Los Angeles, the air stewardess approaches a man sitting at the back of the plane.

"Good evening sir, can I get you anything to drink? Would you like some TWA coffee, TWA chocolate or a TWA cordial?"

The man looks up at her and grins.

"I'd like some TWA tea, please."

A real sleaze-bag walked into a bar and sat down next to a very attractive woman. He ordered a drink and for the next five minutes sipped at it slowly, continuously looking at his watch.

The woman was so intrigued she finally spoke.

"Excuse me, I couldn't help but notice you keep looking at your watch. Has your date not turned up?"

"Oh no," he replied, "It's nothing like that. I'm looking at this special watch I've just bought. It talks to me."

"Really! What's it saying?"

"It says you're not wearing any knickers," he replied.

"Well it's wrong," she retorted somewhat taken aback.

"Oh damn," he cursed, "it must be an hour fast."

As the man twirled his partner around the dance floor, he whispered in her ear.

"Hey Tracy, do you shag?"

Tracy ignored the question and carried on dancing.

"Come on Tracy, do you shag?" he asked again.

She turned to him in anger.

"Don't you dare talk to me like that. Is that the way you talk to all the girls you dance with?"

"Oh yes," he said, quite unmoved by her anger.

"Well I bet you get a lot of girls telling you where you can get off!" she exclaimed.

"Oh I do," he said, "but I also get a lot of shags."

A man walked into a bar and ordered a beer from the very attractive barmaid. He engaged her in conversation.

"I bet I can bite my own ear," he said, putting £5 on the bar.

She accepted the bet and the next moment, he took out his false teeth and nipped his ear. He picked up his winnings and then said,

"I'll give you another chance. For another £5, I bet I can keep an eye on my beer while I go to the loo."

The barmaid hesitated. She didn't want to lose any more money but she knew the toilets were outside.

"Okay," she said, "you're on."

The man took out his glass eye and put it by his pint as he went outside for a pee. Again he collected the money, smiled at her and said,

"Listen, I'll give you a chance to win back all your money. I bet I can make love to you so gently, you won't feel a thing."

She agreed immediately. There was no way she wasn't going to feel him. They disappeared into the storeroom and got down to it on the floor.

As he thrust in and out, she declared with glee. "I can feel it, I can feel it."

"Oh well," he gasped, continuing his humping. "You win some, you lose some."

PRESIDENTS

The ex President of the USA woke up one morning to find a red ring around his todger. Immediately he went to the doctor who prescribed a course of pills and told him to come back in a week if there was no improvement.

Alas, the red ring still remained so on his next visit, the doctor gave him some antibiotics but this still had no effect.

"Ah ha," said the doctor, examining it more closely. "I think I have an idea. Take this tube of cream and rub it on every night for a week and let's see what happens."

So the ex President did as he was instructed and a week later rushed into the doctor's surgery full of joy.

"It's gone, it's gone," he said, "what wonderful cream. What was it?"

"Lipstick remover," came the reply.

At last Jeremy landed the star part in a stage show at the Adelphi Theatre in London. He was to play the part of John F. Kennedy.

Overjoyed, he spent the next month researching every aspect of the President's life. He spoke like him, dressed like him and had his hair styled like him. On the Monday morning, rehearsals were due to start. Unfortunately, he was assassinated on the way to the theatre.

Bill Clinton and his wife were asleep in bed one night when she woke up suddenly and prodded her husband in the ribs.

"Bill, Bill," she whispered, "I'm off to the bathroom, I won't be long."

"What!" exclaimed the President, "You wake me up just to tell me that!"

"No, no," she replied, "I just wanted to ask you to save my place."

Snow White, Tom Thumb and Valentino were discussing their merits.

"I must be the most beautiful woman in the world," said Snow White proudly.

But the other two argued that she couldn't prove it.

"At least I know I'm the smallest man in the world," said Tom Thumb.

"How can you be sure?" asked the others.

And of course, Valentino boasted he'd had the most lovers.

Again, the other two wanted proof.

So the arguments continued and then Tom Thumb had a great idea.

"Let's ask Merlin, he knows everything."

All agreed and they went in search of his house.

Snow White went in first and after a couple of minutes emerged triumphant.

"It's official," she said. "I am the most beautiful."

Then Tom Thumb went in and skipped out moments later, punching the air with his fist.

"Yes, yes!" he chortled. "I am the smallest."

Valentino entered and was gone some time. When he eventually returned, he looked confused and angry.

"So who is this Bill Clinton?" he demanded.

60 years on and Monica Lewinsky is a grandma showing one of her grandchildren a history book of the last century. They were looking at a chapter on American Presidents.

She points to one of them and says, "And look here, this is the man who brought me to my knees."

Bill Clinton was walking down the corridors of the White House when he bumped into a girl.

"Hello, are you new?" he asked.

"Yes," she replied. "I've only been her two days."

"I thought so," he continued. "I didn't think I'd come across your face before."

You may get AIDS from sex, but Bill Clinton gets sex from aides.

The British Prime Minister, the Russian President and the American President meet for drinks in Paris.

The waiter addresses the Prime Minister

"Ze pint of beer?"

"Yes," he replies.

Then he looks at the Russian.

"A vodka."

"Ya," replies the President.

Finally he looks at the President of the USA.

"Le whisky?"

The President replies angrily,

"Don't fucking mention that bitch!"

How will Bill Clinton be remembered in history?

He was the President after Bush.

PUBS

A man walks into a pub and orders a pint of beer.

"That's a great shirt you've got on," comments the barman.

"Thanks," he says. "I got it from Colin Mathers."

A little later another man walks in.

"Nice pants," says the barman.

"Yeah, I got them from Colin Mathers" he replies.

"Nice shoes and socks," remarks the barman to a third man who walks in.

"Thank you," he says. "They came from Colin Mathers."

Thirty minutes later, a naked man runs into the bar.

"Who are you?" asks the barman.

"I'm Colin Mathers," came the reply.

Jack said to the man in the pub,

"My wife's a wrestler."

"Really?"

"Yeah, I thought you might have seen her wrestle."

"No, but I've seen her box a few times," came the reply.

Steve walked into the pub sporting a cut lip and a black eye.

"What happened to you?" said the landlord.

"That little sod Jimmy Cormack did this," he replied angrily.

"Never!" exclaimed the landlord, "but he's such a weedy bugger, you should have pummelled him."

"Yeah, but he had a baseball bat in his hand," came the reply.

"Well, you must have had something in your hands, surely."

"Oh yes, his wife's tits."

Two men talking in a pub.

"Your round," said one.

"Yeah! Well you're a fat bastard as well," replied the other.

A man walked into a pub and ordered 13 pints of beer. As the publican lined them up along the bar, he drank the first, the third, the fifth, the seventh, the ninth, the eleventh and the thirteenth. Then he pocketed his change and got up to leave.

"Hold on," said the publican, "aren't you going to drink the rest?"

"No thanks," said the man. "My doctor ordered me only to have the odd drink."

A pile of dog shit had been deposited on the pavement right outside the entrance to the pub. As the little man walked in, he slipped on it and skidded across the floor. Moments later, a big burly man came in and slipped on the shit as well.

"I just did that," said the small man.

So the big man beat him up.

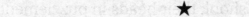

Gregory was determined to improve his social skills so the next time he met 'man-about-town' Harvey Wilkins, he asked him for a good joke that he could tell next time he was in company.

"OK," said Harvey, "here's one. Four separate people spend an afternoon in the park, all meet up at the bandstand. One was a policeman, one was a young woman, one was a horseman and the fourth was a pensioner. Now which of the men knew the woman?"

Gregory looked absolutely dumfounded.

"Well, I have no idea," he stuttered.

"The horse manure," laughed Harvey. "Do you get it – the horseman knew her."

"Oh right," replied Gregory laughing politely but not really understanding. "Thanks Harvey."

The next time Gregory went for a pint in his local, he was determined to tell the joke and become 'one of the lads'.

"I've got a joke," he said. "There were four people at a bandstand in the park. One was an old pensioner, one was a horseman, one was a policeman and the other was a brunette. Which of the three men knew the brunette?"

The group of men shook their heads in puzzlement so Gregory continued,

"The answer is horse shit but I'm not sure why."

A bloke with more money than sense went into a pub and threw down a challenge to the customers.

"If anyone can drink 20 pints of Murphy's straight off, then I'll give them £200. Look here it is on the bar."

Everyone shook his head except one man who left the bar.

Disappointed, the bloke was just picking up his money when the man who had left suddenly reappeared.

"Leave your money where it is," he said, "I'll take up your challenge."

Then to everyone's amazement, he downed the 20 pints, one after another, and picked up the £200.

"So why did you go out?" asked the bloke

"Well first I had to go to the pub next door to make sure I could do it!" he replied.

Q

QUICKIES

Men are like placemats – they only turn up when there's food on the table.

You know you're getting old when lucky means finding your car in the parking lot!

You know things are bad when you fake an orgasm while masturbating.

What's the difference between a woman and a coffin?

You come in one and go in the other.

Why do dogs lick their cocks?

Because they know they're going to lick your face next.

A sign in the toilets of the sex change clinic read:

"We may never piss this way again."

How do you know when you've met the man of your dreams?

You trip over his willy in the pub.

The best thing about a blow job is the 10 minutes of silence.

Why did Superman use a condom?

To protect his dick of steel from rust.

What's the best thing about self abuse?

You don't have to look your best.

What do you get when you cross a donkey with an onion?

A piece of ass that'll bring tears to your eyes.

Did you hear about the woman who only had two chances to get pregnant?

She blew them both.

Did you know that if you're having a bad day, it takes 42 muscles to frown but only four to extend the middle finger and tell them to piss off?

Have you heard there's a new bra on the market called a Sheepdog?

It rounds them up and points them in the right direction.

Did you hear about the girl who jumped out of the cake?

I won't say what she looked like, but no one ate anything!

Did you hear about the ward sister nicknamed Appendix?

All the surgeons took her out.

Did you hear about the man who fell into a tank of paint?

He was overcome with emulsion.

Jimmy Hill was sitting in the bar when the landlord said,

"Hey, why the long face?"

I wouldn't say my wife was ugly but she couldn't lure a man out of a burning building!

What do you say to the person who has everything… and is breathing on you?

Did you hear about the lion that went to see the psychiatrist?

He complained that every time he roared, he had to sit through a 2-hour film.

Why does a Scotsman wear a kilt?

So the sheep won't hear the zipper.

If there are two flies sitting on someone's backside, which one is the drug addict?

The one that's on the crack.

Do you know what happened to the man who had a mole on his willy?

He was reported to the R.S.P.C.A.

What's the similarity between a warm toilet seat and pussy?

They're both nice but you always wonder who was there before you.

Why should you not wear Russian underpants?

Because Cher-nob-ll fall out!

What did the cannibal do after he'd dumped his girlfriend?

Wiped his arse.

What's the difference between a wife and a mistress?

Night and day.

What's the difference between a bucket of shit and an estate agent?

The bucket.

What does a female reindeer do on New Years Eve?

She goes out to blow a few bucks.

What's the difference between a pay cheque and a penis?

You never have to persuade a woman to blow your pay cheque.

If you call nuts on a wall 'walnuts' and nuts on your chest 'chestnuts', then what do you call nuts on your chin?

A blow job!

Why did the simple man not enjoy his honeymoon?

He was waiting for the swelling to go down.

Why did the Irishman ask for a refund on his tie?

It was too tight around his neck.

Did you hear about the girl who asked her boyfriend to kiss her somewhere dirty?

He drove her to a coal mine.

What do Christmas trees and priests have in common?

The balls are just for decoration.

If one synchronised swimmer drowns, do the rest have to drown as well?

Why do nymphomaniacs drive cars with sunroofs?

There's more legroom.

Did you hear about the woman who was so ugly, the only people who ever asked her to go to bed were her parents!

Here follows a lesson on ornithology:

What bird is associated with stalking and aggression?

The Eagle.

What bird is associated with love and peace?

The Dove.

What bird is associated with children?

The Stork.

What bird is associated with larceny?

The Jackdaw.

What bird is associated with birth control?

The Swallow.

How do you tell an old man?

It's not hard.

★

Why did the bird fall out of the tree?

Because he was dead.

Did you hear about the man with the big dick?

It was so big you could toboggan down it.

Men who paint toilets are not necessarily shit house painters!

Men are like cement. After getting laid, they take ages to get hard.

What do you get when you cross a piranha with a prostitute?

Your last blow job.

What goes in pink and hard and comes out soft and mushy?

Bubble gum.

What would you find on a nun's tombstone?

"Returned – unopened."

Why are puppies like near-sighted gynaecologists?

They both have wet noses.

What did the hurricane say to the palm tree?

Hang onto your nuts; this is no ordinary blow job.

What do you get when you cross a prostitute with a computer?

A fucking know-it-all.

Did you hear about the constipated maths teacher?

He worked it out with a pencil!

What has two grey legs and two brown legs?

An elephant with diarrhoea.

"Hello," said the woman, "are you a pole vaulter?"

"Why yes I am a Pole!" he exclaimed in astonishment, "but how did you know my name is Walter?"

How does a Welshman find a sheep in long grass?

Very satisfying.

What do you get when you cross a rooster with a Malteser?

A cock that melts in your mouth, not in your hand.

What's the different between an oral and a rectal thermometer?

The taste.

"Get your hand off my knee!" demanded the girl in the cinema.

"No, not you… you!"

"Oh look," she said, "isn't that Hortense?

"Oh no, I don't think so, she seems quite relaxed to me."

Why do the Irish have potatoes and the Arabs have oil?

Because the Irish had first choice.

There's a girl down our street called 'Doorknob' – she's been handled by so many men!

"Doctor, doctor. I've only got 59 seconds to live."

"Wait a minute please."

Did you hear about the man who went into a bank and asked the teller to check his balance?

She pushed him!

What does a dog do, that a man steps into?

Pants.

R

REAL MEN

How many real men does it take to change a light bulb?

None. Real men aren't afraid of the dark.

The latest group of men from earth had arrived at the Pearly Gates and were waiting to enter. The men were supposed to be queuing behind one of two signs. The first read: 'Henpecked husbands here', and the queue went on for miles. The second sign read: 'Independent husbands here', and behind this stood one forlorn looking man. When the keeper of the gate saw this, he asked the man standing alone why he was standing behind the 'Independent husbands' sign.

"My wife told me to," he replied meekly.

What's the similarity between a weak wally and an old car?

They both need a great deal of touching up to get them going.

A cowboy rides into a rough frontier town and walks into the saloon.

"I'll have a shot of whiskey," he demands from the barman and downs it in one gulp. After another couple of drinks, which he takes more slowly, he leaves the saloon only to return seconds later shouting at the top of his voice:

"Whichever one of you damned critters stole my horse, if it's not back by the time I've had another drink, I'll do what I did in Coyote Creek."

So the man has another drink and goes back outside to see his horse has been returned.

As he mounts to ride away, the barman comes rushing up to him.

"Hey, mister, just out of interest, what did you do in Coyote Creek?"

"I had to walk home," replies the man.

"Bob," whispered his wife urgently, "I think I can hear someone moving around downstairs. Are you awake?"

"No," he replied.

The man was so henpecked, he had to wash and iron his own apron.

What do men and rolls of carpet have in common?

Lay them properly the first time and you can walk all over them for the rest of their lives.

The man behind the bar said to Colin:

"You really are a typical example of a spineless, henpecked man."

"Now look here," replied Colin, "you wouldn't say that if my wife was here."

"Darling," said the husband, "what's your favourite sexual position?"

"Across the street," she replied.

The best way to get a man to do something is to suggest he's far too old to do it.

What is the smartest thing a man can say?

"My wife says..."

Women – what have you got when you have two little balls in your hand?

A man's undivided attention.

What's the difference between pink and purple?

The woman's grip.

An old woman is sitting quietly in her garden when suddenly a genie appears and grants her three wishes.

"I would like to be very rich and live in a mansion," she says.

Wooosh! Her house turns into a mansion and fantastic gold jewellery adorns her body.

"Secondly, I would like to be young and beautiful so I can enjoy my new found wealth."

Wooosh! And her wish is granted.

"Finally," she says seeing her trusty dog lying on the lawn, "I would like my dog to be turned into the most handsome man that ever walked the earth."

Wooosh! And there in front of her is the most perfect man. The woman can't believe her eyes.

"Oh, my, you're incredible," she whispers.

He replies, "Now don't you wish you'd never had me castrated."

A man who had pleaded not guilty beforehand was now in court watching the jury of nine women and two men take their seats. All of a sudden he turned to his barrister and whispered frantically in his ear.

"Your Honour," said the barrister rising, "my client would like to change his plea to guilty."

"And may I ask why he has changed his mind?" demanded the judge.

"Of course. When he pleaded not guilty he didn't realise there would be so many women on the jury. He tells me he can't fool one woman so there's no chance he'd fool nine of them."

"Is your husband easy to please?"

"I don't know, I've never tried."

"Well, isn't that a coincidence?" she said. "You look just like my fourth husband."

"Fourth!" he gasped. "How many have you had?"

"Three."

The man sat staring morosely into his pint of beer.

"What's wrong, mate?" asked the sympathetic barman. "Is it woman trouble?"

"Too right," replied the man. "I've just had an awful fight with my wife."

"What happened?"

"She came crawling over to me on her hands and knees..."

"Oh, no," interrupted the barman, "what happened next?"

"She said she'd put me in hospital for a week if I didn't get out from under the bed."

★

Women's Lib is making him sleep on the wet bit.

Behind every great woman there's a man who's disappointed her.

"Every man who is high up likes to feel that he has done it all himself; and the wife smiles, and lets it go at that. It's our only joke. Every woman knows that."

J M Barrie 'What Every Woman Knows'

Our dad thinks he wears the trousers in our house, but it's mum who tells him which pair to put on.

No man is really successful until his mother-in-law admits it.

The henpecked husband said he couldn't bear to sit through porno movies.

"Why not?" asked a mate.

"Because I can't stand to see one guy enjoying himself more in ten minutes than I have in twenty-five years."

A businessman is walking along the beach when he spots an old bottle washed up on the shore. When he opens it, a genie slowly emerges and whispers, "Hello, I am the genie of the bottle, but I'm not so well, so I can only grant you one wish – and it'd better be an easy one."

"I wish for an end to the recession in this country."

"Oh, that's hard," replies the genie. "Can you give me something easier?"

"OK, can you make my mother-in-law respect me?"

The genie replies, "So you want an end to the recession, do you?"

Many a wife has helped her husband to the top rung of the ladder – and then left him there for a while until she's decided whether the picture would look better somewhere else.

The children were being asked questions in their Sunday School lesson.

"Now," said the teacher, "who is it that we all tremble before, bow our heads and declare our unworthiness?"

A little boy at the back put his hand up. "Please miss, it's my mum. Because that's what I see my dad do every Saturday night when he wants some beer money."

A wife and her henpecked husband are having dinner in a restaurant. The waiter comes over to take their order.

"I'll have the lamb steak with garlic butter," says the woman.

"And the vegetable, madam?" asks the waiter.

"Oh, he'll have the same as me."

Two men talking over a pint in the pub:

"My wife and I had an awful argument on Tuesday. She wanted to go to the opera and I wanted to go bowling. Anyway, we sorted it out in the end."

"Good. So what was the opera like?"

"Doctor, doctor, my wooden leg is giving me such a lot of pain."

"Don't be silly, man," replied the doctor. "How can a wooden leg give you pain?"

"My wife keeps hitting me on the head with it."

The President of the world's most successful international business, accompanied by his wife, stop for petrol at a small out-of-the-way garage. As the garage attendant comes out to help them, the wife looks up and screams with pleasure.

"John, oh, no! I can't believe it!" She jumps out of the car and rushes to embrace him. Then after a few minutes of animated conversation, she returns to the car looking very thoughtful.

As they drive off, the husband looks at her with interest and asks, "Who was that, sweetheart?"

"That was an old boyfriend of mine. We were together a long time. In fact, we almost got married."

There is a moment's silence and then he says, "Ah, well. I guess you're glad you married me instead."

"What makes you say that?"

"Because I'm the President of an international company."

"That's quite irrelevant," she replies with scorn. "If I'd married John, he would now be President."

How do men sort their laundry?

"Filthy" and "filthy but all right for another couple of days".

A beautiful young woman goes to see her psychiatrist because she keeps getting recurring nightmares. The psychiatrist asks her to lay down on the couch and the next moment he's on top of her and they make love. When it's over, he says:

"Right, that takes care of my problem. Now let's hear what your trouble is."

"Doctor, doctor, can you come round and see my wife as soon as possible? She is so ill. I had to carry her downstairs to make my dinner."

A married man went on business to London and met a beautiful young girl. They spent five idyllic days together and at the end of his stay, he bade her farewell and offered to leave her some money.

The girl shook her head. "No thanks, darling, you go back to your wife. I don't want anything, I'm a good sport."

Time went by and it was four months later that the man received a phone call from her.

"Oh, thank goodness I've found you," she sobbed. "I've discovered I'm pregnant. I can't believe it! I'm going to do away with myself."

"My goodness," replied the man admiringly, "you really are a good sport, aren't you."

Two men were talking about their sons over a pint of beer.

"My son must be the laziest bugger in the world," complained Alan. "He never does a thing."

"No," argued Bob. "My son is the laziest."

After discussing this problem for a while, they decide to go to each other's houses to check it out. When they get to Alan's house, they find his son lying on the sofa, watching TV and surrounded by sweet papers.

"Hey, son, pop down the road and get me an evening paper."

"No chance," replied the boy.

"Go on, I'll give you a couple of quid for going."

"Leave me alone, go away," came the reply.

So the two men went over to Bob's house and discovered his son lying on the sofa, watching the TV, the fire full on, the boy dripping with sweat, but also crying."

"What's up, son?" asked his father.

It took a while for his son to answer but eventually he replied, "I can't change channels, dad, the remote's fallen off the back of the sofa."

The angry husband stormed into the pub and confronted a man, quietly drinking at the bar.

"You bastard!" shouted the husband. "Thought you could get away with it, did you? Well, think again. I've got proof right here that you've been carrying on with my wife."

He took some photographs out of his pocket and showed them to the man.

"See," he continued. "This is a picture of you and my wife drinking together in the pub. And this one shows you kissing her in the back of your car...and look at this, in this one she's half undressed. What have you got to say for yourself?"

The man studied each of the photos for a few minutes and then replied,

"I'll take six copies of photo number three."

Why are men so quiet when they have sex?

They don't talk to strangers.

"My bloody stupid boyfriend is going to die of syphilis!" cried the distraught woman.

"Oh, no," replied her friend. "No one dies of syphilis anymore."

"Well they do, if they give it to me," she retorted.

A man returned from the doctor's with some very bad news. He had been told that his sex life was nearly over because he had simply worn out his tackle.

"I would estimate that you have about 30 sessions left," said the doctor sympathetically.

When the man told his wife she was shocked.

"Oh, no, how can this be? Only 30 left! We must make every one of these very special. Let's make a plan now."

"I have," he said. "I made a schedule on the way home and your name isn't on it."

A wife rang up her husband in anguish.

"Jack, Jack, the doctor says I'm pregnant. Why didn't you use a condom?"

"But I always use a condom," he argued. "Anyway, who is this?"

When a woman says...

"Come on Shaun, this place is a hovel. You and me need to clean it up. Put away everything lying on the bed, and then all the stuff on the floor ought to go into the washing machine immediately or we'll have no clothes left."

The man hears...

"Na na na you and me na na na on the bed na na na immediately na na na no clothes."

★

A despicable husband was travelling round the country buying new merchandise for his department store. His trip lasted much longer than usual, so he would keep in touch with his wife by sending her telegrams saying, "Still travelling, still buying".

After two more weeks had passed, the wife eventually sent a message back to him.

'Come home at once or I'll be selling what you're buying!'

"If I say no to going to bed with you, will you really commit suicide?"

"Well, that's my usual procedure, yes," he said.

Did you hear about the innocent young girl who met a man in a raincoat?

Later, she recounted the event to her friend.

"Coming back from the supermarket this morning, a man stopped me in the car park and showed me the lining of his raincoat."

"That's odd," mused her friend. "Are you sure he only wanted you to see his raincoat?"

"Oh yes, he wasn't wearing anything else."

When man was first made, he only had twenty years of normal sex life. To him, this was horrifying. Meanwhile, the monkey had also been given twenty years normal sex life but he said he only needed ten years, so he gave the other ten to the man.

Likewise, the lion, also with twenty years, gave ten years to the man as well. He agreed that ten years was plenty.

Finally the donkey, agreeing with the other animals that ten years was enough, gave the man another ten years.

So all this explains today's modern man. He has twenty years of normal sex life, ten years of monkeying around, a further ten years of lion about it and finally ten years of making a complete ass of himself.

"I'm leaving you!" screamed the man's wife. "You've messed around just once too often. I overheard that tart from number 38 tell her friends that you had a small penis. Oh the shame!"

"The truth is," replied the husband, "that she has a big mouth."

After their honeymoon, the husband brought his wife breakfast in bed. On the tray was fresh orange juice, cereal, bacon and egg, toast and coffee.

"Mmm, thank you darling," she said. "This looks lovely."

"Good," he replied, "because that's how I want it every morning."

The doctor received a call from one of the local farmers.

"If you have a moment, would you mind popping in to have a look at the wife, doctor?"

"Of course," replied the doctor. "Is she feeling unwell?"

"I'm not sure. This morning she got up, as usual, at 4.30, milked the cows, took the sheep up to the top field, cooked the breakfast for myself and the lads, prepared the books for the accountant, cleaned out the barn, made dinner, sorted the hens, went to market, got my supper, cleaned up and then organised events for next week's harvest festival. When she finished at midnight, she complained she felt a bit tired. Maybe she just needs a pick-me-up."

Two men shared a flat in Fulham. On Saturday night, one of them arrived home to find ten crates of beer, four bottles of scotch and a loaf of bread on the kitchen table.

"Hey, mate," he said. "You didn't tell me we were having a party?"

"We're not," replied the second man.

"Then what's the bread for?"

Said the wife to her lazy husband:

"Listen Bert, you're going to make yourself ill, sitting there all day thinking up excuses for not working."

A young newly wed girl was telling her friend how she had been teaching her husband to have better manners.

Suddenly she was interrupted by him rushing into the room and shouting,

"Come on, love, how about a quickie?"

Shocked, the girl's friend remarked, "I thought you were teaching him better manners?"

"I am," she stressed. "A month ago, he wouldn't have asked."

What will you never hear a man say?

I think we're lost, I'll pull over there and ask for directions.

RELIGION

A woman was having a conversation with God. She asked him,

"What does a million years mean to you?"

"Oh, about a minute," he replied.

"And what does a £1 million pounds mean?"

"About a penny."

"Well, do you think I could have £1 million please?" she asked.

"In a minute," came the reply.

Recently a teacher, a bin man, and a lawyer wound up together at the Pearly Gates. St. Peter informed them that in order to get into Heaven, they would each have to answer one question.

St. Peter addressed the teacher and asked, "What was the name of the ship that crashed into the iceberg? They just made a movie about it."

The teacher answered quickly, "That would be the Titanic."

St. Peter let him through the gate.

St. Peter turned to the bin man and, thinking that Heaven didn't REALLY need all the odours that this guy would bring with him, decided to make the question a little harder: "How many people died on the ship?"

Fortunately for him, the trash man had just seen the movie, and answered, "1,228."

"That's right! You may enter into Heaven!"

St. Peter then turned to the lawyer. "Name them."

A priest walked into a pub and addressed the man standing at the bar.

"You, Seamus, do you want to go to heaven?"

Seamus nodded.

"Then come and join me," said the priest, "join me over here."

Eventually all the men had joined the priest except Paddy.

"What's wrong, don't you want to go to heaven?" asked the priest.

"I do, Father," replied Paddy, "but I'm too young to be going just yet."

When you see a priest you call him Father. When you see a Bishop, you call him Your Grace. When you meet a Cardinal it's Your Eminence, and when you see a gorgeous man, it's oh My God!

A couple had been trying for children for many years without any luck. One day their parish priest told them that he was going to Rome for five years but that while he was there he would pray everyday for them and keep a lighted candle in St. Peter's.

So a few years went by and eventually the priest returned home. He went round to see the couple and as he walked up the garden path, he spotted a pair of twins playing on a swing. As the door of the house opened, he saw the poor harassed woman, heavily pregnant, with two small babies in her arms.

"Why Father!" she exclaimed, "we didn't know you'd returned."

"Yes, a week ago," he replied, "and I thought I'd come round to see how you are. I see you've been blessed with children. Where's your husband?"

"He's gone to Rome," she replied, "to blow out that bloody candle!"

A miserly old vicar decided to save money by painting the outside of the church himself. He bought a large can of paint and set to work. But after finishing two walls, he realised he didn't have enough paint to finish. He was determined not to spend any more money so he thinned the paint down with water and just managed to finish the job. Unfortunately, during the night there was a terrific thunderstorm and when he went to inspect the church the following morning, the two walls which had been painted with thinned down paint, had streaked badly.

"Oh what shall I do?" he said in despair, and a voice boomed out from the heavens, "repaint and thin no more."

An atheist was walking through the jungle when he was confronted by a huge lion. He stood rooted to the spot, fear oozing from every pore. The lion growled and got ready to pounce.

"Oh God, please help me," he pleaded.

A voice from the heavens boomed out,

"Help you! You've spent all your life denying my existence, why should I help you now?"

Then the atheist had an idea.

"Please God, if you won't help me, then perhaps you could make the lion a Christian instead."

"Yes, alright," agreed God.

The next minute there was a sudden flash of light and the lion got down on all fours and began to pray.

"Oh thank goodness for that," muttered the frightened man, until he heard what the lion had to say.

"For what we are about to eat may the Lord make us truly thankful."

The Pope flies to New York for a very important conference but the plane is late so he hasn't got much time. He flags down a cab and gives the driver the address as they move out into heavy traffic.

The Pope looks at his watch in exasperation.

"Can't you go faster?" he asks.

"Oh no," replies the cabbie, "it's more than my job's worth to get picked up by the traffic cops. I could lose my licence."

Another ten minutes go by and they are still miles from the conference venue.

"I've got a good idea," says the Pope, "let me drive, then if we get stopped, it won't be your fault."

The two men change places, the Pope grabs the wheel, puts his foot down on the accelerator and away they go. All of a sudden, sirens are heard and a police car flags them down.

"Excuse me Sir," says the officer, "did you realise you were well over the speed limit?"

"Yes, I'm very sorry," replies the Pope, "but we have to get to a very important conference in less than 15 minutes."

"Well, in that case follow me," says the officer, and the two cars take off at speed.

"Lieutenant," says the officer, reporting in on the radio. "I'm escorting a very important person to that big conference down town."

"Who's that then?" asks a voice over the mike.

"Don't know, sir," replies the officer, "but he must be a big shot 'cos the Pope's driving him!"

A man is out practising golf when he hits his ball into a wooded area at the side of the fairway. Muttering to himself, he goes looking for it and stumbles across a funny little gnome sitting cross-legged on the ground.

"Good day to you," says the man, politely.

The little gnome nods his head, then says,

"I see you're not having a good day. I bet you wish you could be the world's greatest golf player?"

"If only," replies the man wistfully.

"Well perhaps I could help you. I have magic powers. But it will mean your sex life will become virtually non existent."

"A champion golfer, instead of a champion lover. Yes please," says the man.

Suddenly, a terrific wind swirls through the trees and the next moment the man is back on the fairway as if nothing has happened. Over the next year, his game goes from strength to strength and he becomes one of the leading golfers in the world.

One day, as he walks the old familiar fairway where his success first began, he steps off into the woods to see if the gnome is still there. Sure enough, he's sitting cross-legged on the ground.

"Ah, ha, I hear you're the best in the country," says the gnome. "But how's your sex life?" he smirks.

"Not so bad," replies the man.

"What!" exclaims the gnome? "What do you mean? How many times did you have sex last year?"

"Oh, I think it was five times."

"And you call that not bad?" sneers the gnome.

"Well, it's not bad for a Catholic priest with a small congregation!"

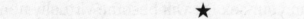

A man decides he would like to become a monk so he goes along to the local monastery for an interview.

"If you want to be a monk, you have to pass two tests," says the Abbot. "In the first test, you will be put into a locked cell where you will live on bread and water for a year, praying to God and reading the Bible. Then, if you are still determined, you will take the second test. This time, a bell will be hung from your John Thomas and a nude woman will be placed in front of you. If the bell doesn't ring, we will welcome you as one of our brothers. Do you agree to the tests?"

The man agrees and prepares himself for the first test. A year later, he emerges from the cell, still determined to become a monk. So arrangements are made for the second test. A bell is tied to his willy and a beautiful nude woman is placed in front of him. Immediately, the bell starts to ring.

"I'm so sorry," says the Abbot "but I'm afraid you've failed the test."

"Now wait a minute," protests the man. "I defy anyone to pass the second test. I demand to be shown proof."

"Very well," says the Abbot and he calls the other 12 monks into the room, tells them to strip and ties bells to their willies. The naked woman returns and not a bell rings except the poor man who demanded the test. In fact, the bell rings so frantically it falls off onto the floor. As he bends down to pick it up, the other 12 bells begin to ring.

A very old Irishman is lying sick in bed. He's only got hours to live so the family are gathered solemnly around his bed, heads bowed in prayer. Suddenly, the old man beckons to his daughter.

"Mary, my daughter," he whispers in her ear. "I haven't long to go, please fetch the Protestant minister."

"But Pa," she protests, "you're a good Catholic, you were born and bred a Catholic, why would you be wanting a Protestant minister now?"

The old man looks at his daughter impatiently and says,

"Mary, Mary, please! Just go and get the minister. And hurry," he croaks, "there's not much time."

Now being a dutiful daughter, Mary rushes off to the minister's home and knocks frantically on the door.

"Why! It's young Mary O'Connell. What are you doing here!"

Mary explains about her father and the amazed minister rushes around to the old man and converts him. Not long after, the old man worsens and minutes from death, the family priest arrives. He is distraught to learn about the old man's dying wish.

"But why, Sean? You of all people! I can't remember the last time you missed church. Why would you want to turn your back on our faith?"

"Well, Father," whispered the old man. "I realised if somebody had to go, it was better to be one of them, than one of us!"

A priest and a Rabbi find themselves sitting opposite each other on a train, travelling from Glasgow to London. Now the priest, a young and very enthusiastic man, attempts to convert the Rabbi to his religion, telling him it's the one and only true faith. Suddenly, to everyone's dismay the train screeches to a halt, there's an almighty crash and their carriage overturns. Luckily no one is hurt and all the passengers scramble clear. As the priest searches out the rabbi, he sees him cross himself.

"Ah ha," he says smiling, "I see you listened to me seriously and have had a change of heart."

The rabbi looks puzzled. "I don't understand. What do you mean?"

"I saw you make the sign of the cross."

"No, no, I was checking my glasses, fly, wallet and cheque book."

A man was seriously ill in hospital so his family called their priest to offer him comfort. As the priest stood at the side of the bed the man started thrashing around frantically and turning blue.

"I think he wants to tell us something," said the priest, "get him a piece of paper."

Within moments, he'd written something on the paper and handed it back to the priest but before it could be read, the poor man had died.

Some time later, as the bereaved family left the hospital, the priest suddenly remembered the piece of paper that he'd put in his pocket.

"I think it may be the right time to read his last words," said the priest. "It says, get off the fucking oxygen pipe, you're standing on it."

"I hear you were playing golf last Sunday," said the vicar to one of his parishioners.

"Er... yes, that's right," replied the man a little embarrassed, "it's not a sin to play on a Sunday, is it?"

"It is, the way you play it," retorted the vicar.

A man was in the park practising penalty taking. He kicked straight at the net but the ball flew up right over the top.

"Dammit, I missed," he cursed.

Just then a priest was walking past and on hearing the man's words, he stopped to speak to him.

"Do not curse," he said, "God is listening."

"Bugger off," replied the man "What's he going to do anyway, send a thunder ball down to get me?" he sneered.

All of a sudden there was a mighty boom from the skies and a huge shaft of fire hurtled to the ground, killing the priest stone dead.

"Dammit, I missed," boomed a voice from above.

A disillusioned priest addressed his congregation one Sunday morning before the service started.

"I have, in my hands, three sermons," he said. "The first costs £200 and lasts four minutes. The second costs £100 and lasts fifteen minutes or the third costs £30 and lasts 65 minutes. Before I continue, we'll take the collection to see which sermon I should use today."

A middle-aged couple had drifted apart and the end of their marriage came one Friday night over a plate of fish and chips.

"It's no good Sonia, this marriage is a sham, I'm leaving you. I may be 57 years old but I've met a 19 year old girl who wants to be with me and I want to be with her," said the husband proudly.

"Well, well, well," replied the wife scornfully. "She's welcome to you. By the way, I've met a gorgeous young man of 19 who goes for older women. I may be 57 as well but he says I've got the body of a 25 year-old. So stuff you, Bob, and just remember this. 19 goes into 57 a lot more times than 57 goes into 19!"

The local vicar was always referring to the bible when talking to his parishioners.

"Please remember," he said, "that all human life can be found in the Bible, it's as relevant today as it's always been."

"But what about PMS?" retorted one woman. "Where in the Bible does it refer to that?"

For a moment, the vicar was unable to speak.

"Well... erm..." he eventually said, "I'll show you when you come to church tomorrow."

For half the night, the vicar read and re-read passages from the Bible and lo and behold, his hard work paid off. The following morning he met the woman with a triumphant smile on his face.

"Here," he said, reading from the book. "It says 'and Mary rode Jesus' ass all the way to Bethlehem'!"

About a century or two ago, the Pope decided that all the Jews had to leave Rome. Naturally there was a big uproar from the Jewish community. So the Pope made a deal. He would have a religious debate with a member of the Jewish community. If the Jew won, the Jews could stay. If the Pope won, the Jews would leave.

The Jews realised that they had no choice. So they picked a middle-aged man named Moishe to represent them. Moishe asked for one addition to the debate. To make it more interesting, neither side would be allowed to talk. The Pope agreed.

The day of the great debate came. Moishe and the Pope sat opposite each other for a full minute before the Pope raised his hand and showed three fingers. Moishe looked back at him and raised one finger. The Pope waved his fingers in a circle around his head. Moishe pointed to the ground where he sat. The Pope pulled out a wafer and a glass of wine. Moishe pulled out an apple. The Pope stood up and said, "I give up. This man is too good. The Jews can stay."

An hour later, the cardinals were all around the Pope asking him what had happened. The Pope said, "First I held up three fingers to represent the Trinity. He responded by holding up one finger, to remind me that there was still one God common to both our religions. Then I waved my finger around me to show him that God was all around us. He responded by pointing to the ground and showing that God was also right here with us. I pulled out the wine and wafer to show that God absolves us from our sins. He pulled out an apple to remind me of original sin. He had an answer for everything. What could I do?"

Meanwhile, the Jewish community had crowded around Moishe.

"What happened?" they asked. "Well," said Moishe, "First he said to me that the Jews had three days to get out of here. I told him that not one of us was leaving. Then he told me that this whole city would be cleared of Jews. I let him know that we were staying right here."

"Yes, yes… and then ???" asked the crowd.

"I don't know," said Moishe, "He took out his lunch, and I took out mine."

REVENGE

A woman opened her handbag to pay for lunch in the department store's riverside café and a TV remote control fell out onto the floor.

"Excuse me, madam," said the waiter, "that's a very odd thing to carry around with you."

"Indeed," she said, "but it's the most evil thing I can do to my husband."

A girl and boy grew up together and naturally started to date when they reached the age of 14. They promised they would stay true to each other always and save themselves for when they got married. However, the girl had a chance to go away to university and it wasn't long before she had discovered a whole new life. She no longer wanted the boy she'd left behind and when he wouldn't stop nagging her, she took drastic steps to warn him off. One morning in the post, came a photo of his ex love with her new boyfriend. They were both naked and she was giving him a blow job. Underneath, the girl had written: 'Get the message! Now leave me alone.'

Well, the boy certainly got the message, as did the girl's parents. The jilted boyfriend sent the picture to the girl's mum and dad with a note that read:

"Having a great time, learning lots but hope you can send me some more money."

A husband and wife got into a crowded lift and the wife was annoyed to see him pressing up against a beautiful blonde. All of a sudden, the blonde smacked him across the face, shouting,

"How dare you pinch me!"

As the couple got out of the lift the shamed husband turned to his wife and said,

"I didn't pinch her, Doris, you must believe me."

"I know you didn't," replied the wife.

A husband and wife are getting all snugly in bed. The passion is heating up. But then the wife stops and says, " I don' t feel like it. I just want you to hold me." The husband says "WHAT???" The wife explains that he must not be in tune with her emotional needs as a woman. The husband realises that nothing is going to happen tonight and he might as well deal with it.

So the next day the husband takes her shopping at a big dept. store. He walks around and had her try on three very expensive outfits. And then tells his wife, We'll take all three of them. Then goes over and gets matching shoes worth $200 each. And then goes to the jewellery department and gets a set of diamond earrings. The wife is so excited (she thinks her husband has flipped out, but she does not care). She goes for the tennis bracelet. The husband says, "but you don 't even play tennis, but OK if you like it then lets get it." The wife is jumping up and down. So excited she cannot even believe what is going on. She says, " I'm ready to go, lets go to the cash register. " The husband says, " no – no – no, honey we're not going to buy all this stuff." The wife's face goes blank.

"No honey – I just want you to HOLD this stuff for a while." Her face gets really red she is about to explode and then the husband says, "You must not be in tune with my financial needs as a MAN!!!!!!!!."

"I'm afraid I have some bad news for you Mr. Kenley, you have a fatal form of rabies," said the doctor.

"Can you get me a pen and paper?" asked Mr Kenley. "I need to write a list of people I want to bite."

The old builder was on his deathbed, the final moments ticking away.

"Marjorie," he croaked, "when I die I want you to marry Bob Higgins."

"But why?" she asked.

"Because he cheated me out of a plot of land," came the reply.

At three o'clock on a wet and windy night, the doctor was called out to attend a man who lived fifteen miles away in the back and beyond. After administering to him, the doctor returned home and told his wife he'd got the family to ring for the lawyer to make a will, as well as the priest, and all the patient's friends and relations.

"Oh no," said the wife sadly, "he must be really bad."

"No," replied the doctor, "but I didn't want to be the only one called out on such a bad night."

A woman walked into the hairdressers and said to the stylist,

"Can you cut my hair so that it's longer on one side than the other. Then can you dye it bright orange and make it go all frizzy?"

"Well, madam, I'm not sure," replied the stylist.

"You managed to last time I came in," she retorted.

Said one woman to another,

"I collect antiques, you know."

"Yes, I've seen your husband," came the reply.

Clever Clive enjoyed making personal remarks about people.

"I say Peter, you've got a bit of a paunch there old chap," he said, patting Peter's stomach. "If that was on a woman I'd say she was pregnant."

Peter replied calmly, "it has been, and she is."

Clever Clive took a pot shot at Henry. He rubbed Henry's bald head remarking loudly,

"By jove, your head feels as smooth as my wife's backside."

Henry slowly rubbed his hand over his head and replied,

"My goodness, so it does."

Two ex lovers bump into each other in a restaurant and start slagging each other off very loudly. They soon have quite an audience.

"So, you little shit," said the man, "how does your new lover like your old, worn out pussy?"

"Oh, he really likes it," she answered. "Once he's got past the old, worn out bit."

A man decides to join his local gun club so he goes down to take a look around and soon gets talking to one of the members.

"Here, take a look through this," says the member proudly, "it's got the most up to date, high powered sight, fitted. There's none better." The man looks through the sight and scans the surrounding housing estates. Suddenly he drops the gun and starts to shake.

"What's wrong?" asks the member somewhat alarmed at the state of the man.

"I just saw my wife in the bedroom of our house and she's got a man with her. The bastards!"

He grabs the member by the shoulders and with a wild look in his eye, says,

"Listen, I'll give you a thousand pounds for each bullet, just shoot the two of them dead. Shoot him in the balls and shoot her in the head, the cheating bitch."

The member peers through the sight and locates the bedroom.

"Come on, come on!" urges the husband, "shoot the buggers!"

"Now hold on," replies the gunman. "I'm trying to save you a grand."

There was only one barber in town so Jack was forced to go to him even though the man was arrogant and self-opinionated. Whatever Jack said to him, the barber always had to go one better.

One morning Jack arrived for his usual 9 o'clock appointment in his brand new BMW.

"How do you like your new car?" asked the barber.

"Oh, it's great, I'm very pleased with its performance," he replied.

"Hmm," mused the barber, "of course you should have gone for the new Jaguar, like mine. That's the car, this year."

Jack refused to be baited and remained silent.

"So did you have a good weekend?" asked the barber.

"Yes thanks," replied Jack "it was the wife's birthday so we went to the French restaurant on the High Street."

"Oh, that's a pity," came the reply, "the chef who made that restaurant so popular has moved on. If I'd known, I could have given you the name of his new venture, he's a friend of mine, you see!"

Jack fumed silently.

"So I hear you're off on your holidays?" continued the barber.

"Yes. We're off to Rome next Wednesday."

"Oh no, I wouldn't go there, the exchange rate is dreadful," complained the barber.

"Well, I really want to see the Pope," replied Jack defiantly. "Maybe, I'll even get to speak to him."

The barber laughed loudly, "In your dreams."

"I bet you a year's free haircuts you don't speak to him."

"Okay," said Jack hotly, "Let's shake on that."

A few weeks later Jack returned for his haircut and the barber asked him about the holiday.

"So did you see the Pope?" he asked.

"Oh yes," replied Jack.

"And did you speak to him?"

"Oh yes," grinned Jack.

"What!" exclaimed the barber "What happened?"

"Well I was just strolling around St. Peter's Square when I spotted the Pope walking towards me. Then to my amazement he engaged me in conversation."

"Never!" exclaimed the barber "What did he say?"

"He said, where did you get such an awful haircut!"

Doris was a very jealous and possessive wife. She hated seeing her husband talk to other women, always believing something was going on. It so happened that one day they were invited to the opening of a new art gallery in the village, owned by a voluptuous blonde called Trudi. Doris's husband was full of praise for the new venture and made a short speech to the assembled guests. "I think we ought to give warm applause to our delightful host, Trudi, who has worked so hard to make this successful."

Trudi blushed shyly and replied humbly,

"Oh please, thank you, but I couldn't have done it without the help of all the men in the village. Their help in the refurbishment and hanging of pictures was invaluable."

Doris's jealousy overflowed when she saw her husband smile fondly at Trudi's words. She swore to get even.

It was almost a year later that Doris gave birth to their first son. Her husband was so thrilled, he invited the whole village to his house for a celebration. Doris was warmly congratulated, as was her husband. Then Doris raised her voice for all to hear and said spitefully,

"Really, my husband can't take all the credit you know, I did have a lot of help from all the men in the village!"

A man was sitting despondently at the corner of the bar nursing a full pint of beer. He was about to put it to his lips when a quarrelsome 6' thug snatched the pint from his hands and drank it straight off.

"So what are you going to do about that?" said the thug challenging the poor man.

"Nothing," replied the man sadly. "I should have guessed something like that would happen to me today. First I wake up this morning to find the wife has left me and taken the kids with her. Then I'm involved in an accident and my car's a right off. So I get to work late and the boss fires me. But if that isn't enough, just as I get the nerve up to kill myself, you go and drink my last dose of arsenic."

S

SEA STORIES

It was the HMS Victory and only moments to go before Nelson's death. He beckoned Hardy forward and said,

"Kiss me Hardy."

"Now he asks me," muttered Hardy, "after all this time on board!"

The night was inky black. Up ahead, the Captain of the warship saw a light on collision course with his vessel. He immediately ordered a signal to be sent saying 'change your course 20° east." But the light signalled back 'change your course 20° west."

The Captain was furious.

"I am the Captain of one of Her Majesty's Warships," he signalled, "change your course immediately."

"That may be so," came the reply, "but it is you who must change course."

The Captain was beside himself with rage. He signalled,

"How dare you challenge my orders, I am the keeper of the country's defences."

"Yes, and I'm a lighthouse," came the reply.

A young woman was so depressed that she decided to end her life by throwing herself into the ocean. She went down to the docks and was about to leap into the frigid water when a handsome young sailor saw her tottering on the edge of the pier crying. He took pity on her and said, "Look, you've got a lot to live for. I'm off to the States in the morning, and if you like, I can stow you away on my ship. I'll take good care of you and bring you food every day." Moving closer, he slipped his arm round her shoulder and added, "I'll keep you happy, and you'll keep me happy." The girl nodded yes. After all, what did she have to lose? That night, the sailor brought her aboard and hid her in a lifeboat. From then on every night he brought her three sandwiches and a piece of fruit, and they made passionate love until dawn. Three weeks later, during a routine inspection, she was discovered by the captain. "What are you doing here?" the Captain asked. "I have an arrangement with one of the sailors," she explained. "I get food and a trip to the States, and in return, he's screwing me."

"He certainly is," replied the Captain. "This is the Mersey Ferry!"

SEX

Two mates were sharing drinks while discussing their wives.

"Do you and your wife ever do it doggy style?" asked one.

"Well... not exactly," his friend replied, "She's more into the trick dog aspect of it."

"Oh, I see, kinky, huh?"

"Well... not exactly.... I sit up and beg, and she rolls over and plays dead."

A woman went to the doctors looking worried.

"My husband has a preference for anal sex," she said "is that alright?"

"Oh yes," replied the doctor, "that's okay as long as you like it as well, and as long as you don't get pregnant."

"Pregnant?" she queried. "I didn't think you could get pregnant doing it that way."

The doctor looked at her with pity and replied,

"Now where do you think all the estate agents come from?"

After examining her, the doctor said she was run down and needed rest.

"Stop having sex with your husband for a couple of months," he suggested.

"Okay," she replied. "I've got a couple of boyfriends who could stand in for him."

The girl sighed and said to her friend,

"Sex is like social security. You get a little each month but it's never enough."

"Look at these," said the man enthusiastically, "they're called Olympic condoms because they come in gold, silver and bronze!"

"And what are you going to wear?" asked his wife.

"The gold, of course."

"Well it would be nice if you wore a silver one and came second for a change," she replied bitterly.

In a lecture on sexual behaviour the professor commented on a woman who'd had more than 100 orgasms in one session.

"Bloody hell," remarked one of the men, "who was she?"

"Oh never mind that," retorted a woman. "Who was the male?"

"Oh Steve," she whispered seductively. "Fuck me with your 12" dick and hurt me."

So he fucked her three times with his 4" dick and punched her in the face.

There once was a nymphomaniac who lived in the land of Nursery Rhymes. She was forever out and about looking for new conquests and her behaviour was getting so bad that the Fairy Godmother came to visit her.

"You've been warned many times to stop screwing every man in sight," she said angrily, "so there's only one way to stop you," and with that she waved her magic wand and turned the girl's pussy into a pumpkin.

Some time later, the nymphomaniac returned home with a big smile on her face.

"Hi everyone," she called, "meet my new man, Peter, Peter."

How can you tell if you're making love to a nurse, a teacher or an air hostess?

A nurse says, "this won't hurt a bit."

A teacher says, "we're going to have to keep doing this until we get it right."

An airhostess says, "now just hold this over your mouth and nose, and breath normally."

A woman is concerned that her husband is lonely so she decides to buy him a pet. The pet shop owner shows her a frog.

"Not only will this frog be a good companion, it also gives a great blowjob," said the man.

The woman buys the frog thinking that if the frog is as good as he says, then her husband will be less demanding in bed.

That night, the wife goes to bed, happy in the knowledge that the frog will give her husband a blowjob and so she will be left alone. However, about 3 o'clock in the morning

she is woken by the clattering of pans in the kitchen. She goes downstairs to discover her husband and the frog busy cooking.

"What's going on?" she asks.

"Well if I can teach this frog to cook, then you can start packing your bags," he replies.

As Holmes and Doctor Watson strolled down the street, they passed three women sitting on a bench eating bananas.

"Good day," said Holmes as he walked by.

"I say Holmes, do you know those women?" asked Watson.

"You mean the nun, the whore and the newlywed? No I don't."

"But that's astonishing," said Watson "you say you don't know them yet you know what each of them are!"

"Elementary, my dear Watson. I can tell by the way they eat their bananas. The first woman holds the banana in one hand and breaks pieces off it with the other – so she's the nun.

The second woman stuffs all the banana in her mouth at the same time so she's obviously the whore, and the third woman holds the banana with both hands and leans her head towards it."

A policeman on the beat discovered a couple doing the business in the park. As he watched, he started to get the urge himself and recognising the woman as one of the local tarts he said,

"Mind if I have a go next."

"Oh, I'm not sure," replied the man. "I've never done it with a copper before."

Maureen had been away at university for two months when she rang her mother one Monday night.

"I just have to tell you that finally I've lost my virginity," she said.

Mum replied,

"Well that's alright. You're out in the big world now, looking for romance and possibly a husband. How is everything?

"Well the first ten guys were okay, but I'm a bit sore now!"

A nun was walking through the park on her way home when she was attacked and raped. Afterwards the man said to her

"You'll be off to see the Mother Superior now, won't you? Telling her you've been raped."

"Oh yes," replied the nun. "I'll tell her I was raped twice."

"Twice!" he exclaimed "but I only did it once."

"Well, of course, if you're too tired…"

"Go and get a good story," demanded the news editor. "Go sniff out some local culture and don't come back until you've got something."

The young journalist drove into the ancient part of the city and spotted an old man sitting in a rocking chair on his porch.

"Evening Sir," he said "I'm writing some stories on the way things used to be, I wonder if you've got any good experiences from the past?"

"Aye lad, park yourself down here," replied the old man, "now let me think."

There was a few moments of silence and then the old man began.

"Well there was this one time when me and the boys had drunk a lot of whisky and we lost our old donkey. It took ages to find the daft bugger but when we did, we all shagged it unmercifully."

The journalist blushed deeply and said he didn't think that was quite what the newspaper was looking for.

"Well there was another time when we'd all had a couple of bottles of rum and I lost my wife. But it was alright, an hour later we found her and screwed her rigid."

"Oh no, no," said the journalist, paling at the thought, "no I couldn't use that."

Suddenly, the old man looked very sad.

"You know, there was another time when I got lost..."

"How are you feeling?" the Theatre Manager asked his leading man.

"Not so good," replied the man, "I've got a terrible sore throat."

The manager took him aside and whispered in his ear.

"Listen, this may sound odd, but when I had a sore throat, my wife gave me a blow job and it cleared up almost immediately. Why don't you try it?"

"Yeah, thanks, I will," said the man gratefully. "Do you think your wife can do it for me tonight?"

A young man and a beautiful young woman answered the wanted ad for a lion tamer and went along to the circus for their interviews.

"Let me warn you," said the circus owner, "that this lion is uncontrollable. The last 6 tamers have quit on me, so I don't hold out much hope."

The woman went into the cage and faced the wild beast. He growled menacingly and walked towards her, but as he got close she undid her coat to reveal a stunning naked body underneath. The lion was immediately silenced. He crawled up to her, licked her legs and laid his head on her feet.

The circus owner was astonished. He turned to the man and said,

"Can you do better than that?"

"Just let me show you," said the man, "but first get rid of the lion."

Every Christmas, Marty would dress up as Father Christmas and visit all the houses in the village, leaving the children a toy for their sacks He'd just been to Mrs Fishers and was now heading back into the village centre when he popped into Grove Cottage. He tiptoed into the bedroom on the right and was startled to see a young woman sitting up in bed looking at him. Her sheer see-through nightie left nothing to the imagination. She spoke in a small voice,

"Hello Santa. Won't you come over and stay with me awhile?"

"Er no... no," he stuttered. "I'm so sorry," he continued. "I thought this was little Peter's room."

"It usually is," she replied "but we've swapped for the holidays. Oh please come over and keep me warm," she said coaxingly as she slipped off one of her shoulder straps.

"I must go," he replied, "I've... erm... lots to do."

She slipped off her other strap and let her night dress slip to the waist.

"Oh Santa, just for a little while."

Marty looked at the woman and then at his sack of toys.

"Oh fuck it," he murmured, taking off his beard. "I'd never get back up the chimney like this anyway."

Colonel Hawty had spent most of his time in India and was only 6 months from retirement. He decided to ask his wife to join him for the remaining time out there and she was delighted to accept. On their first night, he told his wife he had to be up early the next day but he would meet her for lunch.

"Don't be in a hurry to get up," he said, "you'll be tired after your trip so have a relaxing morning."

The Colonel left at 7am and half an hour later his batman strode into the bedroom, smacked the sleeping figure on the backside and said in a loud voice, "Okay Miss, time to get up, grab some breakfast and then go home."

A young girl walked into a hardware store and as her eyes met the old storeman's across the counter, a magic moment occurred. It was love at first sight. Within a week, the happy couple were married and spent their honeymoon on a round-the-world cruise. When they returned home, the old storeman went down to his local for a quick pint and bumped into his cribbage partner.

"Welcome home Ernie," he said "did you have a good time?"

"It was wonderful Gerald, everything was so romantic, we made love almost every night, we…"

"Really!" interrupted his friend, "to make love almost every night is fantastic at your age."

"No, no, you didn't let me finish. I was going to say we almost made love on Monday, we almost made love on Tuesday, we almost…"

On the first day of his holidays a young man walked into a Spanish bar and caught the eye of a blonde woman sitting in the corner. She smiled at him so he sauntered over.

"I'm selling," she murmured provocatively, "are you buying."

"Why not?" he replied, and they went off to his room for an afternoon of pleasure. And so it happened that over the next two weeks they spent many hours together and he spent many pesetas. The following year, the man returned once again to the Spanish resort and on the first day he cruised the bars. Lo and behold there in the third bar he visited, was the same blonde woman. She smiled in recognition and walked over to him.

"Are you buying?" she whispered.

"And what are you selling this year, AIDS?" he replied angrily.

"Oh Doris, guess what. I've got this complaint that every time I sneeze I have an orgasm."

"Golly, what are you taking for it?"

"Pepper."

For the past hour, a man and woman had sat at opposite ends of the bar, staring morosely into their drinks. Eventually, the man got up and went to sit next to her.

"Hey, cheer up, it can't be that bad," he said.

"Oh yes it is," she replied, "My husband's left me because he thinks I have extreme sexual behaviour."

"Really?" replied the man excitedly. "I've just lost my girlfriend because she thinks I'm too kinky. Maybe meeting here is fate and we were made for each other."

The couple finish their drinks and go back to her flat.

"I'll be back soon," she tells him as she disappears into the bedroom. "I'm just going to change into something more appropriate."

Five minutes later, she returns, dressed in suspenders and high heels, wearing a teacher's gown and mortar board, and carrying a long cane.

"I'm coming you naughty boy," she says entering the room but the words die on her lips as she sees him walking out of the door.

"What's wrong, where are you going?" she asks.

He replies. "Hey, I've fucked the cat and peed in your shoes, so I'll be off now."

★

A new commanding officer was sent off to run a desert outpost, situated miles from civilisation. All went well for a couple of months but then the C.O. started to crave female company. He called in his second in command.

"I say Jenkins, what do you do for sex round here?"

"We use the camels sir," came the reply. The C.O. was utterly dismayed at the suggestion and tried even harder to keep his feelings in check. However, after another month had passed, he gave in to weakness and headed over to the camel enclosure. He put a ladder up to the back of one of the female camels, climbed up and started thrashing away. All of a sudden, his second in command appeared and exclaimed in astonishment.

"Commander, Sir, what are you doing?"

"Well you told me to use one of the camels if I wanted sex," replied the C.O.

"Yes, that's true," said the officer, "but I meant we use the camels to travel to the nearest village. It's forty miles away in that direction."

A couple undress ready for bed and the man is surprised to see his wife cover her private parts with half a tube of Vaseline.

"My goodness," he mutters to himself. "Um… darling, may I borrow your diamond necklace for a while?" he asks her.

The wife passes over the necklace and is amazed to see him put it on.

"Harry, what are you doing?"

"Well darling, with all that slipperiness, you wouldn't expect me to go in without chains on, would you?"

"Oh come on," said the inadequate man. "I may not be the world's greatest lover but at least I'm fast!"

A lorry driver drove round the bend to discover a couple having sex in the middle of the road. He sounded his horn wildly and put on the emergency brakes, managing to stop just inches away from the busy couple.

"You bloody idiots," cursed the lorry driver, "didn't you see me, you could have been killed."

"Sorry mate," apologised the man, "but I was coming, she was coming and you were coming. But you were the only one to have any brakes."

Two old men are on their way back from the park when one looks at his watch and exclaims,

"Blast! Is that the time, I've got to get home to make love to my wife."

"Love to your wife," says the other astonished. "But you're nearly 82 years old."

"I know," replies the other, "but it doesn't stop me making love to my wife three times a day."

"What? But how do you manage it?"

His friend smiles and winks. "Sultana scones, my friend, sultana scones." Some time later, the old man muses on what his friend had said and decides to try some sultana scones for himself. He searches out the nearest bakery and asks the assistant if she has any sultana scones.

"Lots of them," she replies. "How much do you want?"

"I'll take it all" he says, thinking how much this will change his life if it works.

"All of it!" she exclaims, "It will go very hard."

"Bloody hell," he curses, "how come everybody knows about it except me!"

Mabel was an avid football fan. She was well known in all the team dressing rooms doling out her favours quite generously. One afternoon, she visited the doctor with abdominal pains.

"When did you last have a check up?" he asked, examining her.

"Oooh, let me see" she mused. "I don't think I ever have, I've had a Scot, an Italian, a Norwegian and a Dutchman..."

Why does a bride smile when she walks up the aisle?

She knows she's given her last blow job.

Have you heard about KFC condoms?

They're finger licking good!

Men who snatch kisses when young, kiss snatches when old.

"What sort of a week have you had?" asked the receptionist to the chambermaid.

"Well, a bit funny really. Take yesterday, for instance. The bell went for room 32 and when I went up to see what was wrong, a man pulled me inside, stripped me naked and had his wicked way with me… And the odd thing is, I never did find out why he rang the bell."

Two sixty-year-old men are chatting over their lunch in the work's canteen. Fred grins at his mate and says,

"You know George, I made love to my wife three times last night."

"Never!" exclaims George, "how did you manage that?"

"It was easy really. I made love to her once, then slept for half an hour, then I woke up and made love to her again, had another 30 minutes sleep and made love to her a third time."

"Wow!" says George impressed, "that sounds good, I think I'll do the same."

So that night George gets into bed, makes love to his wife and turns over to sleep for half an hour. He wakes up, makes love again and goes back to sleep. Thirty minutes later, he wakes up once more, makes love and falls asleep.

In the morning, he wakes up in a panic to realise he's 45 minutes late for work. He throws on his clothes, skips breakfast and rushes down to the factory. As he gets to the gates, the boss is standing there looking very angry.

"Sorry I'm late boss," he gasps, "give us a break. I've worked here for 40 years and I've never been late before. Come on, it's only 45 minutes."

The boss replies in disbelief.

"45 minutes! Where were you yesterday, and the day before?"

A chicken and an egg were lying in bed. The chicken was smiling contentedly and smoking a cigarette while the egg was looking depressed and tearful.

"Well, I suppose we answered that question," muttered the egg.

"I'm not feeling myself tonight," said David.

"Well that's good," replied his wife, "you can feel me for a change."

"Today, we will talk about human sexual positions," said the professor to his social behaviour students. "Who's going to start the ball rolling?"

A voice at the back called out, "I know at least 150 positions Sir."

"Yes, you probably do Jack," said the professor somewhat alarmed, "but first let's start with the more common ones. For instance, the most well known position is the woman underneath and the man on top."

At that point, there was a frantic waving of hands from the back of the class.

"Yes Jack, what is it?"

"Now that makes 151 positions I know, Sir."

Why is sex like a game of bridge?

You don't need a partner if you have a good hand!

A man went to the doctors complaining that his pubic hair was turning red.

"How often do you have sex?" asked the doctor.

"Now and again," said the man.

"Twice a week?"

"No."

"Twice a month?"

"No."

"Well, how often?"

"Twice a year."

"Ah ha," said the doctor. "Now I know what's wrong, you've got rust."

"Doctor, doctor, sex with my wife is like November 5th," said the man.

"Oh you mean, full of excitement, plenty of rockets, ooohing and aahing?"

"No, no, I mean only once a year!"

A young couple are on a walking holiday far away from civilization when they are lucky enough to witness a UFO landing and see two strange people emerge from the craft.

"Come on," whispers the husband, "this is our chance to be good ambassadors, let's go over and introduce ourselves."

The odd foursome spend all afternoon together learning about each other's cultures and as it gets dark, they decide to swap partners for the night to experience different sexual practices. The woman disappears with the alien man and they both strip off.

"Oh," says the woman disappointed when she sees his very small todger. But the man smiles confidently, wiggles his right ear and it grows to an enormous length."

"Ooooh!" exclaims the woman and she watches in delight as he wiggles his left ear and sees his todger thicken six times over.

The following morning, the couples meet up, say goodbye and go their separate ways.

"So how did it go?" asks the man to his wife. "Did you have a good night?"

"Fabulous," she says dreamily. How about you?"

"I don't know," he replies, "it was a bit odd, she kept trying to wiggle my ears."

75 year old Gloria, walked into the lounge of the old people's home and said loudly,

"If anyone can guess what's in my hand, then they can have sex with me tonight."

No one answered.

"Come on" she urged "let's have some guesses."

"Okay," sighed one old man, reading his newspaper, "it's a 3-piece suite."

Everyone laughed, but the old woman thought for a moment and then said,

"Okay, that's close enough."

The bank manager looked up in horror as the masked gunman crashed through the door into his private office.

"Don't move," hissed the gunman as he put his gun to the manager's head.

"Now, very slowly, lift the phone and tell one of your employees to bring £50,000 in here as soon as possible. Just make sure you don't make them suspicious."

After thinking up a good story, the money was brought to the office and stuffed into a carrier bag. Thinking his ordeal was over, the manager began to relax when the gunman said,

"Now drop your trousers and turn round."

"Oh no, not that, please," begged the manager but the gun was put to his head, so he had no choice. When he was finished, the robber told him to turn round and give him a

blow job. Again, the bank manager asked for mercy but he was helpless against the armed robber so he complied. Moments later, the gunman started to get carried away and let his guard down as his arms moved around uncontrollably. Suddenly, the manager stopped and said to the gunman,

"For goodness sake, put the gun back to my head," he gasped, "in case one of my colleagues comes in."

Mavis went to see the vicar on some personal business.

"I have to know whether my husband and I will be told to leave the church," she said nervously. "Last Friday, I was bending over when he came up behind me and gave me a good rogering."

The vicar looked a little embarrassed. He coughed and replied.

"Well, I've not been asked anything like that before but what you and your husband do is your own business. No, you won't be thrown out of church. What made you think that could happen?"

"Well, we got kicked out of the supermarket."

SHAGGY DOG

The lecture theatre was buzzing with anticipation. Professor Golightly had cloned a human being and was going to exhibit him that afternoon.

After a 10 minute introduction, the clone was brought onto the stage and the professor described the technique. But after 5 minutes, the clone began shouting and stamping his feet.

"Stop that at once," shouted the professor who eventually got him under control. The lecture continued for another 15 minutes before the clone began disrupting the proceedings again with bad language and cursing. This time, it took longer to quieten him down.

Now the professor was an impatient man and after the fourth disruption, he lost his temper and threw the clone out of the window where it fell 15 storeys. All hell broke loose and eventually the police were called.

"I'm arresting you on a charge of murder," said the officer to the professor.

"Oh don't be such a damn fool," replied the professor. "That wasn't a human being, it was just a clone."

The officer thought for a moment and answered, "In that case you're charged with making an obscene clone fall."

Caesar was at the peak of his popularity in Rome and much of this was due to his great warrior, Brutus. Time after time, Brutus would set out on another campaign and always come back victorious.

Each time he returned to Rome, Caesar presented him with another medal which he kept in a special chest next to his bed – Brutus loved medals and every day he would get them all out and polish them.

However, the mines that produced the gold to make the medals eventually ran out of metal.

"Brutus," said Caesar, "you are to be presented with another 5 medals but this time they will be made of chocolate."

"That's alright," said Brutus. "I will cherish them as much as I cherish all the others."

Then one tragic day, Brutus got out his medals to discover that three of the chocolate ones were missing. He ranted and raved around the house, accusing everyone in sight.

"Brutus, Brutus," said his wife gently, "you know that no one here would dare touch your medals, but I did see Caesar creeping out of here earlier this morning."

Blind with rage, Brutus high-tailed it over to the Emperor's quarters, ran in and stabbed Caesar through the heart.

As Caesar fell to the ground, his last dying words were. 'Et tu Brutus'.

"You fucking liar," yelled Brutus, "you ate three!"

A man moved 500 miles across country to buy a secluded cottage and a small piece of land. Once he'd settled in and got the house in order, he decided to buy some animals for his smallholding. One morning he set off early to visit a neighbouring farm.

"I wonder if I might buy a rooster from you?" he asked the old farmer.

"Aye, that's alright," said the farmer, "but round here, we call them cocks."

"OK, thanks. May I also buy a chicken?"

"Here we are," said the farmer showing him a fine bird "but round here we call them pullets."

The man was just about to set off with his two birds when he noticed a donkey grazing nearby.

"Would you be willing to sell the donkey?" he asked.

"Certainly. You won't be disappointed with him. He's a good little worker but sometimes if he gets stubborn, you need to scratch him between the ears. Oh, by the way, round here we call them asses," said the farmer.

So off the man went with his new purchases but as they neared his cottage, the donkey suddenly stopped in his tracks and no amount of persuasion would make him move.

"Damn," cursed the man under his breath, but just then he noticed a smartly dressed woman walking by.

"Excuse me Madam," he called "would you hold my cock and pullet while I scratch my ass?"

When human life began, the parts of the body competed against each other as to whom should be boss.

"Well, it's obviously me," said the heart because I keep all the body working."

"Not at all" replied the brain "I'm the one who controls all the different parts, without me there would be no organisation."

"No, no," said the hands, "we should be boss because we do all the work."

"Rubbish," said the feet, "we should be boss because without us, you wouldn't get around and do all the things you're supposed to do."

And so the arguing went on with every part of the body claiming superiority.

Last to speak was the arsehole but everyone else laughed at such an absurd idea. So the arsehole reacted in the only way he could. He blocked himself up. Time went by, the face began to sweat, the eyes began to bulge, the hands clenched and the legs crossed…

"OK, OK," they said in unison, let the arsehole be boss… so the motion was passed and while the rest of the body did all the work, the boss just sat there and passed out the shit! So the moral of this story is: you don't need brains to be the boss, any arsehole will do.

Whoosh! The firework factory exploded with a mighty roar and the flames could be seen for miles around. Ten fire engines were sent to the scene and battled for 10 hours to get the blaze under control.

"Anyone know how this happened?" the boss asked his employees.

"It was Jack Higgins, Sir," came the reply, "he lit up a cigarette in the powder room."

"Jack Higgins!" exclaimed the man, "I can't believe it, he's been with me for 15 years. Lighting up a cigarette! Well that's the last thing he'd have done."

It was his daughter's 14th birthday and dad asked her what she would like as a present.

"Oh daddy, there's only one thing I'd really like and that's a picture of the Great Pyramid," she said. "There's nothing else I want."

So her father bought and wrapped up a picture of the Great Pyramid and the daughter was absolutely delighted. However, strangely enough, it disappeared the following week, never to be seen again.

So a year went by and his daughter's 15th birthday was fast approaching. Again he asked her what she would like and this time she asked for 12 pictures of the Great Pyramid.

"12!" he exclaimed "but why?"

"I can't tell you yet" she replied "but I will one day." So 12 pictures were bought and after a couple of weeks they disappeared as well.

"What would you like for your 16th birthday?" asked dad a year later.

This time the daughter asked for a gross of Great Pyramid pictures and dad bought them without questioning her. Once again, they all disappeared.

On her 17th birthday she asked for a truckload of pictures and on her 18th birthday, a whole warehouse of them. Within a few weeks they had all disappeared. Then one evening tragedy struck and the daughter was rushed to hospital with a deadly virus. The doctors shook their heads sadly and informed dad that his daughter was dying. She opened her eyes one more time as her father kissed his daughters forehead.

"Oh my darling," he whispered, "all these years I have bought you hundreds and thousands of Great Pyramid pictures. You said that one day you would tell me why you wanted them."

"Yes, dad," she replied faintly. "You have always done as I asked and it's only fair that I tell you now, why those pictures were so important. I needed them because..." But at that moment, she died.

SHIPWRECKED

Two men had been stranded on a desert island for 2 months and were getting very frustrated.

"Listen Geoff," said Matt "who knows when we might see another woman, so do you fancy doing it man to man."

"Now hold on a minute," said Geoff looking alarmed, "that isn't my scene at all."

"Nor mine, but needs must," replied Matt.

"Listen, if you don't like it, make a noise like an animal, but if you do, then start singing… and I'll do the same."

So they started doing the business and almost immediately Geoff called out

"Moo, Moo, moon river wider than a mile…"

A man has been marooned on a desert island for 15 years. In that time he has learnt to adapt completely to his surroundings. He's built a good shelter, grown his own food and tamed some of the wild animals. After 15 years of never seeing another human being, a beautiful young woman is washed ashore one morning, barely clothed and clinging to a small bag, containing all her worldly goods. She's delighted to see the man and is amazed at his stories of survival on the uninhabited island.

"Gosh!" she exclaims, "you're quite a man, I bet you could do with a cigarette?" The man agrees and she pulls a packet of cigarettes out of her bag and hands one to him. As he savours the moment, she asks him if he would like a drink.

"I'd love a drink," he says. "I used to like a tot of whisky."

"Well look here," she says, and pulls out a bottle of malt whisky.

The man can't believe his luck. There he sits, smoking a cigarette and drinking the finest scotch. Moments later, the woman looks coyly at him and says,

"I guess after 15 years there's other things you haven't done either. Do you fancy playing around?"

The man jumps up with joy. "Oh no, this can't be true. Do you mean you've got a set of golf clubs in that bag as well?"

A 'good time' girl went on a round-the-world cruise but the liner went down in a freak typhoon and she found herself washed up on a desert island. Fortunately, the island was inhabited by one other person – a handsome blonde boy of 22.

"How long have you been here?" she asked.

"I'm not sure," he replied. "I know I was only a small boy when I first arrived."

"Wow, that's incredible!" she exclaimed, eyeing him up and down. "So how come you've managed to stay alive?"

"I eat cockles," he replied. "Everyday I dig for cockles in the sand."

"And what about sex?" she said, smiling.

"Sex? I don't know what you mean."

So she showed the naïve boy, and 20 minutes later turned to him and said

"So what do you think of that?"

"Um… it's OK I suppose, but now you've gone and damaged my cockle digger."

SHOPPING

Three women, on a shopping trip, walked into a pet shop and came face to face with a parrot.

"Pink, blue, green," he squawked.

"Well that's amazing!" they exclaimed, "he's just named the colour of the underwear each of us is wearing."

The following day, they returned to the shop, hoping to catch him out.

"White, white, white," he squawked. Once again, he was absolutely right.

For a third time, they returned and this time he said,

"Bald, curly, straight."

The three women left immediately, never to return.

"Come here Jenkins," said the arrogant Sales Manger. "Watch an expert in action and just remember that if you want to get on in this business, you need to think fast."

Jenkins followed the manager into the D.I.Y department where they found a man looking at the paint brushes.

"Can I help you Sir?" asked the Sales Manager.

"Well, I was just about to buy this brush to freshen up the gloss paintwork in the spare room."

"Well, this is a good choice Sir," came the reply, "but you know, the gloss might show up the 'tiredness' of the walls. With a roller and tray you could have it all done in no time."

"Yes," considered the man, "I think you're right. I'll take a roller and tray as well."

"And have you seen our new range of Spring colours?" persisted the manager. "Lilac is particularly popular."

"Mmm, it's nice," said the man. "I'll take 2 cans."

"A nice choice Sir, thank you for shopping with us and may I just draw your attention to the furnishing department on the first floor which has a comprehensive range of ready made curtains to match all our Spring colours."

The man left with his purchases and the manager turned to Jenkins saying,

"There, that's how you do it. They come in for one item and leave with four!"

The following week Jenkins was transferred to the chemist department.

"A box of tampons, please" said the man coming up to the counter.

"Certainly Sir, and while you're in the store, why not buy a can of paint?"

"What!" exclaimed the man. "Why would I want to do that?"

"Well, you're not going to get your leg over this weekend so you might just as well do some decorating!"

A red Indian girl went to buy some toilet paper from the local store. There were two choices. A special deluxe roll or a cheaper pack of two that didn't have a name. The girl bought the cheaper 2-pack but returned angrily the following day.

"This stuff is rubbish." she complained, "but I'll give it a name. It ought to be called John Wayne because it's rough, it's tough and it takes no shit from Indians."

A woman was examining the fruit in the grocer shop and spent some time looking closely at the cucumbers.

"Come on Madam, please," said the greengrocer impatiently. "You're not at home with your hubby now, you know. They don't get bigger the more you handle them!"

Two blonde girls walk into a department store. They walk up to the perfume counter and pick up a sample bottle. Nancy sprays it on her wrist and smells it, "That's quite nice, don't you think, Kathy?"

Kathy takes a sniff and replies, "That is nice. What's it called?"

"Viens a moi," replies Nancy.

"Viens a moi? What the heck does that mean?"

At this stage the store manager offers some help. "Viens a moi, ladies, means 'come to me' in French."

Nancy takes another sniff, then offers her arm to Kathy again, and remarks, "That doesn't smell like come to me. Does that smell like come to you?"

An extremely curvaceous young woman was trying on a low cut dress and asked the shop assistant for her opinion.

"Hmm," said the assistant thoughtfully, "do you have hair on your chest?"

"Of course not!" she replied.

"Well, in that case, the dress is cut too low on you."

"I'd like a Barbie doll for my daughter," said the woman to the sales assistant "can you show me what you have?"

"Certainly madam. This is Barbie with her scuba diving at £9.50, here's Barbie dressed for the disco at £12, this is Barbie ready for the beach at £12 or there's divorced Barbie at £150."

"What!" exclaimed the woman, "why is divorced Barbie so expensive?"

"Oh that's easy to explain," replied the sales assistant, "divorced Barbie comes with the house, Ken's car, Ken's trailer and all Ken's other possessions."

"I'd like to try that skirt on in the window," said the woman to the shop assistant.

"I'm sorry Madam, you'll have to try it on in the dressing room like everybody else!"

A man walked past a shop which advertised that it 'sold everything' so he went in to test it out.

"I'd like a pair of glass pants," he said.

The assistant shook his head in dismay. "We don't have any glass pants" he replied, "there's no such thing as glass pants."

"Oh yes there is," said the man and the following day he returned wearing a pair of glass pants.

"See!" he said triumphantly. The assistant looked at him in amazement and remarked, "yesterday I thought you were crazy but now I see you're nuts."

A man went up to pay for his goods in the supermarket but as the girl gave him the bill, he suddenly remembered he'd meant to buy a packet of condoms.

"That's no problem," said the girl "what size are you?"

"I don't know," he stammered. So the girl asked him to unzip his flies while she had a feel. "OK" she said after a moment, "that'll be a size 4." The man bought the packet and left.

A few shoppers down the line was another man who had also forgotten to buy some condoms.

"Size please," asked the girl, but this man didn't know either. Again she asked the man to undo his flies. She put her hand in, felt his todger and said, "that's a size 5."

Now watching all this was a boy of 17. He decided to take advantage of the girl's good nature, so he stood in line waiting his turn. When he got to the checkout, he told her the same story so, as with the others, she asked him to unzip. She put her hand inside and seconds later exclaimed "Whoops... Doris can we have a mop and bucket over here please," she called.

A pretty young woman went into the department store for some dress material and was served by a cocky young man. When she asked how much it was, he replied,

"A kiss per yard," winking at her slyly.

"OK," she replied "I'll have 5 yards."

The man cut and wrapped the material, handed it to her and said "that'll be 5 kisses please."

The young woman pointed to a wrinkly old man standing next to her,

"Granddad's paying," she said, walking away.

A man walked into a shop and asked for a sexual sofa.

"I think Sir means a sectional sofa" said the assistant.

"Sextional, schmectional, who cares," he replied. "I just want an occasional piece in my living room."

A woman went to the butchers to buy a chicken. She lifted it up, sniffed under one wing, sniffed under the other wing and then sniffed between the legs.

"I'm not having this," she complained. "It's not fresh."

"Madam," said the butcher impatiently. "Would you pass such a test?

SHOWTIME

"Joey," says the agent of the Four Diamonds strip club. "I've got a great new act for you."

"Oh yeah?" replies the manager, "what is it this time?"

"It's Luscious Linda. She'll make the club famous. She's got a 78" chest."

"Okay, what does she do? Sing, dance, tell jokes?"

"Oh no," replies the agent, "she doesn't do anything like that. She just crawls onto the stage and tries to stand up!"

SICK

Three medical students were the best of friends but one of them smoked very heavily and every morning would start the day with a terrible bout of coughing.

"You'll cough your guts up one day," the others would say.

One night they went out to celebrate the end of exams and came home plastered. Dave, the smoker, collapsed on the bed but the other two were still wide awake. They decided to try and put an end to his smoking. They sneaked down to the laboratory and picked up a jar of intestines which they spread all over Dave's bed. The next morning, all three arrived down for breakfast but Dave looked particularly sick.

"You alright?" one of the others asked

"No, not really," he replied, "a terrible thing happened last night. I coughed my guts up, just as you said would happen."

"Never!" they exclaimed, "that must have been awful."

"It wasn't that so much," he replied, "it was when I had to stuff them all back in again."

★

The young man burst through the doors of the surgery and shook the doctor by the hand.

"Thank you doctor, thank you so much," he said. "You couldn't possibly imagine how much I've benefitted from your treatment."

The doctor looked puzzled. "But you're not one of my patients," he said.

"That's right," replied the man, "but my mother-in-law was, and I've just come from her funeral!"

SOLDIERS

The general was not a drinking man but on the occasion of the reunion dinner, he hit the brandy bottle quite seriously. In fact he drank so much, he couldn't remember getting back to his quarters.

The following morning, he woke with a blinding headache and was unable to get out of bed. At 8 o'clock his batman arrived and picked up the general's clothes which were strewn all over the room.

"I'm afraid your regimental tunic is badly marked," said the batman, holding up the jacket.

"Oh dear, yes," said the general acutely embarrassed. "Some silly chap bumped into me last time and was sick all over the front of my clothes," he lied. "When I find out the name of the bloody man, he'll be confined to barracks for the next two months."

"Well I'd make it four months Sir," replied the batman, "the bugger's also had a crap in your trousers."

A man rang to tell his wife that his platoon had been posted to a remote island in the Indian Ocean. It was deserted except for a few wild animals and some native

girls. The following week, a harmonica arrived in the post for him, accompanied by a note from his wife.

"This will be something for you to learn to play, when you're not working," she said.

Two months passed before the man returned home. He gave his wife a passionate kiss and suggested they go upstairs.

"Before we do, you'd better be able to play that harmonica," she said.

An old hillbilly was called away to fight in the war and many months later, received a letter from his family. As he couldn't read, a fellow soldier read the letter out loud to him. It brought him up to date with all the news but afterwards, he sat there looking very sad.

"What's up?" asked his mate, "is there something wrong?"

"Yeah," he replied. "You say my sister's in bed with arthritis." The hillybilly gathered his thoughts and continued "... And I know that Ritus family well, they're a read bad bunch, especially Art."

The commander of the fort received a message, warning him that a massive Indian attack was imminent and he should get the men well prepared. Immediately, there was a great flurry of activity as everyone was called back to base including an old Indian scout. Lookouts were posted and a few hours later came a shout that something was moving on the horizon.

"Tell me what's happening," the commander asked the old scout, so the Indian put his head to the ground and informed him,

"200 Indians are coming straight towards us, in the front is Running Bear and his three mighty warrior sons. They have guns as well as bows and all are painted with white stripes and four red spots across the forehead."

The commander was very impressed.

"You can even describe such small details, just by putting your head to the ground?" he asked in amazement.

"I can see under the gate," replied the Indian.

A man was posted to a remote outpost in the middle of the desert and after three months, all he could think about was sex. He needed it so much that eventually he went to see his C.O. in the hope that something could be done.

"Yeah, I can help you," replied the C.O. "There's an old traveller, lives in a tent about two miles from here, and when the men get restless, they go and see him. You get a good time down there if you spend a little money."

"Oh no!" gasped the man. "I don't go in for things like that."

However, three months on, the man was so desperate, he enquired about the traveller again.

"How much does it cost?" he asked the C.O.

£200," came the reply.

"Bloody hell, I don't call that cheap!" exclaimed the soldier.

"Well it's £50 for the old traveller and £50 each for the three men who hold him down. You see, he's not into that sort of thing either."

The situation is critical. The Welsh Guards have been fighting the Zulus for more than 24 hours and there's no sign of them retreating. Suddenly Lloyd stands up in defiance and begins tosing 'Men of Harlech' at the top of his voice. But it makes no difference, the Zulus surge forward. Then someone shouts,

"For fuck's sake, Lloyd, sing something they know!"

A General and a Colonel were walking across the base and each time they passed one of the private soldiers, he would salute and the General would reply with the words 'and the same to you'.

After this had happened half a dozen times, the Colonel turned to the General in puzzlement.

"Why do you always say 'and the same to you'?" he asked.

"Simple," came the reply. "I was a private once so I know what he's thinking every time he salutes someone like me."

Back in the First World War a group of new recruits was sent for training to an army camp on the Yorkshire Wolds. Now the war had been raging for some time and stocks and provisions were running short. The last recruit to be kitted out was told they had run out of rifles so he would have to use a broomstick.

"Don't worry lad," said the C.O. "When the enemy approach, just say bangety bang, bangety bang."

The poor recruit was even more alarmed when he discovered they had also run out of bayonets and that he would have to tie a stick of celery to the end of his broomstick.

"When the enemy get up close, just say stabbity stab, stabbity stab," instructed his C.O.

The training ended and the soldiers were shipped out to the front. It was a desperate time for the young man who was armed only with a broomstick and a stick of celery. However, he did as he was taught and when the enemy came into view, he lifted his head above the trenches, pointed his broomstick and yelled 'bangety bang, bangety bang'. To his astonishment, the enemy soldiers fell to the ground.

Some time later, the enemy managed to break through, so the soldiers were forced to use their bayonets. The young recruit stabbed his enemy with the stick of celery shouting 'stabbity stab, stabbity stab' and with a look of utter astonishment on his face, he watched his enemy fall to the ground. The recruit was overjoyed at his success. He began to seek out the enemy more and more. Suddenly a soldier started advancing towards him and he raised his broomstick. But no matter how often he yelled 'bangety bang, bangety bang', the man continued to approach until he was only a couple of feet from him. Quickly, the new recruit stabbed him with the stick of celery. 'Stabbity stab, stabbity stab' he said but it had no effect. The last words he heard as the enemy soldier trampled him to the ground were 'tankety tank, tankety tank'.

SPORT

On a bright Sunday Morning two men were out early on the golf course, eager to get a round in before it became too busy. Unfortunately, Martin's tee shot off the 3rd fairway went badly off-line and careered down a steep ravine. The hapless man took out a 7 iron and scrambled down after it, determined to make his shot. But to his horror, he came across a skeleton and lying next to the bones was a golf club – a 7 iron.

Immediately, he shouted to his partner,

"Hey Mick, throw me down an 8 iron. Looking at this poor bugger here, there's no way you can make the shot with a 7 iron."

A professional golfer had been asked to coach a young couple who had just joined the club. On the first morning, he took them out onto the greens to assess their ability.

"Let me give you some advice," he said, "it's always worked in the past for others. When you hold the club," he said to the man, "imagine you're holding your wife's breasts, not too tight, gentle but firm. Now have a go."

The man did as he was instructed and drove the ball straight down the fairway.

"Well done," said the professional. "Now it's your turn," he said, turning to the wife. "Your grip is a little tight as well, hold the club as you would hold your husband's penis." The woman took his advice but the ball only went a few yards.

"Not to worry," said the professional, "but maybe this time you should hold the club in your hands, not in your mouth!"

The football match had been playing for almost 40, minutes and for at least half of that time, the referee had been constantly heckled by a fan on the front row. Insult after insult was thrown at him until finally he could take it no longer.

The ref marched over to the fan and said,

"Now listen mate, I've had my eye on you for the past 15 minutes…"

"Well that doesn't surprise me," yelled back the fan "'cos you certainly haven't been watching the game."

Did you hear about the girl who joined six men on a fishing trip?

She came home with a red snapper.

The interviewer was talking to the losing goalkeeper after the match.

"So what did the manager say to you all in the dressing room?" he asked.

"Am I allowed to use swear words?" replied the goalie?

"No."

"Well in that case, he didn't say anything."

"Johnson! You're late," said the manager, standing at the door with his hands on his hips.

"Yes Sir, I'm, sorry. I usually dream about my football team and wake up dead on 7.30, but this morning, they had to play extra time!"

Dad was a fanatical football supporter and his happiest day was when his son got chosen to play in the local team. For two seasons, he never missed a match until one fateful day when he slipped over on an icy road outside the ground and had to be carted off to hospital. Some time later, his wife arrived to take him home.

"Our Darren's just been on the phone," she said, "he's broken his nose, got a bad gash above his eye and stud marks all the way up his leg."

"Yes, yes," said dad impatiently, "but did they win?"

One day, when Snow White returned home from shopping she found her house had burnt down.

"Oh no!" she wailed, "where are my seven dwarfs?" She began to walk through the charred rooms calling their names when she heard a voice cry "Wales for the World Cup."

"Oh thank goodness!" she exclaimed, "at least Dopey's still alive."

Poor Morrison! He'd been with the team for nearly three years and had never moved off the substitute bench. Then one Saturday, all that looked as if it was about to change.

The match had been particularly 'bloody' and Morrison's team had used all its substitutes except himself. Now was the chance! The manager looked towards the bench and to the lone figure.

"Shall I go on?" said Morrison eagerly.

"No, get out of the way," yelled the manager. "I'm sending on the bench."

"OK Stoneman," said the wrestler's manager. "You can win this match. I've watched Scarface's last two fights and he's not unbeatable. The only thing to look out for is his 'clawback' hold. Now that could be a winner so don't give him an opportunity to use it. OK, go for it," and with that Stoneman left his corner and faced up to his opponent. The match was fast and furious; first one man had the advantage, then the other. The bell went for the final round and the scores were equal, but the wrestlers were very tired. For a moment Stoneman dropped his guard and in a split second Scarface had him on the floor in the 'clawback' hold. A ripple went through the crowd.

"That's it," they said. "Scarface has got him now."

Then to a roar of sheer amazement, Scarface went flying through the air, Stoneman pinned him to the ground and it was all over. Later in the dressing room Stoneman's manager asked him what had happened.

"Well Jim, I thought it was curtains for me when I suddenly caught sight of this testicle hanging in front of me. So I bit it, and you know, when you bite your own testicle it's amazing what you can do!"

A man walked up to the football official and asked for a ticket for the match that afternoon.

"Sorry mate, there isn't a match today," came the reply.

"But there must be," he argued, "there's always a match on Saturday afternoon."

"Well there isn't today," replied the official impatiently.

"Well I don't believe you," persisted the man. "You're having me on."

"Now look here, you moron, read my lips. There is no M – A– T – F – C – H this afternoon, okay?"

"But there isn't an F in match," retorted the fan angrily.

"That's what I've been trying to tell you!" yelled the official.

The star of the English rugby team was asked if he would appear naked in a women's magazine.

"You'll be our June pin-up," said the magazine editor. "We'll picture you just holding a ball."

"Okay," agreed the rugby player, "but what will I be doing with my other hand?"

An enthusiastic young golfer joins his local golf club, hires a caddy and sets out for his first 18 holes. Half way round, they come to the 10th hole which looks quite tricky. As he steps up to take his second shot, he says to his caddy.

"You know this course well. What would you recommend for this shot?"

"Well, it's probably the longest fairway n the course," replies the caddy. "I would suggest a 2 iron."

He hits the ball as hard as he can but to his dismay, it strays badly to the left and hits his fiancée, who's just popped out to watch him, on the forehead, killing her immediately.

Many months pass by and the young man's grief abates. He decides to take up golf again and visits his club. As luck would have it, he gets the same caddy and off they go. At the second shot on the 10th fairway, the man turns to his caddy and asks him which iron he would suggest.

"A 2 iron," comes the reply.

"A 2 iron!" he exclaims. "You told me that last time and look what happened. I didn't even get on the green!"

Mid field player Chas Pastall was asked why he had requested a transfer to a club in a much lower division.

"Well, Des, it's through illness and fatigue," he replied.

"Is that so?"

"Yeah, the fans are sick and tired of me."

Two worms who live on a golf course have been underground all night and it's time they went to the surface.

"Go on Cliff," urges one of them. "Pop up and see if it's raining."

Now just as Cliff is making his way to the surface, two female golfers are walking down the fairway.

"Ooh! I need a pee," says the first woman.

"Well, pop over there by that tree," says the second. "There's no one around."

So as the woman crouches down to pee, the worm emerges right underneath her and gets soaking wet.

"Wow!" exclaims the worm's friend, when he sees Cliff, "it must be raining really hard up there."

"You're not kidding," replies Cliff "even the birds are building their nests upside down."

Barbara decided to have a few practice shots out of the green before the second round of the woman's competition took place that afternoon. She made her way up to the third green and hit a huge drive up the fairway. However, it veered badly off centre and disappeared into the trees. Ten minutes later, a course official caught up with her on the fourth green.

"Barbara dear, that was a bit of a disaster on the last green. Your ball flew through the trees and hit the windscreen of a passing motorist. It shattered the glass and caused the driver to swerve into the Colonel's driveway and dent his Rolls Royce. At the same time, a milk float coming the other way, stopped so abruptly, 32 crates of milk fell off the back and broke all over the road. The milkman had to go to hospital for stitches to a cut on his forehead. "Oh my goodness!" exclaimed Barbara. "Whatever shall I do?"

The official replied, "Well the trouble is, you're tending to hook the shot, if I were you I'd try not to bend my arm so much."

The avid football fan returned from the match looking very downcast.

"What's wrong love?" asked his wife, "wasn't it a good game?"

"The other side won by five very lucky goals!" he replied furiously.

The furious cricket captain walked over to the referee and hissed, "What would happen if I called you a fucking blind bastard who shouldn't be allowed anywhere near a cricket pitch?"

"I'd report you to the authorities and have you banned for the season," replied the referee.

"OK, but what if I just thought it?"

"Well, if you just thought it and didn't say anything, then I couldn't do much about it."

"Right," said the cricketer, smiling, "that's all I wanted to know."

T

THICK

"I require only three things of a man. He must be handsome, ruthless and stupid."

Dorothy Parker

Why do men like clever women?

Opposites attract.

Why do most men prefer looks to brains?

Most men see more clearly than they think.

The phone rang for the fourth time that night and the husband picked it up in a rage. He listened for a moment and then bellowed,

"How the bloody hell would I know? You want the weather centre, you berk."

"Who was that, darling?" asked his wife, innocently.

"I don't know, some twerp asking if the coast was clear. Bloody pest, that's the fourth time tonight."

"Hey, Charlie," said one of his mates, "you should go on the stage; those jokes you tell really lift our spirits."

"Oh, no, I couldn't," he replied, "People would laugh at me."

A man was kneeling down, praying to God.

"Oh, Lord, thank you for giving me such a wonderful wife. Why did you make her such a good cook and housekeeper?"

"So you could love her," replied God.

"Thank you, dear Lord, and why did you make her so beautiful and young looking?"

"So you could love her."

The man smiled. "And why did you make her so kind and affectionate towards me?"

"So you could love her."

"And just one more question, Lord, why did you make her so stupid?"

"So she could love you."

Three scaffolders were moaning about their lunchboxes. The first one, a Welshman, said to the other two:

"If I have Welsh rarebit and leek sandwiches one more time, I swear, I'll jump off this ledge."

The Italian looked at his box and responded:

"Yes, it is right, if I have to eat any more anchovy pizza, I will follow you off the ledge."

Then the third man, an Irishman said, "Well now, be Jesus, if I have to face any more boiled ham and cabbage soup, count me in, lads."

So the next day, lunchtime came and the three men opened their boxes.

"Aaggh," gasped the Welshman, "leeks again" and he jumped from the ledge.

"Mama mia," cried the Italian, "pizza, pizza, pizza" and he jumped from the ledge as well.

The Irishman opened his box, saw the soup, crossed himself and followed his two mates off the ledge.

Some time later, the three wives arrived at the site to be told the dreadful news. The other scaffolders also recounted what they had heard the three men talking about.

The wives of the Welshman and the Italian cried out in pain, "If only we'd known, we'd have changed the food."

But the wife of the Irishman looked puzzled. "But I don't understand," she said. "My husband always packed his own lunchbox."

Women are more irritable than men, probably because men are more irritating.

Three men were out mountain climbing when they discovered a cave in the side of the rock face.

"Cool! Let's go and explore," said one of them.

So in they went and stumbled across an old lamp.

"Hey, look at this. Wouldn't if be funny if it was a magic lamp!"

The others laughed but suddenly stopped in amazement as the man who had first spoken, rubbed the side of the lamp and out of the spout a genie materialised.

"I am the genie of the lamp and I will grant you one wish each."

"Great," said the first man. "Can you make me twice as clever as I already am?"

"Of course," replied the genie, and immediately the man began to quote great chunks out of Encyclopaedia Britannica.

The second man was so impressed, he asked to have his intelligence increased four times. Whoosh! the next minute the man was chalking fantastic mathematical equations all over the cave wall.

Then the third man spoke:

"This is incredible. Can you make me ten times as intelligent?"

"Are you sure you want that?" replied the genie. "It might be a bit alarming for you."

"Yes, yes, I'm sure," replied the man impatiently.

So the genie granted his wish and the man was turned into a woman.

Why do men like blonde jokes?

They can understand them.

Two men are walking through the jungle, one carrying a garden shed and the other a lump of concrete.

"What are you carrying that shed for?" asked the second man.

"Well if any dangerous animals come along, I can hide in the shed and remain unharmed," he said. "So why are you carrying a block of concrete?"

The second man gave him a knowing wink and replied, "If we meet any man-eating animals, I can throw down the concrete and make a faster getaway."

When a man says "I've got my reasons", he actually means, "I'll think of something in a minute."

Why do men drive BMW's?

Because they can spell the name.

Did you hear about the stupid man who went to the ironmonger's to get some screws?

"How long do you want them?" asked the shopkeeper.

"Well, actually, I was hoping to keep them," he replied.

A young man was riding a bicycle through town when he stopped to speak to his mate.

"Hello, Shaun, I didn't know you had a bicycle?"

"Yeah, I got it this morning when I was walking to work," replied Shaun. "This beautiful girl rode up to me, got off her bicycle and then stripped off until she was completely naked."

"Get away!"

"Really! She then said I could have anything I wanted, so I chose the bicycle."

"Yeah, you did right," replied his friend. "The clothes would never have fitted you."

Did you hear about the stupid man who wanted to impress his girlfriend? He took her out to dinner and ordered everything in French.

She was surprised, and so was the waiter. It was an Indian restaurant.

"My wife looks after me so well," said the simple man to his mate. "Last night I came home early to find a pair of trousers on the bedstead. She said she'd felt like buying me a present."

A very dumb man fell overboard from a cruise ship and was washed up on a deserted island. The only inhabitant was a beautiful young girl. Immediately she administered to his needs – taking him to her shelter, feeding him and supplying him with whisky washed up previously. When he had fully recovered, she asked him if he would like to play around.

He looked at her in astonishment and replied, "I can't believe my luck. All this and you've got a set of golf clubs too!"

"Professor," asked John, "how long can a man live without a brain?"

"I don't know; how old are you?" she replied.

If a man said what he thought, he'd be speechless.

A man stayed out very late drinking, staggered home and crept quietly into bed so he wouldn't wake his wife. Just as it started to get light, he woke up dying for a pee.

"Hey, Betty, there's three pairs of feet in our bed," he said nudging her.

"You daft oaf," she replied scornfully. "You can't see properly with all that booze in you. Get out and count again."

So the man went to the bottom of the bed and counted again.

"Sorry, you're right," he said. "There's only two pairs here and I can see I need my toenails cut."

Women don't make fools out of men. They only conduct the performance.

If ignorance is bliss, why aren't there more happy men?

A policeman was walking through Soho when he spotted a man kicking another man up the backside.

"Now, now, what's going on here?" he asked.

The first man explained, "It all goes back to when I was young. I met this beautiful girl and she invited me back to her place. When we got there, she took off her dress and then later she took off the rest of her clothes. So, of course, I turned down the heating and left. But it was then, as I was closing the door, that she told me one day I would realise what I had done and be so angry that I would ask the first man I saw to kick me up the backside. Well now I understand and I've asked this man to do just that."

"Right oh," said the policeman. "Carry on as you were."

Three women were out horse riding when they came across a magic lamp. On rubbing the lamp, a genie appeared who offered to make them more clever.

"Oh my!" exclaimed the first woman. "I'd like to be twice as clever as I am now", and immediately the genie turned her into a world-renowned doctor.

The second woman wished she could be three times as intelligent and she became a top nuclear scientist.

But the third woman, who was a model, was not interested.

"I get a lot of attention already," she replied, "and the more dumb I act, the more attention I get. So really I'd like to be a hundred times less intelligent."

And she got her wish. The genie turned her into a man.

Did you hear about the dumb man who invented an inflatable dartboard for campers?

How do you keep a man busy?

Put him in a round room and tell him to see in the corner.

"Just remember this!" shouted the angry man, "No woman ever made a fool out of me."

"Oh? Who did then?" she calmly replied.

A young girl went out with a boy who was very naive about lovemaking. When the girl discovered that he didn't know how to use a condom, she demonstrated by putting one on her thumb. Satisfied he understood, they climbed into bed, switched off the light and began their lovemaking. However, after a while, the girl realised something was terribly wrong.

"John," she whispered, "I think the condom must have broken."

"Oh, no," he said, switching the light back on. "Look, here it is, quite safe on my thumb."

What's the similarity between a stupid man and an intelligent man?

They both think they know everything.

What is a man doing when he holds his hands tightly over his ears?

Holding onto a thought.

A husband comes home from work to find his wife in bed with another man. He goes absolutely berserk, ranting and raving for a good few minutes. Then he rushes to the wardrobe, pulls out his rifle and sticks the barrel in his mouth.

His wife jumps up screaming, "Bob! Don't, please."

"Shut up, you bitch!" he bellows. "You're next."

Did you hear about the stupid man who divorced his wife?

He was in the maternity unit waiting for her to deliver their baby when out came the midwife to tell him he had a beautiful set of twins.

The man put his head in his hands in anguish.

"Oh, no, I never thought she'd be unfaithful to me. Our marriage is over."

"But why?" asked the midwife. "There's nothing wrong here."

"Oh, but there is," he persisted. "We only did it once so the other one isn't mine."

A man walks into a take-away and orders a cheese and tomato pizza. When it arrives, the owner asks, "Shall I cut it into four pieces or eight?"

The man thinks for a moment and replies, "I'm feeling very hungry, cut it into eight pieces, please."

What's the similarity between dumb men and herpes?

You can't get rid of either, once you've got them.

A world-renowned professor invented a new lie detector which not only recognised when somebody told a lie, but also kicked the offender across the room.

He spent a day testing it out on people. First through the door came a young woman who was asked what qualifications she had. She told the professor she had a first class honours degree and immediately the machine kicked her across the floor. Then an older woman of 50 years came in and when she was asked her age, she replied 31. Again the machine kicked her across the room.

"Next, please," called the professor.

This time it was a young man.

"Why don't you give me your opinion on the way you view your life?" asked the professor.

"I think..." replied the man, but before he could say any more, he was kicked across the room.

A young couple were driving down a narrow country lane when suddenly the man took a corner too quickly and ploughed into the back of a car that had pulled up into the ditch to mend a puncture.

Badly shaken, the couple got out to inspect the damage but the driver of the other car was nowhere to be seen. Then 100 yards down the road, they spotted a very small man sitting cross-legged on the ground, chanting to himself.

"Excuse me," said the man, "would you happen to know where the driver of this car has gone?"

"He has gone to get help," replied the little man, "but don't go. I must thank you for setting me free. I am a genie and I was imprisoned in that car for many years but now the crash has released me, so I can grant three wishes. One for each of you and the third for me."

Immediately the man said, "I wish for a Lotus Elan, what a beautiful car!"

"Then it will be yours," replied the genie.

"And I would like a house on millionaires' row," enthused the wife.

"Then, that too, will be yours." He continued, "Now it is my turn. I would like to have my way with your wife. It is many years since I had a woman."

Appalled at the idea, but realising their wishes would not come true if they refused, the wife and genie got into the back seat of the car and down to business.

Some minutes later, the genie sat back with a satisfied smile on his face and said, "By the way, how old is your husband?"

"Thirty-three," she replied, looking puzzled.

"Fancy that! Thirty-three and he still believes in genies!"

A man took his cat to the vet's because it seemed to be acting in a strange way.

"It looks to me as if she's going to have kittens," explained the vet. "I'll just do a few tests to make sure."

"But that's impossible," spluttered the man. "We live in a flat, 24 floors up, and she never goes out."

"So what you're saying is that she never comes into contact with any other cats?"

"Absolutely," confirmed the man. "But she's not lonely because we have a tom cat as well."

"But I don't understand," puzzled the vet....

The man interrupted "For goodness sake! it's not him, that's her brother."

A man came home and caught his wife in bed with another man.

"Hey!" he shouted, "what's going on here?"

The wife retorted, "See what I mean? I told you he was stupid."

An alien came down to earth and sought out a scientist that would allow him to take some brains back to his own planet for research purposes.

"This is an ape's brain," said the scientist. "It will cost you £250."

"Very good," replied the alien. "Have you anything else?"

"Yes, this is a woman's brain and it will cost £1,000."

"OK that's fine. And just one more possibly?"

"Well, this here, is a man's brain but it will cost you £5,000."

"Goodness me! Why is it so expensive?" the alien exclaimed.

"Well, it's hardly been used," replied the scientist.

"A man was asked by his boss to start up another office on the other side of the country. It would mean he'd be away from home for three weeks, so he called up his friend and asked him for a favour.

"Hello Matt, I'm going to be out of town on business for a while and I wonder if you'll secretly keep an eye on my wife while I'm gone. I just have these doubts that she's up to no good."

His friend agreed and after three weeks had passed, they met up again in the local pub.

"So what happened?" asked the husband.

"Sorry mate, not so good," replied Matt. "After a couple of days, a man appeared at the door, they kissed passionately and then went inside. It was getting dark by this time and as the light in the kitchen was on, I could see them fondling each other frantically. Then the light went out and I saw them go up to your bedroom."

"What happened?" said the husband in despair.

"He stripped off, then undressed your wife and just at that moment, he came over and closed the curtains, so I couldn't see any more."

"Oh, no!" moaned the husband with his head in his hands. "You see what I mean? There is always the doubt."

Jake was a real wally. When he walked into the pub on Saturday morning, all the regulars burst into laughter.

"Hey, Jake, my old stud, we didn't know you had it in you," they laughed.

"What do you mean?" he replied.

"You wally. Last night, upstairs in your bedroom. You left the curtains open and you and your wife put on a great show for us all."

"Well, you lot are the wallies, not me," he replied with spirit. "I wasn't even at home last night."

What did the stupid man say to his unmarried pregnant daughter?

Don't worry, maybe it's not yours.

A pregnant woman is involved in a serious car crash and ends up in a coma for three months. When she finally awakes, the hospital tell her that they delivered her twins a few weeks earlier and both are doing well. She asks them where they are and is told that her uncle is looking after them and has had them christened.

"Oh, no!" she wails, knowing her uncle is a bit of an idiot. "What has he called them?"

The doctor replies, "He's called the little girl Denise."

"Oh, that's nice," she says thankfully, "and what has he called the boy?"

"De nephew."

Two simple-minded men, deciding to spend a night on the town, were discussing where they should go.

"I've heard of this great pub down the bottom of Market Street," enthused one of the men. "You get free drinks all night and then they take you out the back for some sex."

"Are you sure about that?" asked the other. "Sounds too good to be true."

"Oh, no, I promise you it's right, my sister goes there a lot and she told me."

A rather stupid man is driving along in his car when it gets involved in an accident with a lorry carrying nuts and bolts. The lorry sheds its load all over the car and damages it with lots of little dents.

So the next morning, the man takes it to the garage and explains to the mechanic what has happened.

Now the mechanic is an awful practical joker and once he realises the man is a right 'Herbert', he decides to have some fun. He tells the man to take the car home, blow up the exhaust pipe as hard as he can, and all the dents will pop out.

So the man does as he's told but no matter how hard he blows, the dents remain. Just then his flat mate, another 'Herbert', comes home from work and asks what is going on. After hearing the explanation, he looks at his friend and replies scornfully, "You great dumbo, of course it won't work, you need to roll the windows up first!"

What's the difference between a man and a supermarket trolley?

A supermarket trolley has a mind of its own.

Two simple men were walking through the woods when they stumbled across an old mirror. The first one picked it up, looked in it and said, "Hey, I know that bloke."

The second one took it from him and looked in it.

"Of course you do, you daft prat, it's me."

Big Jake was always being teased by his team mates about his sex life.

"How's it going, Jake?" they asked him one day. "We hear you've been trying out a lot of new sexual positions."

"Yeah, that's true," said the big man proudly. "I'm just about ready to try them out on girls now."

Did you hear about the stupid man who started work on a building site?

After the first day, the boss came to congratulate him on his hard work. When he'd gone, the man turned to his fellow workmates and winked.

"I've really tricked the boss. I've been carrying the same load of bricks up and down the ladder all day."

A policeman came upon a stupid man peeing in the river.

"Stop that immediately!" he shouted, "And put it away."

So the stupid man did as he was told, but he couldn't stop himself from doubling up with laughter.

"OK, what's so funny?" demanded the policeman.

"I really fooled you this time," he laughed. "I may have put it away, but I didn't stop."

"Is that a gun in your pocket or are you just pleased to see me?"

"No, it's a gun."

One mother-in-law said to the other:

"I would never make a fool of my son-in-law. I've always allowed him to do that for himself."

Having just got married, the naive man said to his friend:

"Cor...was my girl dumb! She put the pillow under her bum instead of her head."

Why wasn't the man worried when his car was stolen?

He had the licence plate number.

If there is anything a man does not know, he imagines it.

The old building had fallen into such disrepair that a demolition gang moved in to raze it to the ground. Eventually, only the cellar was left and as they entered the one remaining room, they were horrified to see a skeleton in the corner. All that was left were the bones and a bright green sash, which read: 'Irish Hide And Seek Championship Finals 1949'".

What should you give a man who has everything?

A woman to show him how to work it.

"Mr Peterson, I have listened very carefully to your case," said the divorce judge, "and I have decided to award your wife £450 a month."

"Well, thank you very much, Your Honour, that seems very generous," replied Mr Peterson. "I'll try and throw a couple of quid in myself each month."

The wife turned to her husband and said, "It says here in this article that over 2,000 camels are used each year to make paint brushes."

"Really!" exclaimed her husband. "It's amazing what they can teach animals these days."

A "right Herbert" of a husband was so fed up with his wife telling him he was useless that he decided to give her a surprise. He decided to paint the bedroom. Early the next morning, after she had gone to work, he bought some paint and got down to work.

His wife returned home that evening and immediately smelled the new paint.

"Now what?" she thought. Up the stairs she went and into the bedroom to find her husband lying on the floor in a pool of sweat.

"Are you all right?" she asked, going up to him. "What are you doing?"

He gasped, "I just wanted to show you I'm not as useless as you think, so I decided to paint the bedroom."

She looked around and commented, "Well, it's very nice but why are you wearing your winter coat and your raincoat?"

"Well, it said on the directions 'for best results, put on two coats'."

My husband is so stupid, when he went to the mind reader, they gave him his money back.

He was so stupid, when he heard that 89 per cent of all crimes occur in the home, he moved.

A man arrives home early from work and hears strange noises coming from the bedroom. He rushes upstairs to discover his wife lying naked on the bed, sweating and panting heavily.

"What's going on?" he asks.

"I think I'm having a heart attack," she cries.

"Oh, no!" he gasps, but as he rushes back down the stairs to ring for an ambulance, he bumps into his five-year-old son.

"Daddy, daddy!" says the little boy excitedly. "Uncle Ted's upstairs in the wardrobe and he's got no clothes on."

"What!" roars the man and storms back up the stairs to the bedroom. He opens the wardrobe door and sure enough, Uncle Ted is standing there naked.

"You bastard, you bloody prat!" he screams. "How could you? There's my wife on the bed having a heart attack and all you can do is run around naked, playing hide and seek with the kids."

The man was so stupid, he sold his car for petrol money.

Giles had been shipwrecked on the desert island for more than two years and was missing female company badly. His only companions were a dog and a pig. The time came when the pig looked more and more attractive and one night, he decided to make his move. However, as he started to make his way over to the pig, he was attacked by the dog and stopped from going anywhere near it. Time after time he tried, but the ever-watchful dog would immediately start to growl, so he had to abandon his plans.

Then one day a beautiful young girl was washed up on the beach. The man took her to his shelter and nursed her back to health.

"You saved my life," she said with great feeling. "If there's anything you want in return, you only have to ask."

The man smiled broadly and replied "Oh wow! Great! Thanks a lot."

"Well, what would you like?" she whispered coyly.

"I wonder if you could take the dog for a walk," he replied.

It's a well known fact that you will often see clever men with thick women but very rarely see clever women with thick men.

TRAVEL

The King had a loyal servant who had been with him for more than 20 years and was never far from his master's side. However, this servant had one affliction – he couldn't stop repeating the phrase 'great, really great'.

Now one day, the King and his entourage went hunting. They spotted several pheasants in the wood, the King aimed his gun and fired. Alas, the firing pin stuck, the gun backfired and shot the Kings foot off.

"Arrgh!" cried the King in agony, "help me!"

Everyone gathered round to see to their master and amidst the crowd could be heard the faithful servant saying,

'Great, really great.'

In a flash of rage, the King ordered the servant to be thrown in the deepest, darkest dungeon and left there to rot.

Some months later, the King travelled abroad and went hunting in Africa. Early one morning, he and his hunting party were captured by cannibals and taken back to their camp to eat. However, on seeing the King had no foot, they let him go because their faith had instructed them never to eat anything that wasn't whole. The rest of the party went into the pot. The

King returned to England and ordered his faithful servant to be released.

"The accident turned out to be the best thing that ever happened to me," said the King, "otherwise I wouldn't be here today."

"Great, really great," replied the servant, "because if I hadn't been in jail, I'd have been with you!"

A tribe of cannibals were complaining about the last batch of missionaries they had captured.

"We've roasted them, stewed them, even marinated them but they're still as tough as old boots."

"Wait a minute," said a newcomer, "did you get them from the village at the bottom of Red Stone River?"

"Yes," they replied, "why?"

"Well, that explains why you're having so much trouble. You see they're Friars."

A man gets lost in the middle of the outback and lands up in a very primitive town. He has a drink in the small saloon and then asks for directions to the toilet because he's desperate for a crap.

"Out the back," comes the reply. So the man walks round the side of the building to see two huge piles of shit. He almost vomits with disgust but time is not on his side and he just makes it to the top of one of the piles before dumping his load. As he looks over to the other pile, he sees an old man sitting on top, reading the newspaper. The old man looks up and says,

"Morning stranger."

"Oh... err... good morning," replies the man, "how did you know I was a stranger?"

"Because you're in the ladies'," came the reply.

A cannibal and his son were walking through the jungle looking for food when they came across a beautiful naked woman.

"Shall we take her home to eat, dad?" asked the son.

"We'll take her home," replied dad, "but we'll eat your mother."

A woman, on holiday in Africa, meets Tarzan in the depths of the jungle. She takes one look at him and immediately falls in love with his good looks and wonderful physique.

When she discovers he lives alone she says coyly,

"So what do you do about sex?"

He points to a tree where she can see a hole half way up the trunk.

"Oh goodness!" she exclaims. "I'm sure you'd much rather have this," and she lies on the ground with her legs spread wide.

Tarzan walks over and kicks her hard on the crotch.

"Owww! Why did you do that?" she asks, looking hurt.

"Me check for wasps nests first," he replies.

A woman goes to work on an Indian reservation in Arizona and for 3 months spends her time helping to educate the young children. On her final morning, once more she sits down to breakfast with the Chief and his family and says to the Chief,

"Chief Running Bull, I've been told you have a unique memory. Can you tell me what I had for breakfast on the first day of my stay?"

"Eggs," he replies, and of course he is right. The woman returns home and it's more than ten years before she's able to return to Arizona. In the meantime she's told a lot of people about the amazing memory man but many are cynical about the question she asked. It was too easy they say, you should have thought about something more searching. So when she arrives back at the reservation, she searches out Chief Running Bull, determined to ask him a more difficult question. However, remembering her manners, she enters his teepee and first greets him by saying,

"How."

"Poached," he replies.

The flight to New York has 30 minutes flying time left when lightning hits the plane and it starts to lose altitude. As the passengers sit there dumbfounded at the enormity of what is about to happen, a woman suddenly jumps to her feet in hysterics.

"No, no!" she yells "help me, I'm too young to die."

But the next moment, she realises the futility of it all and instead says,

"Alright, if I'm going to die, then my last wish is this. Is there anyone on this plane who can make me feel like a real woman, and I mean, a real woman!"

No one moves, all the passengers are caught up in this unexpected drama, completely forgetting their own peril.

Then a voice is heard and from the back of the plane a man stands up.

"I can make you feel like a real woman," he says in a deep sexy voice. Slowly he walks towards the desperate woman, unbuttoning his shirt as he goes, revealing a perfect torso, tanned and rippling with muscles. The passengers gasp as he reaches her, the woman breathes heavily in anticipation as he extends his arm and says,

"Just run an iron over this, would you, love?"

A very naïve Irishman was visiting America for the first time. Walking down one of the busy shopping streets he came to a halt at the side of a busy intersection where a traffic cop was directing the traffic. Every now and again, the cop would stop all the traffic and call out,

"Okay, pedestrians," and allow the people to cross over. Thirty minutes later, the cop had called 'pedestrians' at least 20 times when the Irishman tapped him on the shoulder and said,

"Isn't it time for you to allow the Catholics across now?"

An aircraft crashed in the middle of the Australian outback, leaving fourteen badly shaken survivors. For many days they wandered through the rough scrubland but slowly each fell to the wayside until there were only two left – an elderly peer and his faithful servant.

"Bates, I can't go any further," gasped the peer. "I need water, please go and find water."

The servant disappeared into the bush and returned several hours later empty handed.

"Where's the water?" asked the peer.

"I couldn't bring it Sir," came the reply.

"Couldn't? What do you mean couldn't?"

"The river was full of giant crocodiles," whispered the servant.

"Now pull yourself together man. Those crocodiles are just as scared of you as you are of them" said the peer forcefully.

"Oh Sir," he replied miserably, "If that's right, then the water isn't fit to drink anyway."

"Can you tell me when you get to Highfell Woods, please," said the woman to the bus driver. "My cat Tiddles has died and I want to bury him under the beach trees."

She showed him the sack she was carrying under her arm and then went to sit at the back of the bus.

It was more than forty minutes later before they reached the woods and by this time the sack was beginning to give off an awful smell. Suddenly, the driver pulled to a halt and shouted,

"Will the lady with the smelly pussy get off now please."

Four women crossed their legs and three jumped off the bus immediately.

For three months, the man had been attending French language lessons at his local night school and now he was in France to test out how well he had been taught.

On the first evening he visited a small restaurant and ordered onion soup but when it arrived, he noticed a dead fly floating in it.

"Excusez moi," he said to the waiter. "Regardez, le mouche."

The waiter replied,

"Non, Monsieur. Not le mouche. la mouche."

The man was extremely impressed.

"Golly, you have got good eyesight!"

Three men were kidnapped by an elite band of ancient warriors and told that one of them still had a chance to live if he beat the other two at an old competitive custom. A bee would be released into a room and each man in turn had to kill it by using an ancient sword. If all three killed their bees, then the slowest two would die. The first man walked confidently into the room, the bee was released and within seconds, the sword had flashed through the air, killing the bee stone dead.

"The second man achieved an even quicker time.

"Oh no," thought the third contestant, a small Jewish man. "I'll never do this, I've never handled a sword in my life."

He walked into the room, swiped the air several times with his sword and all watched as the bee continued to buzz around the room.

"You have not killed it," pronounced the leader of the ancient warriors.

"No," replied the man, "but if you look very closely, you will see that I have circumcised it."

A naïve young woman was due to travel by aeroplane for the very first time. She rang the airport to ask how long it would take to fly from London to Manchester.

"Just a minute," said the information assistant.

"Thank you," replied the woman as she hung up.

A man and his wife visited Australia for the first time and stayed at a very exclusive hotel in the outback. On their second day, they hired a jeep and drove out into the bush. To their amazement, they came across a man shagging a kangaroo. The husband was shocked that his wife had viewed such a tasteless sight and he drove off as fast as he could, only to find a similar situation around the next bend. Yes, there was another figure shagging another kangaroo.

"Come on Doreen," said the husband angrily, "that's the last time we go out into the bush, let's get back to the hotel."

To their dismay, as they turned into the drive of the exclusive hotel, they notice a man with a wooden leg masturbating at the side of the road.

"Oh John," wailed his wife. "I just want to go home."

They stormed into the hotel and demanded to see the manager.

"In the past hour we've seen two men shagging kangaroos and another man masturbating in the grounds of this very hotel. What do you have to say to that?" he rasped.

"Oh come on mate," said the manager, "have a heart. How do you expect a man with a wooden leg to be able to catch his own kangaroo?"

A wife went off on holiday to Spain on her own. After a week, she phoned her husband and said,

"I'm feeling a new woman, mind if I stay another week?"

"So am I," replied the husband. "Stay as long as you like."

The girl was on her first flight and feeling very excited about it. She found a comfortable seat near the window and settled down to enjoy the trip. However, moments later a man appeared and insisted that she was sitting in his seat. But no matter how much they argued, she would not move. Eventually, the man gave up.

"Alright, fuck you," he said angrily. "You fly the bloody plane!"

A tourist wanders accidentally into a rough part of the city. He goes up to a man lounging in a shop doorway and says,

"Excuse me, can you tell me what time it is or should I just go fuck myself?"

Out in the middle of the dense jungle, the hunting party were captured by a group of native warriors and taken back to their settlement. Turning to their guide, the hunters asked him what was going to happen to them and the answer was chilling.

"We will be ritualistically killed," said the guide, "but first they will torture us."

"What do you mean?"

"We will be made to play Luma Luma roulette?"

"Well I've heard of Russian roulette," said one of the hunters, "but what's that?"

"Each of us in turn will be ordered into the tent. Inside, six holes are cut in the side of the tent and behind each hole stands a beautiful native woman. You will then put your willy into one of the holes and the woman on the other side will suck you off."

After a moment's silence, one of the hunters spoke.

"So why is it called roulette?"

The guide replied sadly,

"Because one of the women is a cannibal."

UNDERPANTS

"Hey darling, black underwear really turns me on," said the man to his wife.

So she didn't wash his underpants for six months.

URBAN MYTH

Yesterday I was on the Underground travelling on the Victoria line. A man of Arabic appearance got off the train and I noticed that he had left his bag behind. I grabbed the bag and ran after him, caught up with him at the top of the escalator and handed him back his bag. He was extremely grateful to me and reached into his bag that appeared to contain large bundles of banknotes. He offered me a reward, but I refused.

So he looked round, made sure nobody was looking and whispered to me:

"I can never repay your kindness, sir, but I will try to. Let me give you a word of advice for you. Stay away from Aberdeen Steak Houses." I was terrified.

"Is there going to be an attack?" I whispered.

"No, sir," he whispered back, "I went there yesterday evening – the food was awful and the dessert selection extremely limited."

V

VETS

A man went to the vets with his sick dog and sat in the waiting room while the animal was examined next door. Fifteen minutes later, the vet came out carrying the dog and said to its owner,

"I'm sorry, I'm going to have to put the dog down."

"Oh no!" cried the man in distress. "Why do you have to do that?"

"Because he's too heavy," came the reply.

VIAGRA

A woman walked into the chemists to enquire about Viagra™.

"Can you get it over the counter?" she asked.

"If I take two, I can," he replied.

"Can I get you some breakfast, darling," said the woman, "if you don't want anything fried, I can get you a nice piece of fresh smoked haddock with a poached egg on top."

"No thanks," he replied. "This Viagra™ seems to have taken my appetite away."

Some time later, she asked him again.

"How about a bit of lunch. I've made some thick vegetable soup and we can have that with crusty bread."

"No thanks," he said. "I'm still not hungry."

So later still, she asked for a third time.

"Let's have some dinner. A bit of sirloin, Yorkshire pudding, roast potatoes... Doesn't that sound nice?"

"I'm sorry love, I just don't have any appetite. This Viagra™'s stopped my interest in food completely."

"Alright," she said impatiently, "but can you get off me 'cos I'm fucking starving."

A man goes to the doctor complaining that since he has been taking Viagra™, he always feels so tired. After examining him, the doctor remarks,

"Well, I can't find anything wrong with you, perhaps you'd better tell me how you spend your days."

"Okay," replied the man. "I usually wake up about 6.30, make love to the wife, doze off for a while, make love again and get up about 8 o'clock. Then after breakfast I usually make love to her again in the kitchen before going off to work. At one o'clock, I drive the four miles home, make love to the wife, have lunch then go back to work. I get home at six, make love to the wife a couple of times, have supper, make love again, pop down the pub for an hour then come back and make love on the sofa. We go to bed about 11.30, have lots more love and then go to sleep. Quite often we wake up a couple of times in the night and have more."

The doctor was dumbfounded.

"Well I think I can tell you what's wrong," he said. "It's too much shagging. It's wearing you out."

"Oh really," replied the man. "For a while I thought it might be all the wanking I do in the office."

★

Why do they give Viagra™ to old men?

So they won't roll out of bed.

★

Have you heard about the new 'Viagra™ Light'?

It's for those who only want to masturbate.

★

What is virgin wool?

An ugly sheep.

★

Did you hear about the theft of a carton of Viagra™?

Police are looking for three hardened criminals. A police spokesman stated that when a judge got his hands on them, they would all receive stiff sentences.

A man asks his pharmacist for half of a Viagra™ pill. The doctor says that half a pill won't do any good, he needs two or three pills.

The man explains, "No, you see the reason I only want half a pill is because I'm tired of peeing on my shoes."

VOODOO

A businessman was getting ready to go on a long business trip. He knew his wife was a flirtatious sort with an extremely healthy sex drive, so he thought he'd buy her a little something to keep her occupied while he was gone.

He went to a store that sold sex toys and started to look around. He thought about a life-sized sex doll, but that was too close to another man for him. He was browsing through the dildos, looking for something special to please his wife, and started talking to the old man behind the counter. He explained his situation.

"Well, I don't really know of anything that will do the trick. We have vibrating dildos, special attachments, and so on, but I don't know of thing that will keeher occupied for weeks, except..."and he stopped.

"Except what?" the man asked.

"Nothing, nothing."

"C'mon, tell me! I need something!"

"Well, sir, I don't usually mention this, but there is The Voodoo Penis."

"So what's up with this Voodoo Penis?" he asked.

The old man reached under the counter, and pulled out a very old wooden box, carved with strange symbols and erotic images. He opened it, and there lay an ordinary-looking dildo.

The businessman laughed, and said "Big damn deal. It looks like every other dildo in this shop!"

The old man replied, "But you haven't seen what it'll do yet."

He pointed to a door and said, "Voodoo Penis, the door." The Voodoo Penis miraculously rose out of its box, darted over to the door, and started pounding the keyhole. The whole door shook wildly with the vibrations, so much so that a crack began to form down the middle. Before the door split, the old man said, "Voodoo Penis, return to box!"

The Voodoo Penis stopped, levitated back to the box and lay there quiescent once more.

"I'll take it!" said the businessman.

The old man resisted, saying it wasn't for sale, but finally surrendered to £738 in cash and an imitation Rolex.

The guy took it home to his wife, told her it was a special dildo and that to use it, all she had to do was say "Voodoo Penis, my crotch." He left for his trip satisfied that things would be fine while he was gone.

After he'd been gone a few days, his wife was unbearably horny. She thought of several people who would willingly satisfy her, but then she remembered the Voodoo Penis.

She undressed, opened the box and said, "Voodoo Penis, my crotch!"

The Voodoo Penis shot to her crotch and started pumping. It was absolutely incredible, like nothing she'd ever experienced before. After three mind-shattering orgasms, she became very exhausted and decided she'd had enough.

She tried to pull it out, but it was stuck in her, still thrusting. She tried and tried to get it out, but nothing worked. Her husband had forgotten to tell her how to shut it off.

 Worried, she decided to go to the hospital to see if they could help. She put her clothes on, got in the car and started to drive, quivering with every thrust of the dildo. On the way, another incredibly intense orgasm made her swerve all over the road.

A police officer saw this and immediately pulled her over. He asked for her licence, and then asked how much she'd had to drink.

Gasping and twitching, she explained, "I haven't had anything to drink, officer. You see, I've got this Voodoo Penis thing stuck in my crotch and it won't stop screwing me!"

The officer looked at her for a second, shook his head and in an arrogant voice replied, "Yeah, right... Voodoo Penis, my ass!"

W

WIVES

A man arrived home from work to find absolute chaos. As he walked up the garden path he fell over toys, strewn all over the ground and a broken milk bottle on the doorstep. Inside, the living room was in uproar. The two small children had up-ended the furniture and pushed over the television. The carpet had food all over it plus an overturned vase of flowers and spilt glasses of milk. The kitchen was even worse. Dirty dishes, covered every work surface, the fridge had been left open so it had de-frosted and the cat was sitting on the table eating left-over food.

"Oh no!" he gasped, turning white. He was really worried that something had happened to his wife. He raced up the stairs, two at a time and rushed into the bedroom. There, sitting up in bed was his wife, reading a book and eating chocolate.

"What's going on?" he asked. "I thought you must be ill."

"Oh no," she replied, "but when you come in every day and ask me what I did... well today, I didn't."

Three women were chatting over tea, one was English, one French and one Italian. They were moaning about their husbands.

"Well I soon sorted mine," said the English woman. "I told him I would do no more cooking until he washed up afterwards. On the first day, I didn't see anything, on the second day I didn't see anything, but on the third day he went into the kitchen and cleaned it until it was spotless!"

Then the French woman spoke.

"That's very good," she remarked. "I have also been successful. I told my husband that I would no longer do any washing unless he did his share. On the first day, I saw nothing, on the second day I saw nothing but on the third day he washed and ironed three loads!"

The other two nodded in approval.

Then the Italian woman spoke.

"Some time ago, I told my husband I would do no more cleaning unless he helped me. On the first day I saw nothing, on the second day I saw nothing, on the third day I could just about open my right eye!"

A man had been stung on his willy by a big bumblebee, so his wife took him to the doctor's surgery. As the man went into the consulting room, the wife whispered in the doctor's ear.

"Doctor, please take out the sting but leave the swelling in."

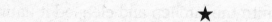

There was a knock on the front door and Mrs Hardcastle answered it to find a woman standing there with a collecting tin in her hand.

"Good evening," she said. "I'm collecting for a home for those inflicted with the demon drink. I wondered whether you'd like to make a donation."

"I certainly would," replied Mrs Hardcastle, briskly, "but my husband's in the pub at present. Come back when it closes and you can have him."

A woman was so suspicious of her husband that she called in a private investigator to have him followed. A few days later, she received the results.

"I'm sorry Madam," said the P.I. "but there is no doubt that your husband is having an affair. He showed the poor wife photographs of the husband with a glamorous woman and video footage of him visiting gambling casinos, exclusive nightclubs and wild all-night parties.

"I can hardly believe what I'm seeing," she gasped.

"Is it because the woman is a friend of yours?" asked the P.I.

"Oh no," she replied. "It's because I had no idea he could be so much fun."

Seeing that the road was clear in both directions, the man began to cross on the zebra crossing. Suddenly, from out of the blue, a car appeared from nowhere and knocked him to the ground. As it sped off, he heard a witches cackle.

The man picked himself up, as a policeman rushed over to check that he was alright.

"Can you tell me anything about the incident?" he asked. "Did you get a look at the driver?"

"I didn't need to," he said wearily, "it was my wife."

"But how do you know?"

"I'd know that chilling laugh anywhere."

WORKING GIRLS

A man was looking through the job vacancies and saw something that he thought would be ideal. 'Caretaker for brothel. £150 per week, including all meals and choice of girl every night.' He rushed down to see the manager and was hired that day. After working his shift he then enquired about a woman.

"Take your pick," came the reply, so he opened the door to room 3 and saw a gorgeous brunette lying on the bed. He stripped off immediately and walked towards her.

"Oh no," she replied "not tonight, you'll have to satisfy yourself in the corner."

The next night, the man tried another room. A sexy blonde was sitting on the bed. Again he took his clothes off and winked at the girl.

"No way," she said "go and see to yourself in the corner."

Every night he got the same response until he was so annoyed, he went to see the manager.

"One of the main reasons I took this job was because of the perks," he complained, "yet none of the women will let me near them. It's been like that for six nights now."

"Oh sorry," replied the manager "I forgot to tell you, it'll be alright on Monday, but you have to work the first week in hand."

A man visited a brothel in Paris and asked for the services of Monique. In return, he gave her £100. The following night he came back again and at the end of the session gave her another £100.

Now Monique was intrigued by this handsome stranger and after the third night when he gave her a further £100 for services rendered, she said to him

"I hope I see you tomorrow, you know I look forward to our time together. In fact, tomorrow's on the house."

"Well that's mighty kind of you," replied the man, "but I'm flying back to the States tomorrow. I came to see you because I know your brother and he asked me to give you £300."

A panda escapes from his cage one night and heads for Soho where he picks up a prostitute. They go back to her place but before the main action begins, the panda eats everything in the kitchen.

"Greedy sod," thinks the prostitute, "that'll all go on his bill."

For the next few hours they do the business, then the panda gets up and prepares to leave

"Hey," calls the prostitute "haven't you forgotten something?"

"I don't think so" he replies.

"I'm a prostitute," she says angrily.

"And I'm a panda," he replies sarcastically.

"Look you dumb animal, in the dictionary here it says a prostitute gives sex for money. Get it?"

The panda takes the dictionary from the woman and turns to the page which describes a panda.

"Look at this," he demands.

"A panda eats, shoots and leaves," she reads.

So the panda left.

A man takes a prostitute back to his flat where she strips off ready to do the business. However, instead of stripping off as well, he asks the woman to put on a raincoat.

"Well, okay," she says, no stranger to unusual requests, plus she also puts on a pair of wellies which he hands to her.

"Now will you go into the bathroom and stand under the shower."

Again she does as he asks.

The man smiles in satisfaction and says,

"With one hand can you turn the light on and off so that it looks like lightning and with the other hand, bang loudly on this box to make the sound of thunder."

"We've got a right one here," she thinks to herself. Nevertheless, she carries out all his wishes and stands there for the next 5 minutes getting soaking wet and pretending it's thundering and lightning. Eventually, her arms begin to ache and she says to the man impatiently,

"Listen mate, don't you think we ought to get down to a bit of business now?"

"What!" he exclaims, "in weather like this! You've got to be joking."

Jack had been told by a mate that if he was ever in Liverpool he ought to look up Luscious Lil who would give him the best time of his life. So, one Saturday night he sought her out and she took him back to her penthouse flat. After stripping him and encouraging his John Thomas to stand to attention, she disappeared for a moment or two and came back with a tray of delicious sweets. First of all she covered his dick in swirls of whipped cream dribbled over some chocolate sauce, sprinkled on a bowl of chopped hazelnuts and put a cherry on top.

"Hey, what's all this?" he asked in astonishment.

"Now my darling," she whispered. "I'm going to suck it all off."

"Now wait a minute," he said quickly, "it looks so good, I'm going to suck it off myself!"

"How about a blow job," said the prostitute to the Irishman.

"Oh no, no, no," replied the Irishman, "it might affect my unemployment benefit."

A prostitute stepped off the pavement without looking and was hit by a passing car. As she lay there dazed, she kept moaning.

"I can't see, I can't see."

Quickly, the motorist held up three fingers and asked her,

"How many fingers do I have up?"

"Oh no," she cried in despair. "I'm paralysed as well."

A son was warned by his father never to set foot in a brothel.

"There will be dreadful happenings," said the father, "and you will surely die."

But many years later, the son found himself in a strange town for the night. Feeling lonely he sought out company and ended up at a brothel. He was taken upstairs to room 4 and there on the bed lay a naked woman.

"Oh no," gasped the son, as his father's warning came back to him.

"Dad was right, I can feel myself going stiff already."

Two men went to see Luscious Lil, the town's most popular prostitute. The first man came out with a silly grin on his face and said to the others.

"Wow! That was something else" he exclaimed. "What a woman! She'll do anything you want for £10 as long as you tell her in three words."

"What did you say?" he asked.

"Fuck me rigid."

The second man went in and reappeared some time later looking quite dazed.

"Bloody hell!" he gasped. "You were right. What an experience. I asked her to 'lick me everywhere'… What a woman!"

Now listening to this was an old skinflint called Jake. He decided to try Luscious Lil for himself.

"I hear you'll do anything I ask for £10 as long as I tell you in three words."

"That's right," she replied.

"And that means anything?" he persisted.

"Oh yes," she said, winking at him.

"Well in that case, decorate my house."

X

XYLOPHONE

You didn't really think there was a joke about xylophones, did you?

Y

YETI

An atheist was hiking through the forest when he was suddenly confronted by a huge Yeti. The monster grabbed him by the head and lifted him high into the air.

"Oh God, help me please," screamed the man, and for a moment time stood still and a voice from heaven boomed, "but I thought you didn't believe in me."

The man replied earnestly,

"Oh come on God, give me a chance, a few minutes ago I didn't believe in Yetis!"

A group of British explorers were hunting for a Yeti in one of the more remote regions of Asia. On the fifth night, their guide told them they were very close to their target but whatever happened, they must not touch one.

"Remember my warning, do not touch the Yeti."

They made camp and settled down for the night but just before dawn, one of the explorers woke to find a huge figure looming over him. In sudden panic, he jumped up and made his escape but inadvertently touched the Yeti on his way out. He raced from the camp and down the mountainside but every time he looked round, the Yeti was coming up behind him. The explorer increased his pace and made it back to the village in a record time of 2 days. He sighed with relief, but as he turned to look back up the hillside, he could see the Yeti still following him. It was his worst nightmare. He caught a bus to the city, 60 miles away, and headed straight for the airport where he boarded the first plane for home. Arriving in London, he began to relax but as he jumped on the Heathrow Express he spotted the Yeti coming through customs. So as soon as he arrived in Central London, he raced off to Euston and took a train to the Scottish isles.

"I'm free, I'm free!" he yelled, as he stood on top of the mountain, but alas, right behind him stood the Yeti. In complete despair, he sank to his knees and awaited his fate.

"I give up," he muttered. "I can't go on."

The Yeti approached, raised his arm and touched the man on the shoulder.

"You're it!" he said.

Z

ZEN QUOTES

Do not walk behind me, for I may not lead. Do not walk ahead of me, for I may not follow. Do not walk beside me, either; just f*** off and leave me alone.

The journey of a thousand miles begins with a broken fan belt and a flat tire.

It's always darkest before dawn. So if you're going to steal your neighbor's newspaper, that's the time to do it.

Don't be irreplaceable; if you can't be replaced, you can't be promoted.

No one is listening until you make a mistake.

Always remember you're unique, just like everyone else.

Never test the depth of the water with both feet.

It may be that your sole purpose in life is simply to serve as a warning to others.

It is far more impressive when others discover your good qualities without your help.

If you think nobody cares if you're alive, try missing a couple of car payments.

Before you criticize someone, you should walk a mile in their shoes. That way, when you criticize them, you're a mile away and you have their shoes.

If at first you don't succeed, skydiving is not for you.

Give a man a fish and he will eat for a day. Teach him how to fish, and he will sit in a boat & drink beer all day.

If you lend someone $20, and never see that person again, it was probably worth it.

Don't squat with your spurs on.

If you drink, don't park; accidents cause people.

Some days you are the bug, some days you are the windshield.

The quickest way to double your money is to fold it in half and put it back in your pocket.

Duct tape is like the force; it has a light side and a dark side, and it holds the universe together.

ABOUT THE AUTHOR

JOHNNY SHARPE has been cracking gags since as far back as he can remember. His family call him the 'giggle machine'. Johnny's comedy show, *The Clown in Me*, was a moderate success when he launched it in County Down in 1978. Well known in his native Crawley for his highly effective practical jokes, he can often be seen chuckling as he orders his next batch of custard pies. Johnny Sharpe is single and currently on tour. He is a Saggitarius.